Experimenting with MSI, LSI, IO, and Modular Memory Systems

Charles W. McKay is also the author of

Digital Circuits

Experimenting with MSI, LSI, IO, and Modular Memory Systems

CHARLES W. McKAY

*University of Houston
at Clear Lake City*

PRENTICE-HALL, INC., Englewood Cliffs, New Jersey 07632

Library of Congress Cataloging in Publication Data

McKay, Charles W
  Experimenting with MSI, LSI, IO, and modular
memory systems.

  Bibliography: p.
  Includes index.
  1. Computer storage devices. 2 Computer input-
output equipment. 3. Integrated circuits.
4. Microcomputers. I. Title.
TK7895.M4M33 1981   621.3819'583   80-16738
ISBN 0-13-295477-X

Editorial/production supervision and interior design
    by Barbara A. Cassel
Cover design by Jorge Hernandez
Manufacturing buyer: Joyce Levatino

Printed in the United States of America

10 9 8 7 6 5 4 3 2 1

Prentice-Hall International, Inc., *London*
Prentice-Hall of Australia Pty. Limited, *Sydney*
Prentice-Hall of Canada, Ltd., *Toronto*
Prentice-Hall of India Private Limited, *New Delhi*
Prentice-Hall of Japan, Inc., *Tokyo*
Prentice-Hall of Southeast Asia Pte. Ltd., *Singapore*
Whitehall Books Limited, *Wellington, New Zealand*

This book is dedicated to all the members of my family
and friends whose help, patience, understanding, and
encouragement have made productive work both possible
and enjoyable. In particular, this one is for my wife and
mother-in-law. A list of the reasons why would triple the
size of the book, and neither time nor space permits,
unfortunately.

CWM

Contents

Contents

Preface

There is no more exciting, dynamic, and challenging field in today's technology than the study of digital systems. Both the theory and applications of these systems have grown far beyond our ability to confine this study to a one- or two-semester course which can hope to lay any respectable claim to being sufficiently exhaustive or comprehensive for the serious student. Furthermore, there is every indication that the field is still in its very healthy infancy and that the best is yet to come. As in most fields, the more dramatic and rapid the changes, the more urgent and imperative that we master the basics. The student who desires to understand and utilize innovations needs a solid foundation built so that each necessary set of concepts and supporting laboratory experiences rests solidly on its prerequisite concepts and experiences. This book is intended to aid the student in constructing the second level of this foundation for the study of digital systems.

Before you begin this book you should have mastered the concepts, techniques, and the applications of number systems, Boolean algebra, combinational circuitry, and sequential circuitry. The level of your mastery should be consistent with the expectations of a first book or course in digital logic, such as the first book in this digital systems series by the author.

In this book we study a number of topics in medium-scale integrated circuits (MSI), large-scale integrated circuits (LSI), and their use in input–output (IO) systems and in modular memory systems. We examine experiments and problems in memory interfacing, memory control logic, fixed program memories, sequential access memories, random access read/write memories, stack operations, organization and construction of memory modules, multiported memory modules, device controllers for secondary storage peripherals, and basic software techniques used in programming memories. We examine stored programs in memories and study the memory operations from the fetching and decoding of a software command through the hardware execution of a command. We study the effects on both the program control and on the memory when subroutines are encountered, when interrupts occur, and when files are copied to and from secondary storage peripherals during direct memory access operations.

The eager student who is understandably impatient to proceed to the study of microprocessors (after all, these devices are the common denominator of so much that is new and exciting in this field) should take heart. This book is intended to provide the last level of our foundation before we can begin a meaningful study of microprocessors. This level of preparation is necessary because a microprocessor by itself can accomplish nothing of any value for us. Without the LSI, MSI, SSI (small-scale integrated circuits), and memory chips which enable the microprocessor to interface to the outside world, it cannot perform its intended applications.

Since the microprocessor cannot "stand alone," the student who tries to proceed directly from an introduction to digital logic into a study of microprocessors without first learning about the necessary support circuitry is going to be faced with a very large and frustrating assortment of new concepts and techniques to be learned concurrently. This has frequently led to a very superficial understanding that hinders students in the long run or causes defeat and withdrawal from the field of study. Fortunately for all of us, such frustrations can be avoided by refusing to waste time and effort on a nonexistent "shortcut" in our learning process, since the study of MSI, LSI, and IO, and modular memory systems is itself a fascinating field. Unlike the microprocessor, systems constructed with MSI, LSI, IO, and modular memory units can be added to circuits that we studied in our first level of digital systems to create a "stand-alone" instrument or system than can accomplish a great deal of useful work for us. Some examples that we study in this book include sampling oscilloscopes, waveform generators, mathematical "look-up tables," and device controllers.

This book is written in a self-paced dialogued learning format. The emphasis is on the development and use of concepts in analysis and synthesis rather than on rote memorization and familiarity with special devices and circuits. The student is repeatedly introduced to a topic, asked to interact with the material and the author through an informal question-and-answer dialogue, prompted to predict circuit behavior under specified conditions, and then presented with both the answers and the opportunity to construct the circuitry and verify the results. For each unit of study, the objectives are given at the beginning and tested at the end of the unit. It is intended that the student completing this book will have demonstrated the ability to creatively and actively pursue advanced study in digital systems and devices.

Charles W. McKay

**Experimenting with
MSI, LSI, IO,
and Modular
Memory Systems**

An Overview
of the Concepts,
Problems, and Experiments
in this Book

INTRODUCTION TO THE ORGANIZATION OF THE BOOK

This book is organized into units, and each unit is subdivided into sections. The first section of each unit introduces the concepts to be covered in the unit and outlines their relationships to previously studied concepts in digital systems. The development of these concepts and of current techniques of applying them is accomplished by studying the materials and working the related sets of problems and experiments in each of the sections that follow. For maximum learning benefits you should conceal the answers that are provided on the same pages as the problems and experiments until you have answered all of the questions in a group preceded by a letter of the alphabet. Then check your answers against the ones provided. (For example, answer all questions in group 3c, then reveal and compare the correct answers to 3c before proceeding on to the questions in 3d.) If your responses are correct, you have reinforced your own learning. If your answers are wrong, stop and discover why rather than proceeding with a mistaken impression.

Each section is organized around the study of a closely related set of applications that rely on the concepts discussed in the unit. Although the majority of applications were taken from industrial settings, the concepts and the techniques being studied also have important implications for the growing number of digital systems used in commercial businesses, government agencies, and other enterprises.

Each section was written with the assumption that you have mastered the materials of the preceding sections. Similarly, each unit is built on the assumption that you have mastered the preceding units. Because such assumptions are too important to be left to chance, a mechanism is used to assure both you and the instructor that you are ready to proceed to the next unit. The mechanism is to provide you with a list of the major objectives to be accomplished in a unit. This list always appears in the first section and should be studied carefully before proceeding to subsequent sections. Not only does this let you know what to look for as you progress through the unit, but at the end of the unit you will be tested on your mastery of these objectives. Typically, the tests will require from 1 to 3 hours of written/oral responses and laboratory demonstration work. If you pass both the written and laboratory portions of the test with 80% accuracy in the time allotted, you have a sufficient grasp of both the concepts and the techniques of applying these concepts to proceed to the next unit. If you do not pass both portions under these conditions, do not be disappointed. Just study the materials again and practice working the problems and experiments until you do pass. For most people the quickest and easiest path to proficiency in digital systems (this means knowing the state of the art *and* knowing how to keep abreast of the changes in the field) is through a highly structured and cumulative learning process. On any such path the important thing is to ensure that the number of times you stumble and fall is at least one less than the number of times you get back up and try again.

You can decrease your chances of being one of the casualties if you remember to avoid a few of the more popular temptations. First, do not waste too much time looking for quick-and-easy shortcuts to doing anything meaningful with computers or any other form of digital system. A hobbyist can have a lot of fun with only a superficial knowledge of the subject matter. However, a serious student may well find himself or herself in a position of responsibility where lives and property depend upon a thorough knowledge of the chosen field and the ability to analyze problems quickly under pressure. Performance under those kinds of conditions is a part of the challenge of working with digital systems, regardless of whether you work in a hospital's intensive care

unit, in a ship's navigation and control room, in a plant manufacturing volatile chemicals, or with any of countless other applications that depend upon automation. Learn your field well one step at a time. Do not be overly concerned if you occasionally fail to pass a test because you "know the material but 'froze' on the test." We all do that from time to time. But do not go on to the next unit! Not until you have gone over the material several more times and have retaken and passed the test. Also, do not be overly concerned if you occasionally fail to pass a test because you "knew the material but just couldn't 'communicate' it all in that short test period." We all do that from time to time, too. But once again, do not go on to the next unit until you have gone over the material several more times and have retaken and passed the test. Do not forget that both pressure and time constraints go with the job and, in the face of both, you must be able to think, to function, and to communicate. Fortunately for all of us, no one is born knowing how to do all these things. We learn these behaviors or, in the case of those of us who really have trouble with freezing on tests and getting rattled under time constraints, it is more correct to say that we "overlearn" them. In other words, if all other factors are equal, the individuals who are the least likely to freeze or rattle are those who learned and then repeatedly studied and practiced the material after it was learned. That is, they "overlearn." Not only does overlearning improve your ability to think, function, and communicate under pressure, but it also aids retention, depth of comprehension, and self-confidence. With this in mind, let us begin our work in this second level of digital systems. Please study the following list of objectives for this unit.

Objectives of Unit I

After reading the Preface, studying the material of this unit, and reviewing the fundamentals of digital logic, you should be able to correctly perform each of the following objectives using only a power supply, a collection of commonly available ICs, an oscilloscope or logic probe, and the notes and data obtained while studying this unit.

1. Briefly explain the meaning of each of the following terms and concepts as it applies to the study of MSI, LSI, IO, and modular memory systems. When terms/concepts are grouped after a letter of the alphabet and separated by "vs.," interpret this as "versus" and take care not only to explain the meaning of each term/concept in the group but to do so in a manner that clearly distinguishes the meaning of each term from that of the other terms in the group.

a. Memory
b. SSI vs. MSI vs. LSI
c. Module vs. system
d. Memory chips vs. memory module vs. modular memory system
e. Primary storage (main memory) vs. secondary storage (mass memory) vs. intermediate storage (scratch pad)
f. Combinational logic vs. sequential logic
g. Memory cell vs. static memory chip vs. dynamic memory chip
h. Volatile vs. nonvolatile
i. Fixed program memory vs. sequential access memory vs. random access read/write memory
j. Cycle time vs. location vs. word
k. Hardware vs. software
l. Microcomputer vs. device controller vs. multitasking operating system
m. ANSI
n. *N*-tuple

2. Explain why a systems approach to analyzing problems is more necessary with MSI and LSI than with SSI.

3. What is the hierarchy of memory in a computer memory system, and why are the levels ranked in this manner? Comment on the cost of memories in modern computer systems relative to other units of computer hardware.

4. List at least four types of information that are typically stored in memory to be processed by the computer.

5. Given any five numbers in any combination of radix 10, radix 16, radix 8, or radix 2, quickly convert to each of the other radixes.

6. Give the symbol and the truth table for each of the following gates and gating combinations. (Use a maximum of two inputs for any gate.) Connect the circuitry and demonstrate the truth of your tables (AND, OR, NOT, NAND, NOR, Exclusive-OR).

7. Give the truth table for a full adder. Connect the circuitry and demonstrate the truth of your table.

8. Give the truth table for (a) an SR flip-flop made from NORs; (b) an SR flip-flop made from NANDs. Connect the circuitry and demonstrate the truth of your tables.

9. Give the truth table for a JK flip-flop. Draw the additional circuitry to make it a type D. Draw the additional circuitry to make (a) an octal up-counter; (b) an octal down-counter; (c)

a 3-bit shift register; (d) a 3-bit ring counter. Connect the circuitry and demonstrate that your answers are correct.

10. List correctly in your own words the major precautions for handling MOS circuitry. Explain why these precautions are so much more important to remember as you progress through this book than they were when you were studying the fundamentals of digital logic circuits.

LIST OF EQUIPMENT AND COMPONENTS USED IN UNIT I

Equipment:

Oscilloscope: dc-coupled, 10-MHz BW
Power supply: 5 V dc at 1 A

Commonly used logic circuits (see Appendix G):

4   bounceless input switches
6   LED indicators

Components:

1   7400   quad 2-input NAND
1   7402   quad 2-input NOR
1   7404   hex NOT
1   7408   quad 2-input AND
1   7420   dual 4-input NAND
1   7421   dual 4-input AND
1   7427   triple 3-input NOR
1   7432   quad 2-input OR
1   7480   full adder
1   7486   quad XOR
2   7473   dual JK flip-flops

KEY TERMS AND CONCEPTS

Hopefully, you have read the Preface to this book and meet the suggested criteria for beginning our study of MSI, LSI, IO, and modular memory systems. This book assumes that you have already mastered fundamental concepts and techniques of digital logic. Therefore, let us examine the relationship of each of these newer terms to the digital logic we are already familiar with.

In its simplest form, memory in a digital system (also called "storage") refers to any device into which information (data) can be entered, retained, accessed, and retrieved for future use. Therefore, a paper tape punched by a Teletype or a cassette containing data written by a computer are both forms of memory. Since both of these devices store the data in a medium that is not directly readable by our electronic digital gates, they are often referred to as secondary memory, secondary storage, or auxiliary storage. (That is, the holes in the paper tape medium and the magnetic fields on the cassette tape medium must first be translated into the appropriate logic 0 and logic 1 voltage levels before they are readable by our elecronic digital gates.)

Our principal concern in this book is with devices that store data which are directly readable by our electronic digital gates and registers. Today, this typically implies a "semiconductor" memory. These solid-state devices can be purchased in integrated circuit form and, depending upon the organization of the circuitry, can store logic 1's and logic 0's in such a manner that single bit or group of bits can be accessed and retrieved. Such integrated circuits can be grouped to form the "primary memory" (also called "main memory" or "primary storage") of a modern digital system. A smaller number of the faster integrated circuit memory chips may be grouped to form the "intermediate storage" or "intermediate memory" of a digital system. By contrast to the larger, slower, and less expensive primary memory, where beginning values and ending values of calculations and operations may be stored, the intermediate memory is a smaller, faster, and typically more expensive high-speed scratch pad that may be used for temporary storage of intermediate values that occur during a calculation routine or other operation.

It is in the study of these semiconductor memory chips that we may be reminded of the relationship of memory to digital logic. You may recall that there are two types of digital logic: combinational and sequential. In combinational logic the output at any time t is a function of the combination of binary inputs (called an N-tuple) at that time t. However, in sequential logic the output at any time t is a function of both the present combination of binary inputs *and* the "memory" of past combination(s). One of the first sequential circuits you studied was the SR flip-flop. This bistable is expanded by additional gating and circuitry to form clocked SRs, JKs, and type D's. When today's semiconductor memory chips rely on such bistables as their storage cells (a memory cell is the smallest subdivision of memory that can be used to retain data for later access and retrieval), the chips are said to be "static memory chips." Because of their importance in modern digital systems, this book will place a heavy emphasis on static memories. Dynamic memories (which store data in their cells capacitively) are covered in Appendix C.

As you might expect from your prior experiences with bistables, the static memory chips suffer from being "volatile." That is, if the power supply voltage is removed and later restored, the chips retain no memory of what was going on before power was removed. In a later unit we shall study techniques of protecting volatile memory against temporary losses of power. Of course, there are nonvolatile memories (such as punched paper tape) where no data are lost if the power is removed. However, there are considerable differences in the respective memory cycle times between the volatile static memory and this non-volatile secondary memory that, among other specifications, help us to decide when each is an appropriate choice for use. (A read cycle time is the interval of time between the start and the end of the cycle which accesses the intended memory cell or cells and retrieves the information stored there. Similarly, a write cycle time is the time interval between the start and the end of the cycle which accesses the intended cell or cells and stores new information in the cell or cells. Cycle times and other comparative specifications will be covered in more depth later in the book.)

Primary and intermediate memories can be classified into three categories, based upon the method of accessing the data and what can be done to modify the data stored in the memories. One category is the fixed program memory to be studied in Unit III. The contents of memories in this category are not intended to be altered during normal operation. These are sometimes referred to as read-only memories (ROMs). Another category is the sequential access memory, which will be studied in Unit IV. In this category, data access is limited to passing through a fixed sequence of locations. In other words, if you have just retrieved the contents of location "n" and now need to retrieve the contents of "n + 20," there are 19 locations that will have to be accessed in sequential order before you arrive at the one containing the data you are interested in. Shift registers are an example of sequential access memories. The third category of memory is the random access read/write memory (RAM), which we will study in Unit V. The contents of memories in this category can be accessed in any order for either retrieval or storage of new information with similar access time for each location.

We started this section with the announced intention of introducing some key terms and concepts that would help relate our study of MSI, LSI, IO, and modular memory systems to the digital logic we have previously studied. Thus far our efforts have centered around the word "memory." We have defined it and related it to sequential logic; primary, secondary, and intermediate storage; and static semiconductor memory chips. We have identified three categories of memory and introduced considerations such as cycle time and volatility. Now let us consider some of the other words in the title of our book and see how they relate to digital circuits we are already familiar with. For example, the introduction to experiments in modern digital logic circuits is typically studied using SSI. That is, we use small-scale integrated circuit chips where each chip contains a maximum of 10 gates (some sources prefer to use 12 or less for the term SSI) or circuitry of similar complexity. MSI refers to medium-scale integrated circuitry, where each chip contains more than 10 (or 12) but less than 100 gates or circuitry of similar complexity. LSI refers to large-scale integrated circuitry, where each chip contains 100 or more gates or circuitry of similar complexity. (Some sources now prefer to limit the term "LSI" to values of 100 to 1000 gates and to use the term "VLSI" for very-large-scale integrated circuits of 1000 or more gates.) In this book we shall study some MSI memories in Units III and IV and some LSI (and VLSI) memories in Units V and VI. Interestingly enough, the emergence of MSI and LSI memories have done a great deal to stimulate the increased production of SSI chips. This is partly because the larger chips have to "interface" with other chips in the system. That is, there must be a boundary that enables the appropriate chips to exchange information. Because of timing, loading, and drive requirements, SSI is often used to construct this boundary or interface circuitry. We shall study interface problems in Unit II.

Thus far we have examined the word "memory" and the acronyms (words formed by combining initial letters) MSI and LSI. At first glimpse it would appear that MSI and LSI are simply larger versions of SSI. However, this is deceptive. As we shall discover later in the book, the techniques for using MSI and LSI require much more of a "systems" approach than does SSI. (A "system" is a group of interdependent elements acting together to accomplish a predetermined purpose.) That is, a MSI or LSI chip may have eight inputs and four outputs. Between those points may be 50 or 500 gates. If just one of those gates is destroyed, the task of finding the problem and deciding upon the appropriate action is made more challenging by the fact that you do not have physical access to most of the interconnections between gates and the intermediate gates' outputs. Furthermore, it is entirely possible that out of the 256 possible input combinations (eight inputs provide 256 possible N-tuples), only one N-tuple causes an error in any of the four outputs. This could mean that a large system could function correctly most of the time with irritating, perhaps fatal transient errors that come and go whenever the N-tuple occurs. Since the cause is usually gone by the time we look for it, we sometimes refer to these problems as "ghosts." Finding such problems without a systems approach would be a lengthy (if not a "lucky") process. With a systems approach it can become a "science."

The American National Standards Institute (ANSI) defines a circuit module as "A packaged functional hardware unit designed for use with other components." In spite of the fact that with each month that passes, manufacturers of integrated circuits seem to find ways to package more and more memory cells into a single chip, industry's needs for larger and larger memories is growing at an even faster rate. Because of this dilemma, a single memory chip used by itself will seldom contain enough memory cells to satisfy the requirements of even a small digital system. Therefore, we frequently take a collection of these chips and organize them to meet the ANSI definition of "module." For example, one popular chip is the 2102, which contains 1024 cells that can be randomly accessed for retrieval or storage. One of the popular minicomputers is built to process 12 bits of information at a time. To construct a memory of 12-bit words [a "word" is a group of "characters" to be accessed as a unit and retrieved (and stored if it is a RAM) as a unit], we could organize 12 of the 2102 static RAMs so that each chip provided one cell of the 12-bit word at any of the 1024 accessible locations. Once such a module is developed, we can add more of these "1K" memory modules to the system as needed. (Note that 1024, which is 2^{10}, is commonly referred to as "1K" in discussing memory modules.) Similarly, we could develop 1K (or any other size) modules of fixed program memory and we could also develop modules of sequential access memory of any desirable size. If our memory needs are large enough, we may even need to develop interface modules which can be added as needed. For any digital system, that portion of the hardware and the software (definitions are provided in the Glossary of Appendix F) that relate to the organization and control of the memory is referred to as the memory system (or "subsystem"). Today, we prefer to use a modular memory system as the most-cost-effective way to meet both the current and the future memory needs of a digital system. In Units V and VI we shall study ways of organizing and using modular memories.

After all this discussion on memories, you might be wondering what kinds of systems are the principal users of these modules. Well, as you might expect, the principal use is in computers and computer peripherals. However, as was pointed out in the Preface, there are a great many applications that do not require a computer. For example, certain "games" for home television sets and certain items of electronic test equipment have been marketed for some time that do not contain a computer but do utilize memory. Since the price of microprocessors continues to drop and their performance capabilities continue to grow, it is probable that these games and test equipment will be modified to a "microcomputer" status in the future. (A microcomputer is a microprocessor plus memory.) In fact, one of the main reasons for studying modular memories is their relative expense in a computer system. Memory is now the second-most-expensive portion of a typical computer system. (It is second only to the cost of the computer peripherals.) It is also potentially one of the biggest performance "bottlenecks," since it typically operates at slower speeds than asynchronous processors can. Therefore, our time and attention in this area are very important if we are to evolve more-cost-effective computer systems.

Since computer systems are the principal consumers for memories, we might ask about the relative importance of certain types of memories in the hierarchy of the memory system. Most important is main memory (or primary storage), because this is the memory that can be accessed directly by the operating registers of the computer for retrieval or storage of information. Second in the hierarchy is intermediate storage. This is the scratch pad needed by the computer to calculate and retain intermediate results while performing its own calculations. Unlike primary storage, which the computer user is interested in since it contains beginning and ending results, intermediate storage is often "transparent" to the user. That is, the user neither knows nor cares what intermediate sums, products, quotients, and so on, occurred during the execution of the program. He or she is merely interested in the end results. Third in the hierarchy is secondary storage, because this provides a cheaper form of mass storage than primary memory. Typically, when the computer needs to operate upon information that is in secondary storage (such as on a disk), the computer will request that the information be copied into primary storage from secondary storage so that it can be directly accessed by the computer's operating registers. After operations on this information have been completed, the computer can then ask for the next blocks to be copied into main memory from the disk or can copy the newly resulted information out to the disk. In Unit VI we shall see how such transfers take place.

A logical question at this point might inquire as to what kinds of "information" the memory system stores for the computer. Well, the memory system is used to store computer programs, the data to be manipulated by the programs, special computer languages, operating procedures for the computer, and so on. Since not all programs, data, languages, operating procedures, and so on, have to be directly accessible to the computer at the same time, you can see how the contents of primary memory can be "rolled out" to secondary storage until they are needed again, while the blocks of information that are needed at that time are "rolled in." Some of the peripherals that support these operations include disk, drum, magnetic tape units, paper tape devices, and punched card devices. Typically, these roll-in/roll-out transfers can be handled by a device controller (a far simpler machine than the computer), which frees the computer to switch its attention to another task that is more deserving of its time and talents than would be a simple transfer of blocks of information from secondary to primary storage, or vice versa. When the transfer is completed by the "less-capable" device controller, the computer can be notified so that it can switch back to the original task whenever it is ready to do so. (A collection of software modules called the "operating system" is responsible for managing the resources needed to execute these tasks.) Both device controllers and multitasking operating systems are examined in more detail in Unit VI.

This concludes the overview of key terms and concepts. In the next six units we shall add considerable flesh to this skeleton framework. Since the next section contains a brief review of some of the more important topics from your previous studies in digital circuit fundamentals, you may want to reread your objectives for this unit before proceeding. This may cause you to decide to reread this section if too many of the terms appear to be new to you. Of all the sections in the book, this one is probably the "driest" and least interesting. After all, our intent was to introduce some key terms and concepts that can be committed to memory now so that in subsequent units, as each concept is fully developed and applied, you can relate it not only to digital circuit fundamentals but also to the overall framework we have just constructed for the study of MSI, LSI, IO, and modular memory systems. Congratulations on starting this study. Your worst section is already behind you.

A REVIEW OF DIGITAL LOGIC FUNDAMENTALS

This portion of the unit is intended to review some of the most frequently used concepts and techniques from your previous study of digital logic fundamentals. All of these are considered to be essential "fingertip" concepts and techniques for beginning your study of MSI, LSI, IO, and modular memory systems. "Fingertip" means that you should know the material from memory without having to consult reference sources. In fact, you should have "overlearned" the material so well that it comes to you quickly and easily even under pressure and you are able to work with both the concepts and the physical circuitry while communicating clearly to others exactly what is happening and why. In a responsible position in digital systems work, it is not enough just to be able to communicate so that others can understand you. While under pressure and time constraints that may endanger lives and property, you must be able to communicate so clearly that your coworkers cannot possibly misunderstand you. Practice this review material until you feel it is permanently at your fingertips.

1. Figure I-0(a) gives some techniques and examples for quickly converting straight-code radix x whole numbers to straight-code radix 10 whole numbers, and vice versa. Study these techniques and examples. Practice making up your own radix 10, straight-code whole numbers to be converted to radix x via the quotient–remainder technique. Check your work by applying the multiply–add technqiue to the radix x value to convert back to radix 10.

2. Figure I-0(b) shows techniques and examples for quickly converting straight-code numbers between radix 16 (hexadecimal), radix 8 (octal), and radix 2 (binary). Study these techniques and examples. Practice making up your own problems. You can apply the multiply–add technique to check the whole-number problems.

3. Figure I-0(d) shows the definitions, symbols, and truth tables for the three major gates and three of the most popular gating combinations. Practice writing these definitions, symbols, and truth tables from memory and practice connecting the circuitry and demonstrating the truth of the tables to others while communicating to them what is going on and why. Use the LED indicators and the multiple input connection techniques shown in Figure I-0(c) as necessary for your demonstration.

4. Figure I-0(e) shows the truth table, block symbol, and the circuitry for a full adder. Practice writing the truth table, and connecting and demonstrating the truth of your table.

5. Figure I-0(f) shows the truth tables for a set–reset flip-flop made from NORs and NANDs. Practice writing the truth tables, and connecting and demonstrating the truth of the tables.

6. Figure I-0(g) shows the block symbol and the truth table for a JK flip-flop. Also shown are the truth tables and additional circuitry to make a JK behave as a type D bistable. Practice writing these truth tables, and connecting and demonstrating the truth of these tables.

7. Figure I-0(h) shows the interconnections of JKs and type D's to make a hexadecimal up-counter, a hexadecimal down-

A Review of Digital Logic Fundamentals:

A straight-code radix x number fits the form

$$(\cdots c_2 c_1 c_0 \quad c_{-1} c_{-2} \cdots) \, RX$$

whole number part ↟ fractional part

radix point

and can be evaluated by $\quad \cdots + c_2 \cdot x^2 + c_1 \cdot x^1 + c_0 \cdot x^1 + c_{-1} \cdot x^{-1} + \cdots$

MULTIPLY-ADD

To convert any radix x, straight-code whole number (x not equal to 10) to its whole number radix 10, straight-code equivalent, use multiply/add. Begin by multiplying the most significant digit (MSD) of the radix x whole number by x. Add the product to the next digit on the right. Multiply this sum by x. Continue this multiply-add procedure until you add to the least significant digit (LSD) of the whole number part.

As an example, convert $(372)_8$ to its radix 10 equivalent. By the definition of straight code, the answer can be found as $(3 \times 8^2 + 2 \times 8^1 + 7 \times 8^0) = (215)_{10}$. Now, in the interest of speed, let us apply the multiply-add shortcut.

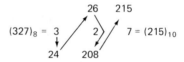

We begin by multiplying the MSD 3 by the radix 8. The product is 24. This product is added to the next digit, which contains a 2. The resulting sum is 26, and is multiplied by the radix 8, which gives a product of 208. This product will be added to the final digit, which contains a 7. The sum is 215 and since it was obtained by adding to the least significant digit we record this as our final answer. With practice, this method will prove considerably faster than application of the straight-code definition.

Let us try another example. First, verify that the binary number $(1011)_2$ is equivalent to the radix 10 number $(11)_{10}$. Now let us apply the multiply-add technique to convert this number.

$$(1011)_2 = 1 \quad 0 \quad 1 \quad 1 = (11)_{10}$$

We begin by multiplying the most significant digit 1 by the radix 2. One times 2 results in 2. This product is added to the next digit 0 to give a sum of 2. The sum 2 is multiplied by the radix 2 to give a product of 4. This product is added to the next digit 1 to obtain a sum of 5. This is multiplied by the radix 2 to give a product 10. This product is added to the least significant digit 1 to obtain the final answer of 11 in radix 10.

Note that this shortcut applies only to whole-number conversion from radix x to radix 10. Thus so far, we have ignored the problem of converting from radix 10 to its straight-code equivalent in another radix. The shortcut for this type of whole-number conversion is referred to as the quotient-remainder method.

FIGURE I-0 Review of key concepts in digital logic.

QUOTIENT-REMAINDER

To convert a whole number in radix 10 straight-code to a whole number in radix x straight-code (where x is not equal to 10), use quotient-remainder. Divide the radix 10 number by x. Record the quotient and the remainder. The first remainder will be the least significant digit (LSD) of the answer. Bring down the quotient. Divide the quotient by x. Record the new quotient and the new remainder. Bring down the new quotient and divide by x. Record the quotient and remainder. Continue this process untill the new quotient is less than x. Record this quotient as the final remainder, or MSD, of the answer.

Let us examine a problem utilizing this technique. We have already established that $(372)_8$ ie equivalent to $(215)_{10}$. Let us see how the quotient-remainder technique will verify this equivalence. Record the 215 as a number over 8.

$$
\begin{array}{llll}
 & & Q & R \\
(215)_{10} = \dfrac{215}{8} & = & 26 & 7 \longleftarrow \text{LSD} \\
26/8 & = & 3 & 2 \qquad\qquad = (327)_8 \\
3/8 & = & 0 & 3 \longleftarrow \text{MSD}
\end{array}
$$

According to the definition, we divide 215 by the radix 8. This yields a quotient of 26 with a remainder of 7. This 7 is the LSD of our answer. We then divide the quotient 26 by our radix 8 obtaining a new quotient of 3 with the remainder of 2. We divide our quotient 3 by radix 8 obtaining a quotient of 0 with a remainder of 3. The 0 in the quotient column tells us we have reached the MSD. The answer is $(327)_8$.

Thus we have shown that quotient-remainder and multiply-add are sufficient shortcuts to the manipulation of whole numbers from one radix straight-code to another radix straight-code using radix 10 as an intermediary. Speed will come with practice.

(a) Multiply-add and quotient-remainder techniques

DIRECT CONVERSIONS BETWEEN BINARY, OCTAL, AND HEXADECIMAL

The table below shows the octal character set and the list of three binary bits equal in value to each character. For example $(7)_8 = (111)_2$, $(6)_8 = (110)_2$, ..., $(0)_8 = (000)_2$.

Since these numbers are all in straight code, we can convert directly from radix 8 to radix 2, by replacing each octal character by its equivalent value in three binary digits. Thus $(704)_8$ becomes $(111, 000, 100)_2$ and $(521)_8$ becomes $(101, 010, 001)_2$. Note that each octal character was replaced by its 3-bit equivalent from the table.

The table also shows the hexadecimal character set and then the list of 4 binary bits equal in value to each character. For example, $(F)_{16} = (1111)_2$, $(E)_{16} = (1110)_2, \cdots (0)_{16} = (0000)_2$.

Since these numbers are all in straight code we can convert directly from radix 16 to radix 2 by replacing each hexadecimal character by the equivalent value in four binary digits. Thus $(F09)_{16}$ becomes $(1111, 0000, 1001)_2$. Note that the commas were inserted simply to call your attention to the fact that F became 1111, 0 became 0000, and 9 became 1001.

FIGURE I-0 (continued)

Conversion table

$(X)_{16}$	2^4	2^2	2^1	2^0	$(X)_{10}$
0	0	0	0	0	0
1	0	0	0	1	1
2	0	0	1	0	2
3	0	0	1	1	3
4	0	1	0	0	4
5	0	1	0	1	5
6	0	1	1	0	6
7	0	1	1	1	7
8	1	0	0	0	
9	1	0	0	1	
A	1	0	1	0	
B	1	0	1	1	
C	1	1	0	0	
D	1	1	0	1	
E	1	1	1	0	
F	1	1	1	1	

Examples of direct conversion:

$(470)_8 =$
$(100, 111, 000)_2$

$(123)_{16} =$
$(0001, 0010, 0011)_2$

$(123)_8 =$
$(001, 010, 011)_2$

$(F1B)_{16} =$
$(1111, 0001, 1011)_2$

$(4700)_{16} =$
$(0100, 0111, 0000, 0000)_2$

(b) Direct conversions between binary, octal, and hexadecimal

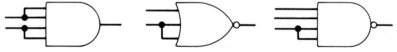

Techniques for converting multiinput gates and combinations to a smaller number of inputs

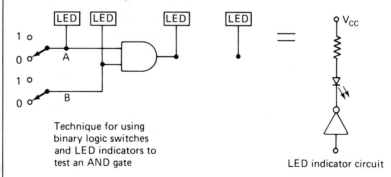

Technique for using
binary logic switches
and LED indicators to
test an AND gate

LED indicator circuit

(c) Test connection techniques

FIGURE I-0 (continued)

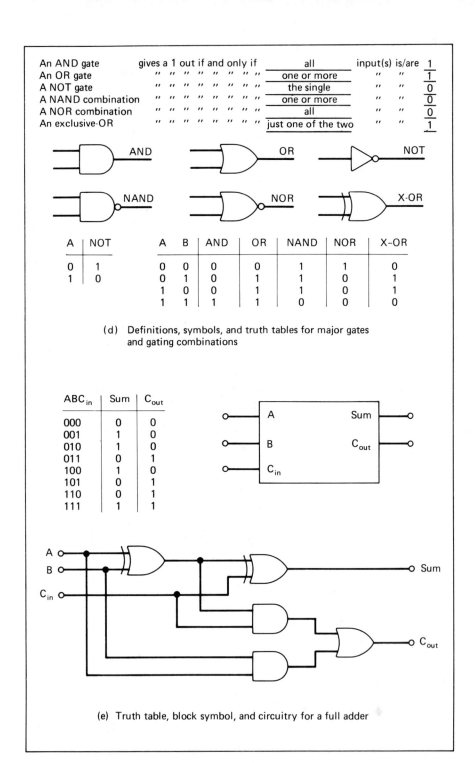

An AND gate gives a 1 out if and only if all input(s) is/are 1
An OR gate " " " " " " " " one or more " " 1
A NOT gate " " " " " " " " the single " " 0
A NAND combination " " " " " " " " one or more " " 0
A NOR combination " " " " " " " " all " " 0
An exclusive-OR " " " " " " " " just one of the two " " 1

AND   OR   NOT

NAND   NOR   X-OR

A	NOT
0	1
1	0

A	B	AND	OR	NAND	NOR	X-OR
0	0	0	0	1	1	0
0	1	0	1	1	0	1
1	0	0	1	1	0	1
1	1	1	1	0	0	0

(d) Definitions, symbols, and truth tables for major gates and gating combinations

ABC_{in}	Sum	C_{out}
000	0	0
001	1	0
010	1	0
011	0	1
100	1	0
101	0	1
110	0	1
111	1	1

A   Sum
B C_{out}
C_{in}

A
B
C_{in}
Sum
C_{out}

(e) Truth table, block symbol, and circuitry for a full adder

FIGURE I-0 (continued)

16

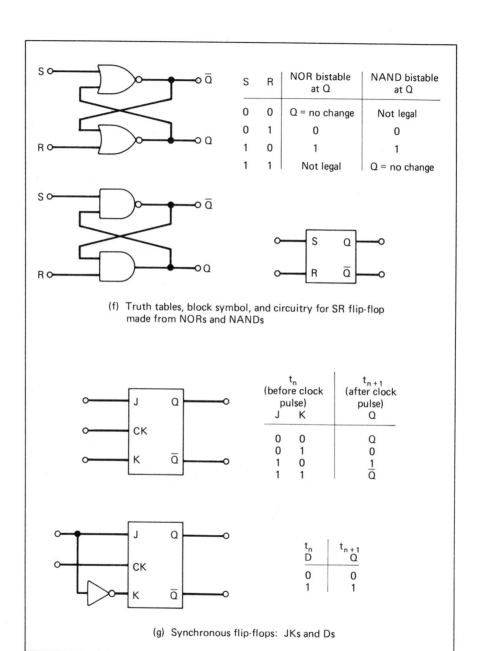

S	R	NOR bistable at Q	NAND bistable at Q
0	0	Q = no change	Not legal
0	1	0	0
1	0	1	1
1	1	Not legal	Q = no change

(f) Truth tables, block symbol, and circuitry for SR flip-flop made from NORs and NANDs

t_n (before clock pulse)		t_{n+1} (after clock pulse)
J	K	Q
0	0	Q
0	1	0
1	0	1
1	1	$\overline{Q}$

t_n	t_{n+1}
D	Q
0	0
1	1

(g) Synchronous flip-flops: JKs and Ds

FIGURE I-0 (continued)

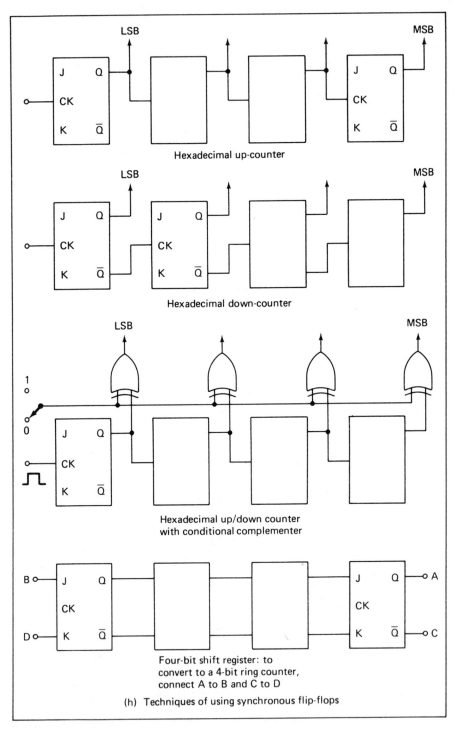

Hexadecimal up-counter

Hexadecimal down-counter

Hexadecimal up/down counter
with conditional complementer

Four-bit shift register: to
convert to a 4-bit ring counter,
connect A to B and C to D

(h) Techniques of using synchronous flip-flops

FIGURE I-0 (continued)

PRECAUTIONS WITH MOS DEVICES

All MOS devices can be ruined by excessive electrostatic charge, such as the charge that builds up on your body as you walk across certain surfaces. For this reason, you should observe the following precautions (Motorola McMOS Handbook, p. 7-1 1974):

1. All MOS devices should be stored or transported in conductive material so that all exposed leads are shorted together. MOS devices must not be inserted into conventional plastic "snow" or plastic trays of the type used for the storage and transportation of other semiconductor devices.
2. All MOS devices should be placed on a grounded bench surface and the operators should ground themselves prior to handling devices. This is done most effectively by having the operator wear a conductive wrist strap. Ground yourself by wrapping a length of conductive foil or wire mesh around your wrist (perhaps under your watch or bracelet). Connect the mesh to a 1-MΩ resistor. Terminate the free end of the resistor at a cold-water pipe if you are sure that metallic plumbing joints are used. Otherwise, connect it to the grounding screw of an electrical outlet.
3. Nylon clothing should not be worn while handling MOS circuits. Wear only antistatic clothing, such as cotton when working with MOS devices. (Synthetics readily build up static charges.)
4. Do not insert or remove MOS devices from test sockets with power applied. Check all power supplies to be used for testing MOS devices and be certain there are no voltage transients present. Always install an MOS device immediately into its circuit after removal from its protective carrier and replace it in the carrier immediately after removal from the circuit. Try to avoid touching the leads. Always install MOS devices last.
5. When lead straightening or hand soldering is necessary, provide ground straps for the apparatus used. To ground your soldering pencil, use heavy solid wire (not stranded) around the tip. Most soldering irons with a three-prong plug already have a grounded tip.
6. Do not exceed the maximum electrical voltage ratings specified by the manufacturer.
7. Double check test equipment setup for proper polarity or voltage before conducting parametric or functional testing.
8. All unused device inputs should be connected to V_{DD} or V_{SS}.
9. All power should be turned off before printed circuit boards containing MOS devices are inserted or removed.
10. All printed circuit boards containing MOS devices should be provided with shorting straps across the edge connector when being carried or transported.

(i) Precautions with MOS devices

FIGURE I-0 (continued)

counter, a hexadecimal up/down counter with a conditional complementer, a 4-bit shift register, and a 4-bit ring counter. Practice connecting the circuitry and demonstrating their operation.

8. Figure I-0(i) lists the major precautions for handling MOS circuitry. Practice writing and speaking the major precautions in your own words. Most of today's LSI and much of the MSI are made in MOS form.

SAMPLE TEST FOR UNIT I

(Closed book. Closed notes. Use only writing materials, templates, and logic circuitry.)

Part A. Answer eight of the following (selected by your instructor or by a random process).

1. Briefly explain the meaning of each of the following terms and concepts as it applies to the study of MSI, LSI, IO, and modular memory systems. When terms/concepts are grouped after a letter of the alphabet and separated by ''vs.,'' interpret this as "versus" and take care not only to explain the meaning of each term/concept in the group but to do so in a manner that clearly distinguishes the meaning of each term from that of the other terms in the group.
   a. Memory
   b. SSI vs. MSI vs. LSI
   c. Module vs. system
   d. Memory chips vs. memory module vs. modular memory systems
   e. Primary storage (main memory) vs. secondary storage (mass memory) vs. intermediate storage (scratch pad)
   f. Combinational logic vs. sequential logic
   g. Memory cell vs. static memory chip vs. dynamic memory chip
   h. Volatile vs. nonvolatile
   i. Fixed program memory vs. sequential access memory vs. random access read/write memory
   j. Cycle time vs. location vs. word
   k. Hardware vs. software
   l. Microcomputer vs. device controller vs. multitasking operating system
   m. ANSI
   n. *N*-tuple

Part B. Answer two of the following (selected by your instructor or by a random process).

2. Explain why a systems approach to analyzing problems is more necessary with MSI and LSI than with SSI.
3. What is the hierarchy of memory in a computer memory system and why are the levels ranked in this manner? Comment

on the cost of memories in modern computer systems relative to other units of computer hardware.

4. List at least four types of information that are typically stored in memory to be processed by the computer.

5. For the given five numbers in radix 10, radix 16, radix 8, or radix 2, quickly convert each number to each of the other radixes: $(83)_{10}$, $(2C)_{16}$, $(3F)_{16}$, $(57)_8$, $(10001101)_2$.

Part C.   Answer two of the following (selected by your instructor or by a random process).

6. Give the symbol and the truth table for each of the following gates and gating combinations. (Use a maximum of two inputs for any gate.) Connect the circuitry and demonstrate the truth of your tables (AND, OR, NOT, NAND, NOR, Exclusive-OR).

7. Give the truth table for a full adder. Connect the circuitry and demonstrate the truth of your table.

8. Give the truth table for (a) an SR flip-flop made from NORs; (b) an SR flip-flop made from NANDs. Connect the circuitry and demonstrate the truth of your tables.

9. Give the truth table for a JK flip-flop. Draw the additional circuitry to make it a type D. Draw the additional circuitry to make (a) an octal up-counter; (b) an octal down-counter; (c) a 3-bit shift register; (d) a 3-bit ring counter. Connect the circuitry and demonstrate that your answers are correct.

Part D.   Answer the following.

10. List in your own words the major precautions for handling MOS circuitry. Explain why these precautions are so much more important to remember as you progress through this book than they were when you were studying the fundamentals of digital logic circuits.

Memory Interfacing:
buses, bus connections,
timing and controls,
temporary storage,
input-output transfers,
demultiplexing, multiplexing,
and sequencing

INTRODUCTION

As mentioned in the overview in Unit I, there are three categories of memory functions: sequential access, read/write, and fixed program. For any of these three functions to be accomplished, there must be an "interface" to link the memory to other portions of the system. Since this interface is a shared boundary between the memory and other portions of the system, it must be designed with electronic components that provide protection to the circuitry on either side of the interface and yet facilitate the exchange of signals and information. In this unit we study the elements that typically comprise the memory interface.

In the author's opinion, the study of memory functions and memory interfacing can be made both easier and more meaningful by frequent references to real-world examples. With this in mind, refer briefly to Figure II-0.

This figure represents a portion of a computer-controlled system

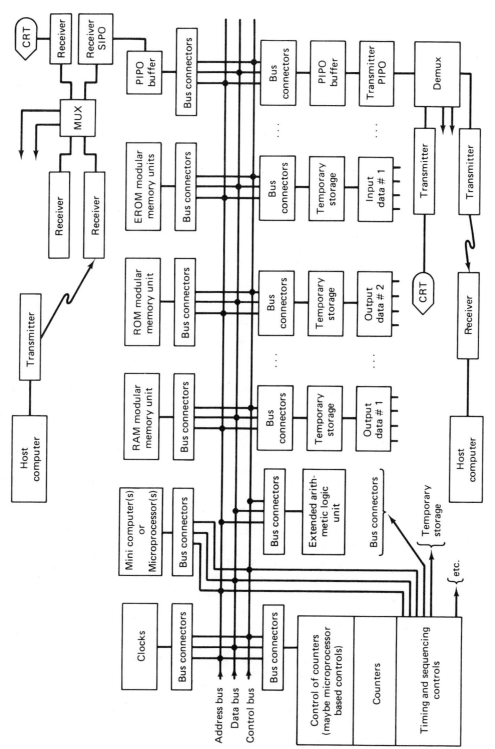

FIGURE II-0 Remote terminal unit.

23

commonly referred to as a remote terminal unit (RTU). In such a system a central computer or computers called the "host" or "master" is responsible for communicating with and coordinating the activities of a number of remotely located RTUs. These remote terminal units may themselves contain one or more minicomputers or, more recently, one or more microprocessors. The host computer(s) is typically a larger, general-purpose computer that:

1. Performs special computation and reporting on data provided by all the RTUs.
2. Supervises the dialogue with the RTUs and provides occasional help on an "as demanded" basis. (For example, if the computer in an RTU fails, the host may assume command and perform the work of the RTU computer until it is repaired and restored to service.)

The remote terminal units, on the other hand, contain special-purpose computers and microprocessors that are "optimized" for the process monitoring and control tasks they are assigned to. The RTUs are usually placed as close to the "action" (the process being monitored and controlled) as possible and are actually in charge of the routine control functions associated with the process. However, if changes in the process begin to overload the RTU or possibly to require special "nonroutine" decisions and actions, the RTU can rely on help from the host for its other processing needs.

Such computer-controlled systems are used in a number of environments. In oil fields and factories, remote terminal units are located at the process or portion of a process they are responsible for (such as pumping stations, assembly lines, etc.) The host computer coordinates the activities of all the RTUs to ensure a completed product. In the cities, the remote terminal units may be located at the electrical power substations scattered throughout the city. The host probably resides at the main power plant. In a separate computer-controlled system, the traffic lights of key sections of the city may be monitored and controlled by RTUs. The host is then responsible for city-wide coordination and control of traffic flow through the RTUs. Such systems can reduce traffic jams, clear paths for emergency vehicles, and regulate the flow of traffic under adverse road conditions by transmitting traffic advisories to electronic street signs, thereby changing the ratio of red-light time to green-light time on major arteries.

Whether we consider the host or the RTU, both contain several applications of memories and memory interfaces. Throughout the next four units of this book, we shall refer back to Figure II-0 and use it to facilitate our studies. For example, in this figure are blocks identified as

PIPO buffers. In Unit IV, we shall study the theory and operation of PIPOs. However, to appreciate the importance of these circuits, we need a frame of reference. That is, we need to know why, where, when, and how PIPOs are used within a system. In addition to their use in RTUs, you will also study other applications of these devices as you progress through this book. However, Figure II-0 is the "common denominator" from which our studies will typically begin.

As shown in Figure II-0, systems employing memory units are typically constructed around "buses." Buses are defined collections of conductors used in the transfer of information from one of a number of information sources to one or more designated destinations. There are three major functions of buses—address, data, and control—to select the address of the destinations (such as the transmitter) that the source (such as the microprocessor) wishes to communicate with and to coordinate and control the input or output transfer of data (commonly referred to as an IOT).

Since only one source can be permitted to use the data bus and address bus at any given time, the timing and control of bus activities is a logical beginning point for our study of interfacing. Accordingly, our first experiments in this unit deal with the operations and controls of the counter circuits from which we derive our timing and sequencing controls. Locate this block in Figure II-0. Notice that signals from this block are routed to bus connection blocks, temporary storage blocks, multiplexers, and other interface elements. By the completion of this unit, you should have accomplished the following objectives.

Objectives of Unit II

For each of the following concepts in memory interfaces:

1. Explain the meaning of each of the following terms.
    a. Asynchronous counter lines to control master reset and parallel load operations
    b. Synchronous counter lines to control up/down counting
    c. Counter presets, rollovers, cascades, carries, and borrows
    d. Buses
    e. Bus connections
    f. Temporary storage
    g. Three major bus functions
    h. Source and destination
    i. Three-state bus connections
    j. Latches
    k. Tracking and holding
    l. Demultiplexers

       m. Multiplexers

       n. Sequencers

       o. Schmitt-trigger logic

2. Explain, draw, connect, and demonstrate the circuitry to preset a counter within three increments of roll over, increment four times, and decrement five times.

3. Explain the use of the address and enable lines of a demultiplexer to transmit information from a single source to destination (5)R16. Draw, connect, and demonstrate the circuitry necessary to accomplish this.

4. Explain the use of a counter, sequencer, bus connector, and temporary storage to quickly load new information and retain it long enough for a "slow" device to respond to. Draw, connect, and demonstrate the circuitry necessary to accomplish this.

5. Pass a closed-book, closed-note, written/laboratory exam over the material of this unit with at least 80% accuracy.

6. Explain the relationship of each of the topics in this unit to the remote terminal unit of Figure II-0.

LIST OF EQUIPMENT AND COMPONENTS
USED IN UNIT II

Equipment:

Oscilloscope: dc-Coupled, 10-MHz BW

Power supply: 5 V dc at 1 A

Commonly used logic circuits (see Appendix G):

4 bounceless input switches

6 LED indicators

6 SPDT input switches

Components:

1	7404	hex NOT
1	7408	quad 2-input AND
1	7475	quad D flip-flops
1	74154	4-to-16 line decoder/demultiplexer
2	74125	quad three-state drivers
2	74193	4-bit up/down counter

PROBLEMS AND EXPERIMENTS

Counters: Controls and Operations

Objectives: By the end of these experiments and the associated problems, you should be able to correctly perform each of the following objectives using only a power supply, logic circuitry, and the notes and data obtained from conducting these experiments.

1. Explain the meaning of "asynchronous counter lines to control master reset and parallel-load operations."
2. Explain the use of the counter's load and clear lines typically encountered in master reset and parallel-load operations. Draw and explain the truth table for the 74193 when used in such operations.
3. Draw and connect the circuitry necessary to demonstrate master reset and parallel loading. Explain the procedural steps and demonstrate how to clear the counter, parallel-load an (A)R16, and then disable subsequent changes on the preset lines from affecting the Q points.
4. Explain the meaning of "asynchronous in conjunction with synchronous counter lines to control up/down counting."
5. Explain the use of the counter's Load, Clear, Up Clock, and Down Clock lines as typically encountered in up counting and in down counting. Draw and explain the truth table for the 74193 when used in such operations.
6. Explain the meaning of the following terms as they apply to up/down counting: rollover, carry, and borrow outputs; cascade counters; counter presets; illegal condition.
7. Draw and connect the circuitry necessary to cascade counters to demonstrate 6-bit up counting and down counting. Explain the procedural steps and demonstrate how to preset the Q points to (00,1100)R2, how to increment to (01,0011)R2, and how to decrement to (00,1110)R2.

Procedures:

1. After studying Unit I and the introduction to this unit, you should be ready to learn how MSI counters work. Although there are many types commercially available to choose from, in these experiments we shall study one of the most versatile, the 74193. This chip is a TTL, MSI, synchronous, 4-bit, straight-code up/down counter with an asynchronous parallel-load and master reset capability.

If we examine this rather long preceding sentence, it tells us quite a lot. For instance, this circuitry is transistor-transistor logic (TTL), so there is no need to worry about the special handling precautions we would use if this were metal oxide semiconductor (MOS) circuitry. Also, this circuit is in medium-scale integrated circuit form, which means that it contains between 10 and 100 gates. Obviously, many internal circuit connections have been made to save us a lot of work in constructing an equivalent circuit out of small-scale integrated circuits (SSI).

The information that the 74193 is a synchronous, 4-bit, straight-code up/down counter means that it is capable of counting up or down within a range of values of $(0000)R2 = (0)R16$ to $(1111)R2 = (F)R16$ and that the change from one count to another is synchronized with the pulses on an incoming clock line.

The information that the chip has an asynchronous parallel-load and master reset capability means that, without regard to any pulses on a clock line, the appropriate manipulation of the Load and Clear control lines will cause the Q outputs to be reset to all 0's or to be loaded with the data currently contained on the four Preset lines. Let us examine this last feature first. Connect the circuit of Figure II-1(a). [Note: For your convenience, the two control lines Load and Clear (abbreviated LD and CL) and the four Preset input lines (abbreviated PA, PB, PC, and PD) are connected to single-pole double-throw (SPDT) switches with the same abbreviations.]

2. Note that QA is the least significant bit (LSB) and QD is the most significant bit (MSB) of the counter. Therefore, the N-tuple $(1010)R2$ implies that QD = 1, QC = 0, QB = 1, and QA = 0 and the value of the N-tuple equals $(A)R16$. Set LD = 1 and reset CL = 0. Toggle CL. (That is, raise CL = 1 and then return to CL = 0.) The LED indicators should now read $(0000)R2$, because the (11) combination on the control lines where LD = 1 and CL = 1 will clear or reset the counter to all 0's.

  a. Use the Preset SPDT switches to establish $(1010)R2$ on the Preset lines (PD = 1, PC = 0, PB = 1, PA = 0). The LED indicators now read (_____)R2. In other words the (10) condition on the control lines (LD = 1, CL = 0) _____ (choose the correct word from: allows, prevents) parallel loading from the Preset lines.

  b. Establish the control lines at the (00) condition (LD = 0, CL = 0). The LED indicators now read (_____)R2. In other

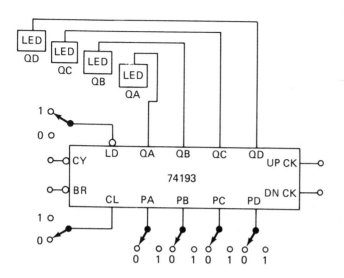

(a) Circuitry for reset and parallel load of an up/down counter (type 74193)

Notes: (1) The circuits for the binary switches are made of:

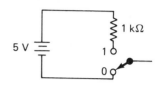

(2) The circuitry for the LED displays:

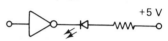

(3) The +5-V and ground-pin connections are not shown. Pinouts are given in Appendix G.

| Inputs | | Output |
LD	CL	results
0	0	Load Qs from Ps
1	0	Disable loads
X	1	Reset counter

(b) Truth table for asynchronous control lines
Notes: (1) Table assumes UP CK = DN CK = 1.
(2) X implies "don't care" whether value is a 0 or a 1.

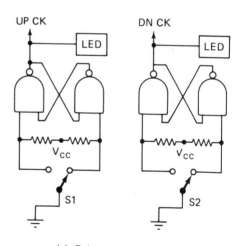

(c) Debounced switches

FIGURE II-1 Up/down counters.

words, the (00) condition on the asynchronous control lines _____ the data on the Preset lines into the Q outputs of the counter.

c. Raise PA = 1. The LEDs now read (_____)R2. In other words, changing data on the Preset lines will continue to be loaded into the Q points (or outputs) as long as the asynchro-

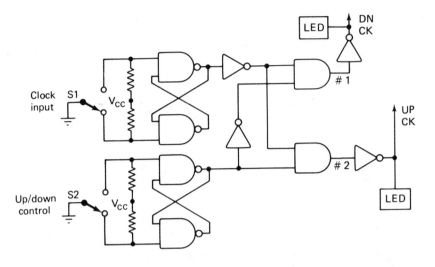

(d) Prevention of simultaneous Os

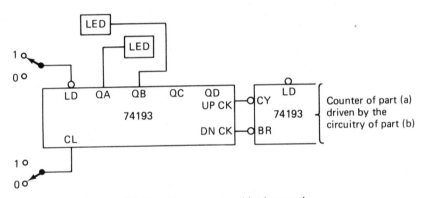

(e) Two binary counter chips in cascade

Asynchronous inputs		Synchronous inputs		Output results at Q's
LD	CL	UP CK	DN CK	
0	0	X	X	Load Q's from P's
1	0	1	1	No change
1	0	CP	1	Increment counter
1	0	1	CP	Decrement counter
1	0	CP	CP	Illegal condition
X	1	X	X	Reset Q's to 0's

Notes: (1) X implies "don't care" if level is a 1 or a 0. (2) CP implies "clock pulse."

(f) Truth table for all control lines of 74193

FIGURE II-1 (continued)

30

nous control lines are in the (00) condition. Return PA = 0. The LEDs again read (_____)R2.

d. Establish (10) on the control lines (LD = 1, CL = 0). From our observation a moment ago, this should disable or prevent subsequent parallel loading of the Q points from the Preset lines. Set PA = 1. The Preset switches now are set to (_____)R2. However, the Q points contain (_____)R2, as indicated by the LEDs. Obviously, LD = 1 and CL = 0 has _____ the parallel-load feature.

e. A moment ago we observed that LD = 0 and CL = 0 (the 00 condition on the asynchronous control lines) _____ the counter from the Preset lines. If we return from our present (10) condition to a (11) condition on the control lines, we expect the counter to be _____. Set LD = 1 and CL = 1. The LEDs now read (_____)R2. Return CL to a low level. This (10) has disabled parallel loading and, as we shall shortly discover, has enabled the two synchronous control lines (Up Clock and Down Clock) to take control of the counter.

f. In our examination thus far, we have neglected one possible condition on our two asynchronous control lines. This is the (_____) condition. The reason for this omission is because the chip is constructed so that once the CL line is raised to a high level, we "don't care" what level is on the LD line. The counter will be reset to all 0's regardless of the setting of LD. This condition can be regarded as (X1), where X signifies that we don't care about the level of LD when CL = 1 because we know what will happen to the counter.

Another thing we have ignored thus far is to discuss the two unconnected output lines, Carry (abbreviated CY) and Borrow (abbreviated BR), and the two synchronous (dependent upon clock pulses) control lines, Up Clock (abbreviated UP CK) and Down Clock (abbreviated DN CK). You may recall that for TTL circuits we cannot predict the level of unconnected outputs (also called "hanging" outputs) unless we know something about the specific circuits inside the chip. However, we can predict the level of input lines that are unconnected or left "hanging." When power is applied to the chip, these TTL inputs will float at a _____ level. (Actually, they typically float at the minimum voltage that can still be considered as a 1. For this reason, just the slightest amount of negative noise voltage such as you might have on your body can, if you touch these inputs, sometimes cause a false 0 to appear. For this reason it is considered to be very poor design practice to install an industrial system with hanging inputs. The inputs should be tied low or high, depending upon the functions you desire to accomplish.)

g. Our observations of the effects of different conditions on the LD and CL lines have taken place with the UP CK and DN CK inputs hanging at a high level. Our results are summarized in Figure II-1(b). Study this truth table until you can remember it, because this counter will often be used in other experiments.

a. (0000)R2, prevents or "disables"
b. (1010)R2, loads or "parallel-loads"
c. (1011)R2, (1010)R2
d. (1011)R2, (1010)R2, disabled
e. loaded, "cleared" or "reset" or "nulled," (0000)R2
f. (01), high or 1

3. Let us now examine the manipulation of the two synchronous control lines UP CK and DN CK in conjunction with the LD and CL lines. To simulate the effects of clock pulses but to allow us to control the starting and stopping of pulses at either level, we can use the two "debounced" switches S1 and S2 shown in Figure II-1(c) (McKay, 1978, p. 253). Connect this circuitry to the UP CK and DN CK inputs of part (a) as indicated.

a. Set UP CK = 1, DN CK = 1, LD = 1, and CL = 1. The counter now reads (_____)R2. Reset CL = 0 and the counter will now be disabled from parallel loads and the synchronous control lines are now enabled to control the counter. Reset UP CK = 0. Note that the counter contents are unchanged. In other words, the transition from a 1 to a 0 (called a _____ edge) did not advance the counter from (0000)R2. Set UP CK = 1. The counter now contains (_____)R2. This counter advances (or increments or counts up) on _____ edge triggering, often abbreviated as LET.

b. Raise and lower (toggle) S1 five more times. The counter LEDs now read (_____)R2. In other words, when LD = 1, CL = 0, and DN CK = 1, the counter is advanced with the _____ edge of each clock pulse (often abbreviated as CP) on the UP CK input.

c. With LD = 1, CL = 0, and UP CK = 1, reset DN CK = 0. The LEDs now read (_____)R2. Therefore, the trailing edge (transition from a 1 to a 0) on DN CK causes no change in the counter. Lower DN CK = 1. The counter LEDs now read (_____) R2. In other words, with LD = 1, CL = 0, and UP CK = 1, the counter decrements or counts down with the _____ of each CP (clock pulse). Raise and lower S2 two more times. These two simulated clock pulses have _____ the counter to a value of (_____)R2.

d. Decrement the counter five more times. These five CPs have caused the counter to contain (_____)R2 = (_____) R16. Notice that the counter can "roll over" from (0000)R2 to (1111)R2 and continue counting when it is being decremented. Let us see if it can roll back over when it is being incremented. Increment the counter five times; that is, let LD = 1, CL = 0, DN CK = 1 and raise and lower S1 five times. The counter now contains a (_____)R2 = (_____)R16. By the way, what do we call the counter transition from all 0's to all 1's or from all 1's to all 0's? _____

a. (0000)R2, trailing, (0001)R2, leading
b. (0110)R2, leading
c. (0110)R2, (0101)R2, LETs, decremented, (0011)R2
d. (1110)R2 = (E)R16, (0011)R2 = (3)R16, rollover

4. There is a practical problem with out present circuit to control the asynchronous control lines UP CK and DN CK: namely, what would happen if S1 and S2 were accidentally reset to 0's at the same time? The manufacturer says "an incorrect count" will occur if both of these lines are low simultaneously. To avoid this illegal condition, examine the circuitry in Figure II-1(d). Note that S1 is now used as the clock input and S2 is used to determine the direction of the count. Also note that the NOT gate connected between the inputs of the two ANDs ensures that one of the control lines will always be at a high level. This is because:

a. An AND gate will have a 1 output if and only if _____ inputs are at the 1 level. Since a NOT gate is connected between one input of the lower AND and one input of the upper AND, one of the outputs of the two ANDs must be a _____, while the level of the other output will depend upon the level of _____. Since at least one of the AND outputs is at the 0 level (and possibly both are), at least one of the two NOTs with their outputs connected to UP CK and DN CK must be at the 1 level. Therefore, the "illegal condition" of simultaneous 0's on the two asynchronous control lines has been prevented, so that we can always predict correctly our output sequence for any given input conditions.

b. Disconnect the circuitry in part (c) of Figure II-1 from the circuitry in part (a). Connect the circuitry of part (d) to part (a). Use S2 and S1 to place a high on both the UP CK and the DN CK inputs. (Lower both S1 and S2).) Clear the counter with LD = 1 and CL = 1. Reset CL = 0. The counter now contains a (_____)R2 and both CK lines are high. Toggle S1 (raise and lower) to provide a clock pulse (CP) to the circuits. The counter LEDs now read (_____)R2. Toggle S1 (raise and lower) to provide three more CPs. The counter LEDs now read (_____) R2 and both CK lines = 1.

c. Change S2 by raising the pole contact. Note that both LEDs on the CK lines are still indicating highs because of the common low going into the two ANDs from the S1 circuitry. Now raise and lower S1. The counter LEDs now read (_____)R2 and both CK lines = 1. Raise and lower S1 five more times. The counter LEDs now read (_____)R2 = (_____)R16 and both CK lines = 1.

d. Lower the pole contact of S2. Note that both CK lines still = 1. Lower and raise the pole contact of S1 five times. The counter LEDs now read (_____)R2 = (_____)R16 and both CK lines = _____ . Note that we can increment and decrement with rollover and without fear that simultaneous 0's will appear on the CK lines.

a. all, 0, its other input
b. (0000)R2, (0001)R2, (0100)R2
c. (0011)R2, (1110)R2 = (E)R16
d. (0011)R2 = (3)R16, 1

5. In our discussion of the 74193, we have thus far neglected to discuss the two outputs Carry (CY) and Borrow (BR). Perhaps the easiest way to understand them is to use them.

   Leave S1 and S2 poles in the lowered position but remove the two LED indicators from the UP CK and DN CK lines. Connect these two LED indicators to QA and QB of a second up/down counter as shown in Figure II-1(e). Also, as indicated in this figure, connect the CY output of the counter on the right to the UP CK input of the counter on the left. Similarly, connect the BR output of the counter on the right to the DN CK input of the counter on the left. This "outputs of one chip" used as the "inputs of the next chip" is an example of "cascading" the 74193s.

a. For both counters, set LD = 1 and CL = 0. For the counter on the right, set PD = 1, PC = 1, PB = 0, and PA = 1. For this counter, lower LD to 0 and restore it to a 1. The four LEDs on the Q outputs of the counter on the right now read (_____) R2 = (_____)R16. For the counter on the left raise CL to a 1 and then restore it to a 0. The 6 bits of the counter now read (_____)R2. We have just "preset" this value into the two counters and are now ready to start incrementing. (By "presetting" the counter we mean that we have parallel-loaded a value into the counter and will begin counting from this value.)

b. Raise and lower S1 to provide a clock pulse (CP) to the counters. The 6 bits now read (_____)R2. Lower and raise S1 again. The 6 bits now read (_____)R2.

c. Raise and lower S1 again. The 6 bits now read (_____)R2. For this to have occurred, what must have happened on the cascade connections? The carry output of the first counter must have provided a clock pulse to the UP CK line of the second counter when the first counter _____ from (_____)R2 to (0000)R2.

d. Raise and lower S1 again. The 6 bits now read (_____)R2. The CY output of the first counter will not provide another CP until the counter rolls over again. When this occurs the next time, the 6 bits should read (_____)R2. Lower and raise S1 until you confirm this.

e. Since the second counter is behaving in a predictable manner, we can conclude that the BR output of the first counter must have stayed high while all of this incrementation has been going on. Similarly, we can conclude that the CY output remained high except for a brief period during rollover when it furnished a clock pulse to the UP CK input of the second counter. (The reasons for these conclusions can be found by reviewing the introduction to the manipulation of the asynchronous control lines in light of our observation of correct straight-code counting in this latest circuit. You can confirm these conclusions by measuring the CY and BR levels as you increment through rollover.)

   Let us now examine the manipulation of the BR output. Raise the S2 pole contact to prepare for decrementation.

f. While the counters still contain (10,0000)R2 and S2 is raised, raise and lower S1. The counters now contain (_____)R2. Since we know something about the manipulation of the CK lines to decrement the counter, we can conclude that during the rollover from (0000)R2 to (1111)R2 in decrementing mode, the CY output remained _____ while the BR output _____ .

g.   Raise and lower S1 again. The counters now contain (_____) R2. Apparently, both the CY and BR outputs remained _____. These two outputs will continue to remain high until rollover occurs again, at which time CY will remain high but BR will issue a CP to the DN CK input. The counters will then contain a (_____)R2.

This circuit behavior is summarized in Figure II-1(f). Please study this carefully to be sure you understand it. Compare it to the partial table of Figure II-1(b). Everything from Figure II-1(b) should be in Figure II-1(f) plus a lot more information.

a.   (1101)R2 = (D)R16, (00,1101)R2
b.   (00,1110)R2, (00,1111)R2
c.   (01,0000)R2, rolled over from (1111)R2 to (0000)R2
d.   (01,0001)R2, (10,0000)R2
f.   (01,1111)R2, high, had a CP
g.   (01,1110)R2, high, (00,1111)R2

6.   Reread the objective for these experiments. Study these experiments until you feel sure that you have mastered and can demonstrate each of the objectives. Reexamine Figure II-0 to be sure you understand how this section relates to the overall operation of the RTU. Remember, these counters are vital to almost every block in the figure (as indicated by all of the output arrows shown coming out of the timing and sequencing logic). You will then be ready to learn about buses, bus connections, and temporary storage for bus information.

PROBLEMS AND EXPERIMENTS

Buses, Bus Connections, and Temporary Storage

Objectives: By the end of these experiments and the associated problems, you should be able to correctly perform each of the following objectives using only a power supply, logic circuitry, and the notes and data obtained from conducting these experiments.

1. Explain the meaning of: buses, bus connections, temporary storage for bus information, three major bus functions, time-shared bus functions, source, destination, source output isolation techniques, Tri-state[1] bus connections, Schmitt-trigger bus connections, latches, tracking, and "holding" or "latching."
2. Explain the use of the Enable line for a Tri-state bus connector to prevent or pass signals. Draw, connect, and demonstrate the circuitry necessary to disable the Tri-state gates while (1001) is prepared for presentation at the outputs. Then enable the gates and demonstrate the predicted outputs.
3. Explain the use of the clock line to track and hold input data for a latch. Draw, connect, and demonstrate the circuitry necessary to track data as they change and then settle to a (1001) and are then latched into temporary storage.
4. Estimate the approximate values of: voltage level of disabled, hanging Tri-state output; voltage level of hanging TTL input; voltage level of disabled Tri-state output connected to TTL input; current drain for TTL input versus Tri-state input; hysteresis threshold levels for Schmitt logic chips. Connect the circuitry and demonstrate the voltage measurements necessary to confirm your predictions.

Procedures:

1. After studying the introduction and the preceding experiments in this unit, you should be ready to learn about buses, bus connections, and temporary storage for bus information. In these experiments we shall study the use of Schmitt-trigger logic and Tri-state logic for bus connections and we shall study the use of latches for temporary storage. It might be helpful if you quickly looked back at Figure II-0 to see how this information relates to the RTU we are using as a vehicle to facilitate our study of memories, memory operations, and memory applications. Then we will examine the operation of Tri-state logic.
2. Buses are defined collections of conductors used in the transfer of information from one of a number of information sources to one or more designated destinations. There are three major bus functions: address, data, and control. Typically, a modern digital system will

---

[1] "Tri-state" is a trademark of National Semiconductor.

use a separate bus for each function. Occasionally, the data function and the address function will be "time-shared" on a common bus. (That is, addresses will be present on the common lines at certain known times and data will be present on the common lines at other known times. Hence the common lines are being shared and are used for different functions at different times.)

The address bus is used to select the designated destination or destinations to which the source is to send information. The data bus is used to send the information from the source to the designated destination or destinations that were preselected via the address bus. The control bus is used to control and coordinate the selection of the designated destination(s) and the transfer of the information from the source to the intended destination(s). The control bus is also used to inform other sources and destinations that an information transfer is taking place so that they know not to try to use the bus until the current transaction is completed. Also, the control bus can be used to signal the source presently using the buses that other sources and destinations want to use the buses at the first available opportunity.

With so many potential sources and destinations connected to the common bus lines, we have to be careful that the outputs of different sources do not cause circuit damage by shorting one another out. In other words, we have to somehow isolate the different source outputs from one another. There have been three major techniques used in the solution of this problem in the last 15 years, as shown in Figure II-2.

a. The major technique used in isolating source outputs from one another when connected to a common line(s) was called "diode isolation" and is shown in Figure II-2(a). Assuming a positive logic system where OV ≤ logic 0 ≤ 0.15 V and 2.5 V ≤ logic 1 ≤ 5 V, if the AND in Figure II-2(a) is acting as the source and if it has a 1 output, this voltage will _____ bias the anode of the diode connecting the AND to the bus line. However, this 1 output will _____ bias the cathodes of the diodes connecting the OR and the NAND to the bus line. These two _____ biased diodes will not allow the signal from the present source (the AND) to pass through the diodes to the other potential sources. In effect, the diodes have isolated the circuits of the potential future sources from the output of the present source. (Note that the gate outputs of potential future sources must be kept at the 0 level until they are given control of the bus line as the present source. In other words, the diode isolation technique requires that only the present source can have a choice of a 1 or a 0 output. Each potential source of the future must retain a 0 output at the anode of its diode until it is given control of the bus.)

b. The second major technique in isolating source outputs from one another when connected to a common line(s) is called "open collector." It is still widely used. The principle of open collector (abbreviated OC) gates is shown in the left-hand side of Figure II-2(b). Here, the output of a gate (it does not matter whether it is a NOT, an AND, etc.) is shown to terminate at a collector of a transistor. The OR and the AND shown in the figure are also going to have their outputs terminated at a collector of a transistor, since the letters OC inside the gate symbols identify them as open collector logic. Somewhere on the bus line a single resistor is connected to V_{CC} and is used to pull up each OC gate except possibly the present source to a logic 1 level. Since all potential future sources are required to maintain their output transistors in cutoff (outputs = 1), it is up to the present source to determine whether the bus is to be left at the _____ level or whether its transistor is to be saturated and hence short the bus line to ground to bring the bus line to the _____ level.

c. One of the latest and fastest-growing isolation techniques is called Tri-state or three-state. The principle of operation of this logic family is shown in the left-hand side of Figure II-2(c). Here the pole contact of S2 can be at either a logic 0 or a logic 1, but unless the gate is enabled (S1 is closed), the data at S2 cannot be passed to the bus. Instead, the bus would view the gate as presenting an "open" or "infinite" impedance to the line. The symbol immediately to the right of S1 and S2 represents the solid-state approximations of these switches. That is, the input data can be either a 0 or a 1, but unless the gate is enabled as the source, only a very high impedance is presented to the bus line by this gate. Obviously, only the _____ source should be enabled at any given time. Each potential future source should be _____ and in its _____ state until it gains control of the bus.

Of the three logic symbols for Tri-state gates shown in this figure, the first and the third gates are enabled by a _____ on the En. control line. The NOT gate shown would be enabled

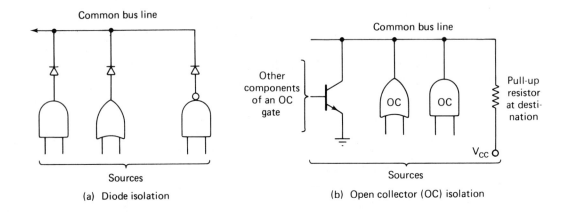

(a) Diode isolation

(b) Open collector (OC) isolation

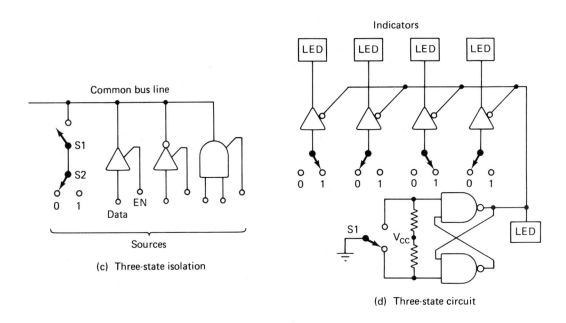

(c) Three-state isolation

(d) Three-state circuit

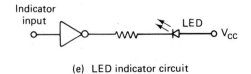

(e) LED indicator circuit

FIGURE II-2 Bus connections and temporary storage.

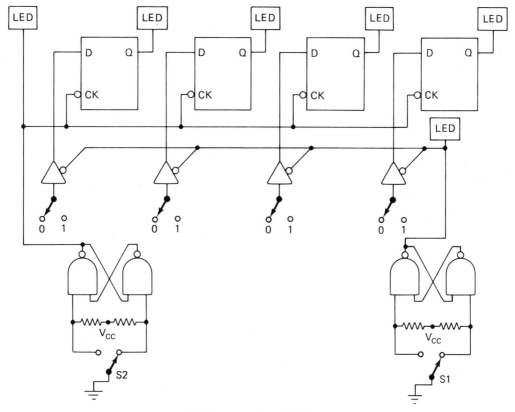

(f) Bus connector and latches

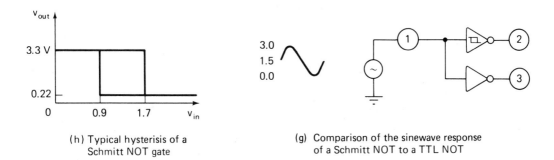

(h) Typical hysterisis of a
Schmitt NOT gate

(g) Comparison of the sinewave response
of a Schmitt NOT to a TTL NOT

FIGURE II-2 (continued)

by a _____ on its En. control line. You can find out whether a 1 or a 0 is used to enable a Tri-state gate to come out of its high-impedance state and present data by referring to the manufacturer's specification sheet.

d. Let's experiment with these Tri-state gates. Examine Figure II-1(d). Note that the LED indicators are not yet shown to be connected to the Tri-state outputs. The inputs to the gates are shown as single-pole double-throw (SPDT) switches which are set to (1010)R2 (you can use the switches connected to PA, PB, PC, and PD of the counter for these inputs).

Set the S1 buffered switch so that a 1 is applied to the Enable line of the Tri-state gates. Since a NOT symbol is shown on the Enable inputs of each of the Tri-state gates these gates can come out of their high-impedance state only if a _____ is applied on their Enable line. Therefore, these gates are presently disabled (not allowed to pass a logic 1 or 0 from input to output).

With a digital voltmeter, measure the voltage from the SPDT switch to the input of the leftmost Tri-state gate. Since you established an input pattern of (1010), this voltage should be approximately +5 V. Reset the switch to 0 and measure the voltage. It should be close to zero volts. Set the switch back to a 1 (+5 V). Now transfer the probe of the digital volt meter (DVM) to the output of this Tri-state gate. The voltage you measure is about _____ volts. In other words, the voltage at the Tri-state input is not enabled to pass through the gate. The voltage at the outputs of the next three Tri-states are _____, _____, and _____.

e. Measure the voltages at the hanging (unconnected) inputs of the LED indicators. These voltages are about _____, _____, and _____. The circuitry for these LED indicators is shown in Figure II-2(e). Note that the indicator inputs are simply the inputs of a TTL inverter (NOT gate). These NOT gate inputs are hanging at the minimum voltage level still recognized by the gate as a 1. Therefore, the output of the gates must be 0's, which are approximately ground potential, and therefore the LEDs conduct current between ground (at the NOT outputs) and V_{CC} in this forward-biased arrangement. Hence the LEDs are lit. If any NOT input is grounded (input 0), the output of the NOT will go to a 1 level and the difference in voltage levels between V_{CC} and the logic 1 level is not sufficient to cause forward bias current to flow and light the LED.

f. Connect the four Tri-state outputs to the four LED indicators. Are the LEDs still emitting light? _____ Measure and record the voltages on the four Tri-state outputs, now _____, _____, _____, and _____.

Notice that the impedance of the disabled Tri-state gates is so high that the hanging inputs of the LED indicators are virtually undisturbed by being connected to the Tri-states.

g. Enable the Tri-states (i.e., reset S1-0). The LEDs now read _____. Measure and record the voltages at the four Tri-state outputs, _____, _____, _____, and _____. Change the switch settings to 0101. The LEDs now read _____. Measure the outputs of the Tri-states. Set S1 = 1. The LEDs now read _____ because _____

_____

_____.

Do you see now why the Tri-state gates are used to drive the buses in Figure II-0? (They are shown as "bus connectors.") There are many circuits that can supply signals to the buses (called "sources"). If they are all tied to the buses through their own set of Tri-state bus connectors and if only one source is permitted to enable its bus connectors at a time; all other potential sources are effectively disconnected from the buses by the high impedance of their disabled Tri-state connectors.

By the way, the preceding paragraph presents the case for using Tri-state bus connectors for circuits that "source" (supply signals or write to) the buses. But what about the destination circuits (the ones that accept or read signals from the buses)? Well, a good case can be made for the use of Tri-states here, too. For example, in Figure II-0 there are over 12 circuits shown connected to the bus and there is the potential for many more in a realistic setting. If the input bus connectors of the destination circuits present even 1 unit of TTL fan-in loading per line, the total number of these circuits will present a sum of fan-in values that may exceed the fan-out capability of most gates. (Remember, most TTL gates only have a fan-out capability of 10 unit loads. Besides 1 unit of TTL load can draw 1.6 mA of current and the sum of these fan-ins would require a multiple of these currents.) So how can we reduce the current requirements

for each bus line input? Easy, just connect the input of a Tri-
state gate such as the 8T95 to the bus line. One of these inputs
only draws 400 μA (which is a big improvement over 1.6 mA).

a. forward, reverse, reverse
b. 1, 0
c. present, disabled, high impedance, 1, 0
d. 0, 0.1 V to 0.2 V typically, since none of the Tri-states are en-
    abled. They should all measure about 0.1 V to 0.2 V regardless
    of whether the inputs to the disabled gates are high or low
e. these four hanging inputs will probably range from 1.6 V to
    1.9 V
f. yes, they now range from about 1.6 V to 1.9 V (about the same
    as the indicator inputs in question e)
g. 1010, 3 V or more, 0.2 V or less, 3 V or more, 0.2 V or less,
    0101, 1111, the Tri-states are disabled and back in their high-
    impedance state, which allows the TTL NOT inputs to "float"
    to a high (as usual when they are "disconnected" from logic-
    level inputs)

Unfortunately, not all bus connection problems can be resolved by
isolating signal sources and minimizing loading (although these are
certainly among our highest priorities in designing bus interfaces). Let
us examine our RTU block diagram in Figure II-0 again to see what
other potential problems are lurking along our buses.

Did you notice that the number of circuit blocks in our RTU
appear to suggest some fairly long bus lines? This is because we often
prefer to work with "modular systems." For example, the counter
circuits have certain jobs or functions to perform that are quite different from the functions to be performed by the extended arithmetic-
logic unit or the read-only memory (ROM) unit. Since these functions
are separate and identifiable, future troubleshooting and/or expansion
and improvement of the system will be facilitated if we place each of
these functional modules on its own circuit board (usually a wire-wrap
card or a printed circuit board). Then if, for example, a circuit malfunc-
tion is detected on the counter board, we can minimize our RTU
system's "downtime for field repairs" by replacing the defective board
with a good spare board and taking the bad unit back to the shop for
repairs.

Okay, let us return to our original point about the long bus lines.
If we place each functional module on its own circuit board, then obviously there are going to be quite a few circuit boards to be plugged
into sockets (for easy board insertion and removal) that are connected
to our bus lines. The more boards we have, the longer our parallel bus

lines will be. Since these lines are parallel conductors separated by a nonconducting material (to keep the lines from shorting together) and since a capacitor is formed by two conductors separated by a nonconductor, we are increasing our capacitive loading as we add bus sockets and line lengths. Unfortunately, capacitive loading slows down our maximum transmission rate of signals along the bus sockets and line lengths which can badly distort both the signal wave shapes and the time-sequencing relationships between signals on the bus. (The recent trends to increase the use of metal oxide semiconductors or MOS circuits makes this particular problem even worse than it used to be.) Also of concern is the fact that long conductors make pretty good antennas for that most unwanted of signals, called "noise." These unwanted electrical signals can result in extra bits which must be ignored or removed from the valid signals.

Although noise can be bad on any bus line we must take particular pains to minimize it on the lines that are connected to ground and to V_{CC} (power supply lines). To understand the significance of this, just remember that every integrated circuit on every circuit board must be connected to these power supply lines. Therefore, if a power supply is physically located at one end of the buses in Figure II-0, there exists a small ohmic resistance between, say, the ground-line connection to the integrated circuit closest to the power supply and the ground-line connection to the last circuit on the last circuit board at the other end of the bus. This small ohmic resistance of the ground line is distributed along the length of the conductor, which simply means that noise signals are free to develop (usually in a cumulative manner) all along the ground line. One way to lower this distributed resistance is to provide several parallel bus lines (some of which are hopefully extra width) for ground and V_{CC}. Unfortunately, this often increases the occurrence of an unwanted feedback of return currents between different ground points in the system. This unhappy state of affairs is said to be caused by "ground loops" and the poor technician or systems designer who has to "chase down a ground-loop problem" is faced with one of the most elusive and frustrating problems to be confronted in a large, high-speed digital system. The malfunctions caused can be sporadic and assume a wide variety of symptoms.

One technique of reducing the noise on the ground and V_{CC} lines is to use small filter capacitors between these lines at several points in the system. In fact, the increased use of large-scale integrated circuits has caused several designers to place at least one filter capacitor as close to every pair of chips (or even every chip) as possible. The intention is for the capacitors to charge to the intended steady-state dc voltage while suppressing the transient noise signals. Unfortunately, this same noise-reduction technique cannot be applied to the information-carrying bus lines, because these lines are intended to carry changing signals rather than steady dc voltage levels. One approach to resolving or at least reducing this noise problem is use Schmitt-trigger logic at the bus connection points. Clear guidelines as to when one should consider the use of Schmitt circuitry are difficult to formulate because so many factors can affect the performance of a system. For example, the author has observed several instances where a system with a bus length of 2 feet operating in an air-conditioned environment containing few if any high-voltage electrical machines would perform well without using Schmitt circuitry for the bus connections. However, the same system can be placed in an environment with wider temperature variances or close proximity to high-voltage equipment or both and depending upon the quality of the design, components, and construction and the extremity of the bad conditions, the Schmitt circuitry may be the key to successful operation.

Let us examine the operation of Schmitt-trigger circuits such as the hex inverters made by Signetics (N7414). Schmitt-trigger NOT gates can recover digital information from bus lines with a very marginal signal-to-noise ratio (SNR) due to "widely separated" (as compared to conventional TTL or MOS circuitry) positive-going and negative-going threshold levels. For example, the N7414 does not recognize a logic 1 input until a positive-going threshold of about 1.7 V has been reached. Once a logic 1 input has been recognized, a logic 0 input will not be recognized until a negative-going threshold of about 0.9 V has been reached [see Figure II-2(h)]. This difference between the two threshold levels is called hysteresis.

h. From Figure II-2(h) the hysteresis of a typical Schmitt-trigger NOT gate can be computed as the typical threshold for a 1 (= _____ V) minus the typical threshold for a 0 (= _____ V) equals a hysteresis of _____ V. Because a Schmitt trigger produces sharp output transitions at the threshold levels, these gates are much less susceptible to false triggering on slow-rising and slow-falling transitions (such as caused by ripple-related noise) than are their TTL or MOS counterparts. The result is a cleaner, more-jitter-free output. Since Schmitt circuits typically contain more temperature-compensation elements than do TTL or MOS circuits, the improved output is even more noticeable with wider temperature variations.

Connect the circuitry shown in Figure II-2(g). Note that a signal generator is used to apply a dc sine wave (from 0 V to +3 V) simultaneously at the inputs of a Schmitt trigger NOT (observe the hysteresis symbol within the gate symbol) and a conventional TTL NOT gate.

i.   Set the signal generator to a frequency of 1 kHz. Use a dual-trace oscilloscope to measure the time relationship between the input at point 1 and the output at point 2. (Remember that many dual-trace oscilloscopes require the use of external triggering to accurately measure time relationships.) Sketch these waveforms below with the output waveform superimposed on the input. Label the threshold points. Your waveforms should closely resemble the ones shown in the answer. Now connect your scope probes to observe the relationship between points 2 and 3. While watching these outputs, begin to slowly decrease

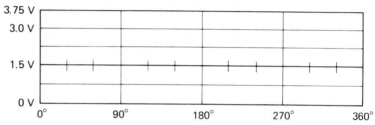

the frequency from 1 kHz to 100 Hz. (This may require checking your amplitudes from the signal generator from time to time to ensure that a change in frequency does not cause a change in the 0 V to +3 V output.) Which output has the sharper transitions and is less subject to jitter? _____ If you slowly decrease the frequency from 100 Hz to 10 Hz, this will become even more pronounced (especially if you apply heat to the circuits, such as the output of a hair drier).

h. $1.7\,V - 0.9\,V = 0.8\,V$

i.   the Schmitt gate (output pictured above) has sharper transitions and is less subject to jitter than the TTL gate.

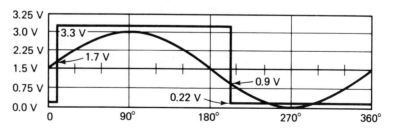

The Schmitt gate

3. Suppose that the first digital-to-analog converter (DAC) in Figure II-0 is responsible for controlling the rpm's of a motor-driven pump. Suppose also that a source on the buses (such as the microprocessor) decides that new information should be sent to this DAC to cause 2% increase in pumping. First, the address bus must be loaded with the correct address of this DAC. When the bus-connection circuitry for this DAC identifies that it is the intended destination for the following data transfer, the circuit must quickly prepare to receive the information on the data bus. Since the DAC and the pump cannot respond to the new information before it would have come and gone (after all, there are a lot of other circuits that need to use that bus and they cannot wait forever on the slow response devices), we need some form of temporary storage to quickly accept and hold the information from the bus. This would free the bus for use by other circuits and retain the information for the DAC to provide the pump until new information is received.

One form of such temporary storage is an array of type D flip-flops called "latches." Examine and connect the bus connector and latch circuitry shown in Figure II-2(f). Set S1 = 1 and S2 = 1.

a. Set S1 = 0. The Tri-state bus connectors are now _____. Establish (1010) at the SPDT switches going into the Tri-states. The LEDs on the 4-bit latch now read _____. Set the SPDT switches to (1001). The latch LEDs now read _____. The latch is apparently _____ the Tri-state outputs as they change 1's and 0's whenever S2 = 1.

b. The SPDT switches at the inputs of the Tri-state gates are intended to simulate the inputs to the bus connector from the source. Set these switches back to (1010). The latch LEDs again read _____. Reset S2 = 0. The latch LEDs now read _____. Change the SPDT switches to (0101). The latch LEDs now read _____. Set S1 = 1 to disable the Tri-states. The trailing edge of S2 has "latched" the values that were present at the D inputs when the trailing edge appeared into the flip-flops. This set of values would be retained for the DAC to respond to until the next time that S1 went low and S2 went high. At that time the Q points of the type D's would follow the input levels (also called "tracking") until a trailing edge at S2 dropped low, which would latch in the new information into temporary storage.

a. enabled, 1010, 1001, "following" or "the same as"
    b. 1010, 1010, 1010

PROBLEMS AND EXPERIMENTS

Demultiplexers, Multiplexers, and Sequencers

Objectives: By the end of these experiments and the associated problems you should be able to correctly perform each of the
following objectives using only a power supply, logic circuitry, and the notes and data obtained from running these
experiments.

1. Explain the meaning of: demultiplexers, multiplexers, sequencers
    demux, mux, preselected address for information transfer.
2. Explain the use of the address and enable lines of a demultiplexer
    to transmit information from a single source to destination (3)R16.
    Draw, connect, and demonstrate the circuitry necessary to accom-
    plish this.
3. Explain the use of a counter, sequencer, bus connector, and tem-
    porary storage to quickly load new information and retain it long
    enough for a "slow" device to respond to. Draw, connect, and
    demonstrate the circuitry necessary to accomplish this.

Procedures:

1. After studying the introduction and the preceding experiments in
    this unit, you should be ready to learn about demultiplexers, multi-
    plexers, and sequencers. It might be helpful if you looked back at
    Figure II-0 to see how this information relates to the RTU we are
    using as a vehicle to facilitate our study of memories, memory
    operations, and memory applications. Then we will examine the
    operation of demultiplexing.
2. Whenever a source needs to transmit information to one of several
    destinations, the circuitry that performs the appropriate routing of
    the data is called a demultiplexer. Functionally, it resembles the
    single-pole multithrow switch [or rotary switch shown in Figure
    II-3(a)]. By appropriate positioning of the pole contact, the source
    can transmit data to the destination that was preselected by the
    signals on the address bus.
         An integrated circuit equivalent of this rotary switch is the

74154 shown in Figure II-3(b). Connect this circuit. Set S1 = 1. Use SPDT switches for the inputs 8 in, 4 in, 2 in, and 1 in. Ground gate input 2 (G2). Establish the SPDT switches at (0000)R2.

a. Reset S1 = 0. Since both G1 and G2 are now 0, the NOTs are both supplying 1's into the AND, which applies a _____ to the Enable input of the control logic. This control logic enables the memory matrix (you will learn in a later unit that this is actually a form of ROM) and it also enables one of 16 different output lines (0 through F). From left to right, the output LEDs on outputs 1 through 5 read _____. Set S1 = 1 and then reset S1 = 0. What effect is observed on the five output LEDs? _____ What binary address is presently on the address bus and what is its hexadecimal equivalent? (_____)R2 = (_____)R16

b. With S1 = 0, set the SPDTs to (0001)R2. What do the output LEDs read? (_____) Toggle (raise and lower) S1 a few times. What effects do you observe on the output LEDs?

_____

_____

What is the hexadecimal equivalent of the current value of the address bus? (_____)R2 = (_____)R16.

In other words, if the input to G1 is the source and if the address bus has preselected line (1)R16 as the destination, serial information can be transferred from source to destination.

c. With S1 = 0, set the SPDTs to (0010)R2. The output LEDs now read (_____), leading us to believe that out of 16 possible output destinations, line (_____)R16 has been preselected by the address to receive the data. Set and reset S1 a few times. What effects do you observe at the output LEDs?

_____

_____

d. With S1 = 0, set the SPDTs to (0011)R2. The output LEDs now read (_____), telling us that line (_____)R16 has been preselected by the address bus to receive the signal from the source. Set and reset S1 a few times. What destinations receive the serial data pulses from the source? _____

_____

Please reexamine Figure II-0 for a moment to locate the demultiplexer (abbreviated as "demux"). Note that serial data are to be transmitted by one source to any of several remote

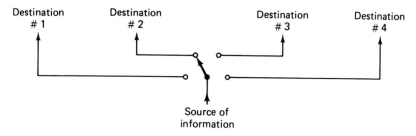

(a) Rotary switch as demultiplexer

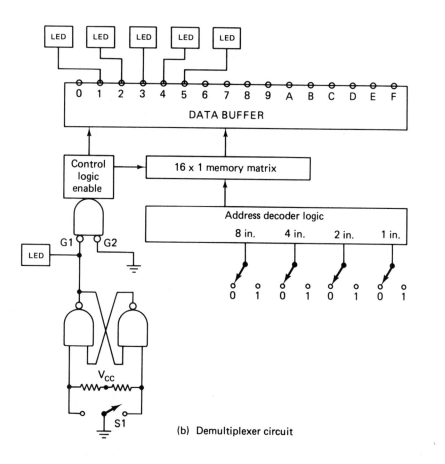

(b) Demultiplexer circuit

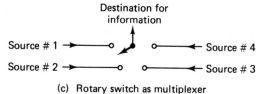

(c) Rotary switch as multiplexer

FIGURE II-3 Demultiplexers, multiplexers, and sequencers.

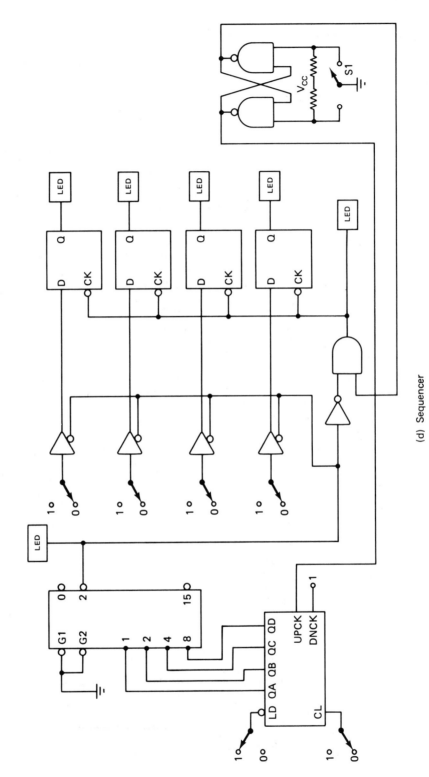

(d) Sequencer

FIGURE II-3 (continued)

52

destinations via some communications link, such as a microwave link, telephone link, radio-frequency link, and so on. The serial information from the PISO register (to be studied in a later unit) will be connected to the appropriate transmitter, which will convert the serial logic data into a form suitable for transmission. (For example, the serial data may be used to frequency-modulate a carrier signal for radio-frequency broadcasting.)

    a. 1, (11111), none, (0000)R2 = (0)R16
    b. (01111), The LED on line 1 follows or tracks S1 while the other LEDs remain high, (0001)R2 = (1)R16
    c. (10111), (2)R16, line (2)R16 tracks the data at G1 while all other LEDs remain high
    d. (11011), (3)R16, only the destination connected to line (3)R16

3. The functional equivalent of a multiplexer is shown in Figure II-3(c). Here a rotary switch (single-pole multithrow) is used to connect one of a number of sources to the single destination. If you locate the multiplexer in Figure II-0 you will see a number of different receivers making source demands on the multiplexer (often called the "mux"). One receiver may come from a microwave link to a host computer. Another receiver may come from a Teletype with signals fed through a telephone line, and so on. At any rate, only one source can input to the destination SIPO register (to be studied in a later unit) at a time. An integrated circuit replacement for this rotary switch would be the 74150, which connects one of 16 sources to the destination.

4. On many occasions in digital electronics, we have need for a sequence of events to be initiated and controlled. An example might be a need for a change of process characteristics in the process, which is monitored and controlled by the RTU in Figure II-0. For instance, we may need to stop certain pumps that have been pumping at maximum capacity for some time. Similarly, we may need to greatly increase our reliance on pumps that have been used very sparingly in the last several months. There may be valves to open and others to close, and so on. At any rate, such a drastic change in the process probably means we need to initiate a sequence of activities that will result in our directing new data to each output bus connector in turn.

    An example of a circuit including the counter, sequencer, output bus connector, and temporary storage is shown in Figure II-3(d).

Examine and connect this circuitry. Notice that by connecting the address lines to the counter and by tying G1 and G2 of our demultiplexer to ground we have converted this circuit to a sequencer. (That is, as the counter increments, one and only one line of the sequencer will go low to indicate it is time for the next event to take place.)

a. With LD = 1 and S1 = 1, clear the counter. (Set CL = 1 and then reset CL = 0.) The only output of the sequencer that should be low is line (_____)R16. Therefore, the Tri-states are _____ by the high on line (2)R16 and a _____ level is applied to the clock line of the latch. Set the SPDT inputs to the Tri-states at (1010).

b. Lower and raise S1. The counter has now advanced to (_____) R16. The only output of the sequencer that should be low is line (_____)R16. The Tri-states are still _____ by the _____ level from line (_____)R16 and the latch is still "holding" its current value.

    Now, in a realistic setting there would probably have been a circuit whose bus connectors would have been enabled during this count of the sequence. The enabling function would have been accomplished during the first half-cycle by output line (1)R16 of the sequencer. The temporary storage connected to the bus connector that is enabled by (1)R16 would have "tracked" the Tri-state inputs during the first half of the cycle and would "hold" or "latch" the input values during the second half of the cycle. In fact, that is what the circuitry you have connected is about to do. Let us see how.

c. Lower S1 to 0. This presents a _____ edge to the UP CK input and the counter contents _____. Raise S1 to 1. This presents a _____ edge to the UP CK input and the counter contents _____. The one output line of the sequencer that is now low is line (_____)R16. This _____ the Tri-states and places a _____ level on the clock inputs of the type D's. The latches are not able to _____ the inputs at the D points. The LEDs at the Q points now read (_____).

d. To prove that the latch can now track the D input values, change the SPDT inputs to the Tri-states to (1001). Lower S1 and leave it low so that the $\overline{Q}$ side of the S1 debounce bistable enables the AND. The LEDs at the Q points now read (_____). Restore the SPDTs to (1010). The LEDs now read

(_____). In other words, the type D's are tracking the inputs as they change levels as long as there is a high on the clock inputs.

e. Lower the S1 switch so that the $\overline{Q}$ side of the S1 bistable = 0. Since $\overline{S1}$ = 0 is connected to the AND whose output drives the clock inputs of the latch, this AND output will be a 0. This means that a trailing edge has just occurred at these clock inputs and the input data have now been latched into temporary storage. Note that a leading edge has been presented to the UP CK input of the counter during this cycle. Therefore, line (2)R16 is no longer low and the Tri-states are disabled. Change the SPDTs to (1100). The LEDs at the Q points now read (_____). In other words, the latch is now "holding" instead of _____.

f. When S1 was raised to 1, this leading edge just _____ the counter and line (2)R16 went high _____ the Tri-states of this particular bus connector. However, the bus connector connected to line (3) R16 of the sequencer would have just been enabled.

Note that the temporary storage now containing (1010) will retain this value so that a slow response device connected to this latch will have ample time to interpret and react to this new information. At the same time that this slow device is beginning to interpret and react, the bus is being used to load other temporary storage locations according to the directions of the sequencer.

a. (0)R16, disabled, low
b. (1)R16, (1)R16, disabled, high, (2)R16
c. trailing, remain the same, leading, advance or increment, (2)R16, enables, low, accept, whatever value originally contained
d. (1001), (1010)
e. (1010), tracking
f. advanced or incremented, disabling

5. Reread the objectives for these experiments. Study these experiments until you feel sure you have mastered and can demonstrate each of the objectives. You will then be ready to take the exam on this unit. After passing the test, you will then be ready to study read-only memories.

SAMPLE TEST FOR UNIT II

(Closed book. Closed notes. Use only writing material, templates, and logic circuitry.)

1. Explain the meaning of the following terms.
    a. Asynchronous counter control lines
    b. Synchronous counter control lines
    c. Counter presets, rollovers, and cascades
    d. Buses and bus connections
    e. Temporary storage and latches
    f. Three major bus functions
    g. Demultiplexers, multiplexers, and sequencers
2. Explain, draw, connect, and demonstrate the circuitry to preset a counter within four decrements of rollover. Decrement six times an increment four times.
3. Explain the use of a counter, sequencer, bus connector, and temporary storage to quickly load new information and retain it long enough for a slow device to respond. Draw, connect, and demonstrate the circuitry necessary to accomplish this.

Fixed Program Memory:
the ROM family

INTRODUCTION

As mentioned earlier in this book, there are three categories of primary memory functions: sequential access (which includes registers), read/write (which includes RAMs), and fixed program (which includes ROMs). In this unit we study that subset of fixed program memories referred to as read-only memories (ROMs).

ROMs are most often used to supply information to microprocessors, computers, or digital controllers. The information that is to be supplied to these devices is usually written into the ROM "off line." That is, the information is inserted into the ROM while it is not electrically connected to the device to which it is to supply the information. Once the information is in the ROM, the ROM is ready to be placed "on line," electrically connected to, and prepared to interact with the microprocessor, computer, or controller. This concept of "on-line" versus "off-line" allows us to define ROMs as follows:

ROMs are a form of memory from which digital data can be repeatedly read (but not repeatedly written into) in an on-line environment.

Those members of the ROM family that can be written into more than once (EROMs) cannot accept new data with the speed and ease of a read/write memory and must typically be taken off-line to reprogram.

There are four basic types of read-only memories. The first type is often referred to as the "basic ROM." It is programmed by the manufacturer during fabrication. That is, the desired information is permanently written into it and there is no way to alter the contents after manufacturing. Such ROMs can usually be classified as "off the shelf" or "custom." The off-the-shelf ROMs are those that would be so useful in a wide variety of applications (such as a decoder for a seven-segment display) that distributors of electronics parts will want to stock quantities of them on their shelves for sale and immediate delivery to their customers. The custom ROMs are made for those customers with a unique application, who therefore must supply the manufacturer with the information they wish to be written into each address. Such customers must be content to wait on the manufacturer's current manufacturing and delivery schedules to receive their custom ROMs.

Because many customers have frequent need for custom ROMs and are not content to wait on the schedules of the manufacturer, we have a second type of ROM, called a programmable read-only memory (PROM) or "field programmable read-only memory." (Note: Although the word "PROM" is commonly used to apply to the products of a number of different manufacturers, the word is actually a trademark of Harris Semiconductor Division.) PROMs can be programmed by the user at his or her location with special circuitry referred to as PROM "burners," "blasters" or "programmers." Once programmed, PROMs cannot be altered further.

A third type of ROM is made for the customer who frequently needs custom-programmed ROMs for a fixed period of time (such as a special project that might last only a few days, weeks, or months) and then would like to reprogram and reuse the ROM in another project. Such ROMs are called EROMs (erasable read-only memories) or EPROMs (erasable field programmable read-only memories). Although these devices can be reprogrammed repeatedly, there is a vast difference between the time required to read the contents of a given address (this typically occurs in an on-line environment in microseconds or even nanoseconds) and the time required to write new contents into a given address (this typically occurs in an off-line environment and requires several minutes to accomplish). One form of EROM is completely solid state and can be reprogrammed only after the old contents are completely erased through prolonged, off-line exposure to ultraviolet light. Another form of EROM uses switches or "patch cords" or "wire straps" as the memory elements and solid-state circuitry to decode the addresses and control when an address is to be read.

The three preceding types of ROMs (base ROM or simply ROM, PROM, and EROM) have an address bus (a defined collection of conductors which carry the signals identifying a location in memory) consisting of A lines (where A can stand for any number of address lines). These devices use "full address decoding" to select one out of 2^A consecutive memory locations whose contents are to be read. For example, a ROM with four address lines (A = 4) would contain 16 consecutively located memory locations $[2^A = 2^4 = (16)R10]$ and every one of these locations could be decoded (recognized by the address selection logic so that its contents could be brought to the data lines to be read). In some applications, not all addresses in a consecutive sequence will contain unique or useful data. Therefore, the number of storage elements can be reduced and "partial address decoding" can be used. For example, a ROM may be needed to convert the 8-bit ASCII code (American Standard Code for Information Interchange) to another code. Since A= 8, a ROM for this purpose might be expected to require $2^8 = (256)R10$ consecutive locations to perform this conversion. However, since ASCII has only $(96)R10$ meaningful codes, obviously many memory elements can be saved and partial decoding of $(96)R10$ rather than $(256)R10$ locations will be all that is required. The type of ROM that accomplishes this conservation of circuitry is referred to as a programmable logic array (PLA).

For any of the four types of ROMs, you might wonder why a user would choose to use fixed program memory rather than read/write memory. After all, a read/write memory could be read with about the same speed and ease as a ROM, and it certainly can be "reprogrammed" with much greater speed and ease! Well, one reason for choosing ROMs over RAMs is that RAMs are "volatile" and ROMs are not. (By "volatile" we mean that the currently stored information will be lost if power is lost.) Therefore, those blocks of information we would like to have readily available without reprogramming each time power is applied should be stored in a type of ROM. For example, code conversions, look-up tables (such as tables of trigonometric functions, logarithms, etc.), frequently used routines in a computer program (such as the solution for the roots of a quadratic equation or the instructions that enable the computer to exchange information with a certain peripheral), and substitution for blocks of combinational logic circuitry are a few examples of likely applications for fixed program memories. It should also be noted that ROMs usually have a much greater storage density in a given amount of silicon.

In reading this introduction you may also have wondered: "What are the parts of a typical ROM?" "How are they made?" The first question is answered in Figure III-0(a). As indicated in this figure, there are four functional blocks to consider in any ROM. First, there is the address decoder logic. This block accepts signals from an address bus, which contains A bits. If the control block has received an appropriate "enable" signal (there are often one or more control lines which are used in some internally gated combination to enable the ROM), the address decoder logic is allowed to select one of 2^A locations in the memory matrix. Each location in the memory matrix has information stored in D data bits. When the address has been decoded and the control block has been enabled, the contents of the selected location will be presented to the outside world for reading.

Figure III-0(b) shows one technique for making a ROM. (There are many techniques used, such as "fusible link" and "avalanche." However the basic functions of any ROM can be understood from this figure.) Note that if a specific address is presented on the address bus, such as $(0 \cdots 000)R2$, only one of the address decoder gates will have a 1 output. In this example, it will be the top left AND gate, with NOT gates on all the inputs. Now, if the Enable line goes to a 1 level, this will allow a 1 output from the two-input AND, which has a 1 input from the address select logic. In this example, the left two-input AND will have a 1 output. Also note that a high level is now present on each of the two-input NANDs in the data buffer. This means that the diode on line 1 is forward-biased by the two-input AND, and therefore the output of the two input NAND on line 1 will go to a 0 output. Since the "fusible link" connected to line 2 and to the diode tied to the leftmost AND has been "blasted" open (probably by a very high current), line 2 is pulled to a low by its grounded resistor, and therefore the NAND output on line D will be a 0.

Study this figure. See if you can explain why the contents of the second location in memory would be read as $(0 \cdots 01)$, why the contents of the 2^Ath word would be $(1 \cdots 10)$, and why all 1's would be on the data lines whenever the Enable line is at a low level.

There are many variations of ROMs available and new applications are being discovered at a very rapid rate. However, an understanding of the four basic types should enable you to readily understand the variations and the new applications. With this in mind, strive to accomplish the following objectives as you progress through this unit. By the end of the experiments in this unit you should be able to perform each of

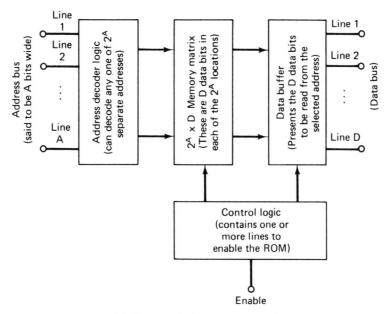

(a) Functional block diagram of a ROM

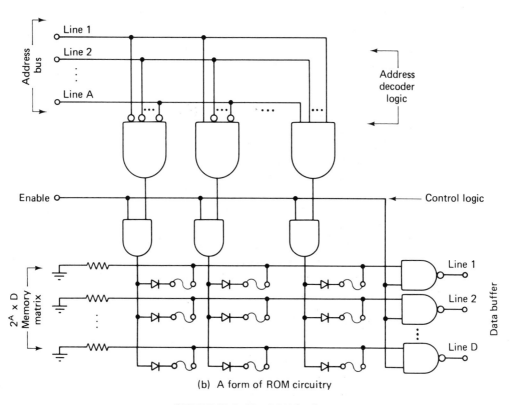

(b) A form of ROM circuitry

FIGURE III-0 The ROM family.

61

the following objectives using only a power supply, logic circuitry, and the notes and data obtained from running these experiments.

Objectives of Unit III

For each of the following concepts in fixed program memory:

1. Explain the meaning of each of the following terms. Give an example of an application for each term.
   a. Fixed program memory
   b. Nonvolatile memory
   c. ROM
   d. PROM
   e. EROM
   f. Table look-ups
   g. Code conversion
   h. Decoder/driver ROMs
   i. Switch register EROM
   j. Party-line operations

2. Draw and explain a functional block diagram for a ROM with 2^A addresses each containing D data bits and a single control line Enable. Label each block and show the flow of signals. Draw the circuitry for each block using diodes in series with fusible links for the memory matrix. Explain how the circuitry works.

3. Explain the manipulation of the individual segments of a seven-segment display to view the hexadecimal character set. Draw the schematic, draw a flow chart of the procedural steps, connect the circuitry, and demonstrate the use of a decoder/driver ROM for a hexadecimal display.

4. Explain the use of a switch register, Tri-state buffer chips, and AND and NOT gates to form an EROM. Draw a schematic, flowchart the procedural steps, and connect and demonstrate the necessary circuitry.

5. Explain the manipulation of the address lines and the construction of the PROM "program" to form a multiplication or a division table for an N-bit multiplicand (or dividend) and an N-bit multiplier (or divisor). Explain how and why a PLA might be considered as an alternative.

6. Pass a closed-book, closed-note, written/laboratory exam over the material of this unit with at least 80% accuracy.

7. Explain the relationship of each of the topics in this unit to the remote terminal unit of Figure II-0.

LIST OF EQUIPMENT AND COMPONENTS
USED IN UNIT III

Equipment:

      Oscilloscope: dc-coupled, 10-MHz BW
      Power supply: 5 V dc at 1 A

Commonly used logic circuits (see Appendix G):

    4 bounceless input switches
    6 LED indicators
    6 SPDT input switches
    8 Mini-DIP SPST switches
    2 seven-segment hex displays

Components:

    1 7400   quad 2-input NAND
    1 7404   hex NOT
    1 7408   quad 2-input AND
    1 7411   triple 3-input AND
    1 7421   dual 4-input AND
    1 7432   quad 2-input OR
    1 74193   4-bit up/down counter

PROBLEMS AND EXPERIMENTS

Code Conversion with ROMs

Objectives: By the end of these experiments and the associated problems, you should be able to correctly perform each of the following objectives using only a power supply, logic circuitry, and the notes and data obtained from running these experiments.

1. Explain the meaning of code conversion with ROMs. Give an example of a typical application.
2. Explain the meaning of decoder/drivers for displays. Explain the use of the control lines typically encountered in decoder/driver operations.

3. Explain the manipulation of the individual segments of a seven-segment common cathode display to view the hexadecimal character set.

4. Demonstrate the procedural steps for displaying the output of a hexadecimal counter with NRZ outputs. Explain and demonstrate how to blink the display, how to blank the display, how to suppress 0's, how to continuously display, and how to freeze the display on a predetermined input or set of inputs.

5. Without consulting any references, from memory draw a flowchart that shows the procedural steps to continuously "read" the contents of a ROM which has been preprogrammed to perform a given code conversion. Using only your flowchart, a power supply, and logic circuitry, connect the circuitry and demonstrate the validity of your flowchart.

Procedures:

1. After reading the narrative on read-only memories, you should be ready to learn how to display the output states of a hexadecimal counter. Let us begin by studying the requirements for displaying each of the 16 characters of the hexadecimal character set on a seven-segment, common-cathode display. Examine Figure III-1.

2. Figure III-1(a) shows the notational order of a seven-segment display. That is, the horizontal segment at the top is referred to as "segment *a*," the vertical segment in the top right position is referred to as "segment *b*," and so on. Figure III-1(b) shows the functional diagram of the seven segments. Note that each segment is composed of diodes. Furthermore, note that each segment has its cathode side connected to a common point (CP), which in turn can be connected or disconnected to ground by the Display Disable switch. (Since the cathode sides of the segments are connected to the common points, this is a common-cathode display. Manufacturers also make common-anode displays.)

   a. Each segment of the display is connected to a current-limiting resistor [for simplicity, only two of these resistors are shown in part (b)] which is, in turn, connected to a source providing either a 1 (positive voltage) or a 0 (ground potential). To light segments *f* and *a*, two things are necessary. A _____ level must be applied to the current-limiting resistors and the Display Disable switch must be _____. When these two conditions are present, the LEDs in the segments are _____ biased.

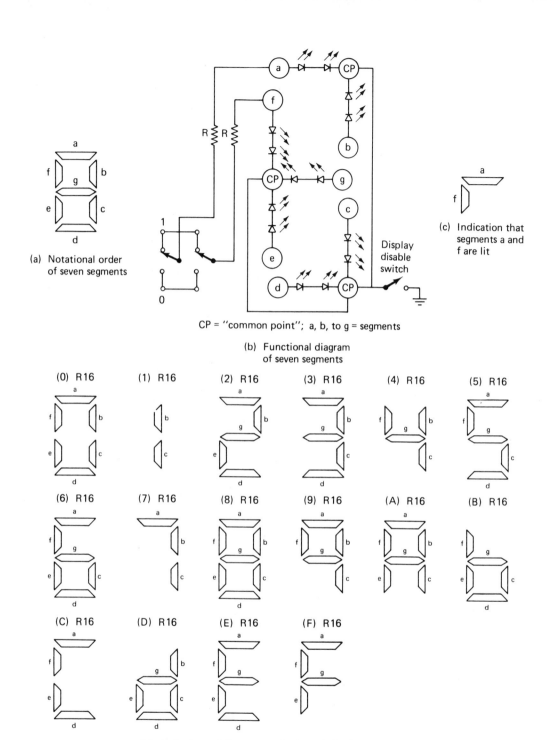

(a) Notational order of seven segments

CP = "common point"; a, b, to g = segments

(b) Functional diagram of seven segments

(c) Indication that segments a and f are lit

(0) R16   (1) R16   (2) R16   (3) R16   (4) R16   (5) R16

(6) R16   (7) R16   (8) R16   (9) R16   (A) R16   (B) R16

(C) R16   (D) R16   (E) R16   (F) R16

(d) Indications of lit segments for hexadecimal character set

FIGURE III-1   Seven-segment display.

65

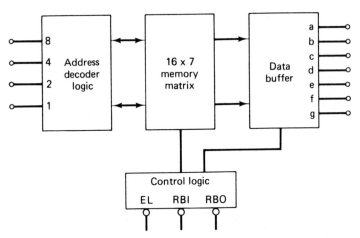

(e) Functional diagram of **9368** (with RBI and RBO unconnected, the control logic can be enabled by EL = 0)

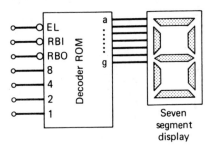

(f) Block diagram of decoder ROM driving seven segment display

FIGURE III-1 (continued)

Therefore, they conduct current and emit light. This is indicated in Figure III-1(c).

b. If any segment has a 0 (ground potential) applied to its current-limiting resistor, then even if the Display Disable switch is closed, the LEDs in the segment are not _____ biased and therefore do not _____. The indication in Figure III-1(c) assumes that 0's are applied to the resistors of segments b, c, d, e, and g while 1's are applied to segments a and f.

c. Examine the indications of lit segments in Figure III-1(d). To display a (1)R16 will require lighting segments _____ and _____. To display an (E)R16 will require lighting all segments except _____ and _____.

    d. To be able to display the entire hexadecimal character set will require that segment *a* be lit for any of the following characters: 0, 2, _____ , and ____ . Segment *f* must be lit for any of the following characters: _____ _____ and ____ .

    a. 1 or high, closed, forward
    b. forward, emit light
    c. *b* and *c*, *b* and *c*
    d. 0, 2, 3, 5, 6, 7, 8, 9, A, C, E, and F; 0, 4, 5, 6, 8, 9, A, B, C, E, and F

Since the hexadecimal character set requires four binary "lines" to represent the 16 *N*-tuples from $(0)R16 = (0000)R2$ to $(F)R16 = (1111)R2$, and since the seven-segment display requires an input line for each segment, there is a need for a code converter to convert from the 4-bit straight code to the necessary 1's and 0's for each of the seven segments. This can be programmed into a read-only memory such as Fairchild's 9368. Because the ROM "decodes" the 4-bit straight-code inputs as an address (assuming the control logic is enabled) and the appropriate seven output levels contained in that address location can then be "read" from the data buffer, this ROM is often affectionately referred to by the "pet" name "Decoder." Because the 9368 has enough power dissipation (typically 225 mW) to "drive" the non-TTL current loads of the display segments, it is referred to as a "decoder/driver." (Many decoder ROMs require separate driver circuits.) The functional diagram for the ROM is shown in Figure III-1(e). In a typical application RBI and RBO may be unconnected (so that they "float" to a high level) or connected to a 1. Then whenever the "Enable Latch" contents line (EL) goes to 0, the 7-bit contents of one of 16 memory locations (which location is determined by the levels on the four address lines) can be read on lines *a* through *g* at the data buffer. (Note: The EL line is sometimes called the LT line for LED Test or the TS line for "To Show.")

    3. Let us study the use of the ROM to decode the *N*-tuple of a 4-bit straight-code counter and to cause the corresponding hexadecimal character to appear on the display. Connect the circuitry of Figure III-2(a). When the Display Disable switch is closed and power is applied, some hexadecimal character should appear on the display.
        a. Raise the Clear (CL) input to the counter to a 1 level and then return it to a 0 level. The display now reads (_____)R16. "Toggle" S2. (That is, change the pole contact of S2 to a new

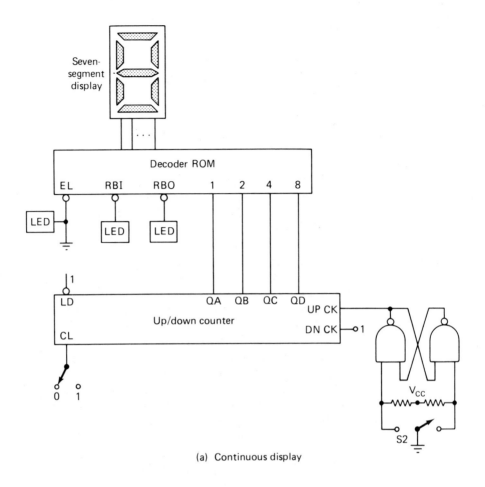

(a) Continuous display

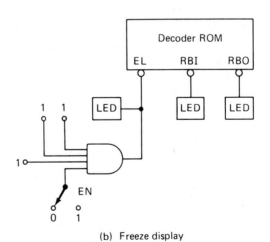

(b) Freeze display

FIGURE III-2 Hex display decoder/driver ROM.

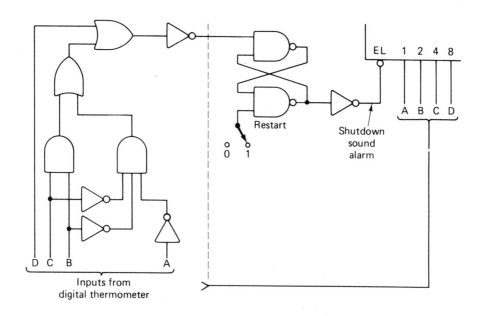

(c) Freeze display of out of limits

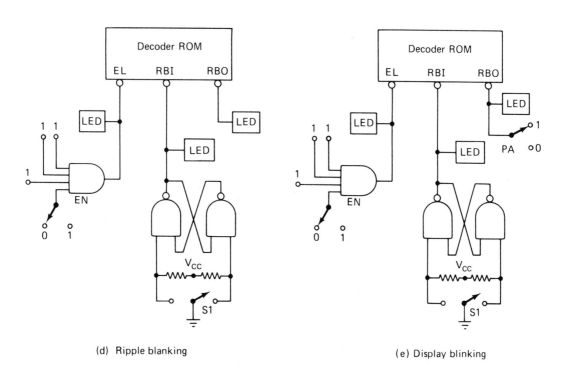

(d) Ripple blanking

(e) Display blinking

FIGURE III-2 (continued)

level and then return to the former level.) The display now reads (_____)R16, indicating that the (_____)R2 N-tuple is on the address lines. Toggle S2 until the display reads (F)R16. Be sure to compare the displayed characters with Figure III-1(d).

b. Now that we have seen the ROM in action, let us stop and check on a couple of things. First, the LEDs attached to RBI and RBO have remained at the _____ level throughout the count. This indicates that these leads are "floating" or "hanging" at the high level. Also, let us confirm the function of the Display Disable switch. Open it. The display is now _____. Close the switch and notice that the display again shows the contents of the counter. (This can be verified by measuring the outputs QA, QB, QC, and QD of the counter.)

c. Remove the connection from EL to ground and replace it with the circuitry shown in Figure III-2(b). Reset the Enable switch (EN) to a 0. Clear the counter (set CL = 1 and then CL = 0). Note that the display again reads (0)R16. Toggle S2 until the display reads (A)R16. Set EN = 1. Note that the LED connected to EL is now at the 1 level just like the LEDs on RBI and RBO. Toggle S2 four times. The display now reads (_____)R16. Reset EN = 0. The display now reads (_____)R16. Set EN = 1. Toggle S2 four more times. The display now reads (_____)R16. Reset EN = 0. The display now reads (_____) R16. In other words, we can "freeze" the display at its current output levels by raising EL = 1.

This can be useful if there are certain N-tuples that should not occur but sometimes do. For example, suppose that we are trying to monitor and control the temperature of a chemical process at $3°C$ (three degrees Celsius), we can tolerate $2°C$ variation in either direction (from $1°C$ to $5°C$ is therefore our control range). Normally, our display should read values between (1)R16 and (5)R16. However, if in our absence the temperature rises or falls below these limits, we would like to "freeze" the display immediately, sound an alarm, and shut the down the process before it either becomes dangerous or we begin to waste our input chemicals. By freezing the display, we can then see whether the process became too hot or too cold and can take steps to prevent its reoccurrence when the process is started again. This is a form of limit control and the circuitry is shown in Figure III-2(c).

d. By applying the laws of Boolean algebra to the ANDs, ORs, and

NOTs located to the left of the dashed line in Figure III-2(c), it can be seen that the output of the NOT which feeds the SR flip-flop will provide a 1 if and only if the digital thermometer indicates between $1°C = (0001)R2$ and $5°C = (0101)R2$. By using the counter as inputs A, B, C, and D, you can easily connect and verify this Limit Detector Logic. Therefore, by manually resetting the Restart switch to 0, the NAND output is forced to a _____ and EL = _____, which allows the thermometer value to be displayed. When the displayed value is within the acceptable limits, the Limit Detector Logic will output a 1 to the SR flip-flop. At this point, the Restart switch would be manually returned to the 1 level. This means that a set of two 1's is applied to the two 1's inputs of an SR flip-flop made of NANDs. This (11) N-tuple causes _____ at the Q point and therefore EL = _____. Future changes of temperature will be displayed as long as the new temperature is within limits. However, if the limits are exceeded (i.e., any value other than 1 through 5), the NOT output from the Limit Detector Logic places a 0 on the upper input of the SR flip-flop. This forces the output of the upper NAND to a 1, which in turn forces the output of the lower NAND to a 0 and hence EL = _____. When EL goes high, the alarm is sounded and the process shutdown procedure is initiated. The out-of-limits value is frozen in the display so that the operator can analyze the faulty symptom. Note that during the shutdown procedure the temperature may drift momentarily back through the acceptable limits. However, even if the Limit Detector Logic does temporarily return to the 1 level, the (11) N-tuple applied to the SR inputs will not change the output and disrupt an orderly shutdown procedure.

a. $(0)R16, (1)R16 = (0001)R2$
b. 1 or high, blank (no segments are lit)
c. $(A)R16, (E)R16, (E)R16, (2)R16$
d. 1, 0, no change, remains = 0, 1

4. Connect the circuit of Figure III-2(d) to the RBI input. With EL = 0 and RBI = 1, toggle S2 until the display reads (E)R16.
   a. Reset RBI = 0 by changing S1. The display now reads (_____)R16. Toggle S2. The display now reads (_____) R16. Toggle S2 again. The display is now _____. Toggle S2

again. The display now reads (_____)R16. Toggle S2 at least 15 more times while observing the display. The only character that is blanked (no segments lit) is (_____)R16. Incidentally, did you notice that the RBO was high (LED was lit) except when the character (0)R16 was blanked?

Try toggling through the characters again to verify this if you missed it the first time.

This blanking of 0's (often called "ripple blanking") is controlled by the Ripple Blanking Input (RBI) line and is very useful if the display is connected to devices with an RZ (return to zero) output format. You may recall that in an RZ format all outputs will temporarily return to 0's before changing to the next set of values. Therefore, if the outputs were slowly changing from a (6)R16 to a (9)R16 and if ripple blanking were not used, the display would read the following sequence: 6, 0, 7, 0, 8, 0, 9. If ripple blanking is used, the display would instead show the sequence 6, blank, 7, blank, 8, blank, 9, which is more visually appealing to the eye and also less confusing to the uninformed observer. Note also that the Ripple Blanked Output Display line (also referred to as RBO) was used as an output line to indicate when a (0)R16 was blanked. In our next circuit we shall see RBO used as an input to control the blinking of the display.

a.   (E)R16, (F)R16, blank, (1)R16, (0)R16

5. Connect the circuit of Figure III-2(e) to the RBO input. With EL = 0, RBI = 1, and RBO = 1, toggle S2 until the display reads (5)R16.
   a.   Use the PA switch to reset RBO = 0. The display is now _____. Toggle the PA switch a few times. Note that the display appears to blinking on and off. Toggle S2 a few times and repeat the blinking to be sure that it works for all characters. (It does!)

   Blinking displays draw human attention more easily than constant displays. Assume for a moment that we want to add a blinking display to our circuit of Figure III-2(c). That is, if an out-of-limits value occurs, we want to shut down the process and display the unwanted value in blinking mode. One way to add this feature would require an astable (oscillating at a slow-enough frequency to allow us to see the blinking) feeding into one input of a two-input NAND. The output of this NAND would be connected to RBO and the other input of the NAND would be connected to the NOT output feeding the EL line.

b. Now, as long as the process is operating within limits, EL = 0 and we are displaying the current temperature. Since our newly added NAND has an input tied to EL, we have forced this NAND to maintain a _____ at RBO. However, when the temperature drifts out of limits, the Limit Detector Logic forces EL = _____. This input to our newly added NAND is now high, which means that the output driving RBO will now go low when the astable output is high and will go high when the astable output is low. In other words, we have frozen the bad value in a blinking display.

a. blank
b. 1, 1

6. The flowchart in Figure III-3 depicts the necessary sequence for using our 9368 ROM as a decoder/driver for a seven-segment common-cathode display. Study it until you are sure you understand how each symbol in the flowchart relates to the operations you have performed in these experiments. While the circuitry of Figure III-2(e) is connected to the control lines of Figure III-2(a), follow the operational steps on your flowchart as you practice: continuously displaying, freezing displays, ripple-blanking 0's from the displays, blanking all displays, and blinking displays. Be sure that you practice until you can demonstrate and explain each step of the sequence.

7. Reread the objectives for these experiments. Study these experiments until you feel sure that you have mastered and can demonstrate each of the objectives. You will then be ready to study PROMs, EROMs, PLAs, party-line operations, and switch registers.

PROBLEMS AND EXPERIMENTS

PROMs, EROMs, PLAs, Party-Line Operations and Switch Registers

Objectives: By the end of these experiments and the associated problems, you should be able to correctly perform each of the

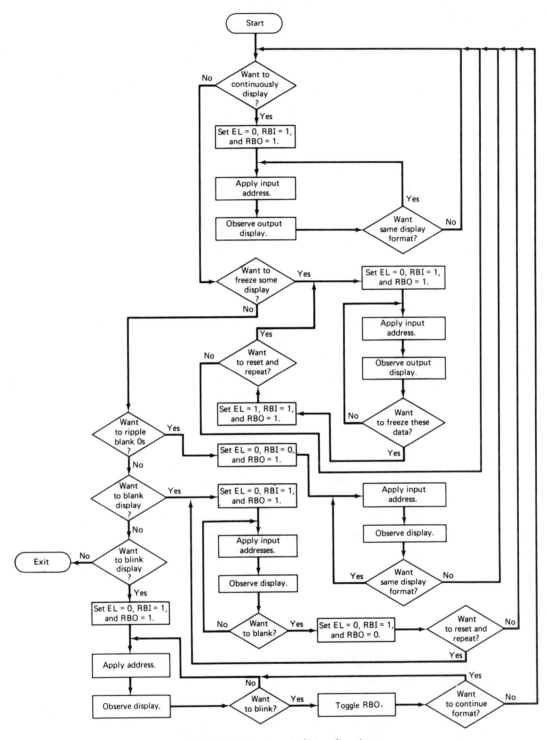

FIGURE III-3 Decoder/driver flowchart.

following objectives using only a power supply, logic circuitry, and the notes and data obtained from running these experiments.

1. Explain the meaning of PROM, EROM, PLA's party-line operations, and switch registers. Give an example of an application of each.

2. Explain the use of the switch register, Tri-state buffer chips, and AND and NOT gates to form a EROM. Draw a schematic, and connect and demonstrate the necessary circuitry.

3. Explain the use of a ROM address decoder in conjunction with switch registers and Tri-state buffers to form a multilocation EROM to initialize set points for a microprocessor.

4. Explain and demonstrate the procedural steps for "writing" a sequence of "set points" into an EROM made of a ROM decoder, switch registers, and Tri-state buffers. Explain and demonstrate the procedural steps for "reading" the sequence of set points from this EROM.

5. Without consulting any references, from memory draw a flowchart that shows the procedural steps to read set points into a microprocessor, to change the set points, and to interrupt the microprocessor to read the new set points. Using only your flowchart, a power supply, and logic circuitry, connect the EROM portion of the circuitry, and demonstrate the validity of this portion of your flowchart.

Procedures:

1. After reading the narrative on read-only memories and performing the experiments on code conversion with ROMs, you should be ready to learn about PROMs, EROMs, and switch registers. Remember that ROMs are programmed at the factory at the time of construction (either in a popularly used pattern of data or in a special pattern requested by the customer). Once you obtain the ROMs, the contents of any location can be read but cannot be altered. By contrast, a PROM is not programmed by the manufacturer at the time of construction. Instead, the customer with a PROM "burner," "blaster," or "programmer" (different terms often used for the same device) can write a program into the PROM. Once the PROM contains the program, it cannot be modified and at that point it becomes a "read-only" device or "programmable read-only memory."

An EROM (or EPROM) is a form of erasable read-only memory.

The customer with the appropriate equipment can write a program into the EROM. The contents can then be considered "read only." For the customer desiring to change the program, it is usually necessary to remove the EROM from use, erase its former contents, and then reprogram. The process of erasing and reprogramming is a lengthy one compared to the process of reading the contents from memory, but the EROM is reusable! As you would expect, EROMs are more expensive than PROMs.

There are different ways of forming EROMs. One popular technique is to make the EROM out of light-sensitive solid-state materials so that its entire contents are erased by prolonged exposure to ultraviolet light. Another technique is to use switches arranged in "groups" or "registers" combined with gates and buffers to provide the equivalent function of an EROM. Let us examine this with the aid of the circuitry in Figure III-4.

2. For convenience, the single-pole single-throw switches (SPSTs), the pull-up resistors (so called because they pull the normally open switch contact to a high level whenever the switch is opened), and the DSO, DS1, . . . inputs of the Tri-state buffers should be preconnected to the power supply and logic circuitry. In fact, the SPSTs are in small dual-in-line package (mini-DIP). Connect the remaining circuitry of Figure III-4(a).

   a. Clear the counter by setting CL = 1 and then resetting CL = 0. The display now reads (_____)R16. Set EN = 1. The output of the AND will now be high for two N-tuples (_____) R2 = (_____)R16 and for (_____)R2 = (_____) R16. Note that if we do not want a high for (F)R16, we should have decoded a 1 from Q _____ as well as the outputs of the other three Q points. The fact that we did not fully decode all outputs is called "partial decoding," and this practice can lead to problems of conflicting outputs during certain addresses if the designer is not careful.

   b. Since the display reads (0)R16, the AND output is a 0 and the NOT output at LED 4 is a _____. The LEDs 0, 1, 2, and 3 all read _____ 's, since the Tri-state buffers are disabled by the NOT output. (Since the Tri-states are at their high-impedance levels, the inputs of the TTL drivers of the LED indicators are allowed to float to a high level. To prove this, set the DS0, DS1, DS2, . . . switches to alternate 10101010. Note that none of the four LED indicators show 0's, which indicates that these levels are not yet enabled to pass through the Tri-states.)

c. If we leave EN = 1 and toggle S2 (change its level and then
    return to its original level), the NOT output at LED 4 will
    remain high until the counter reaches (_____)R16. At this
    time the low indicated by LED 4 will enable the Tri-state
    drivers to come out of their high-impedance levels. Now the
    value displayed by LED 3 through LED 0 is (_____). To
    prove that, we can now transmit any N-tuple through the Tri-
    states, close all the SPST switches. LEDs 3, 2, 1, and 0 now read
    (_____). Open all the SPST switches. LEDs 3 through 0
    now read (_____). Reestablish the N-tuple (1010).

d. Toggle S2. LEDs 3 through 0 now read (_____) because

_____

_____

a. (0)R16, (0111)R2 = (7)R16, (1111)R2 = (F)R16, QD
b. 1, 1's
c. (7)R16, 1010, 0000, 1111
d. (1111), the high at LED 4 has returned the Tri-state outputs to
    their high-impedance level, which allows the inputs of the TTL
    drivers of the LED indicators to float back to a 1 level

Note that this circuit is in the ROM family because:

1. if the appropriate address is presented to the address decoder
    logic [see Figure III-0(a)], and
2. if the appropriate enable signal is present at the control logic,
    then
3. the contents of the decoded address can be fetched from the
    memory matrix and presented at the outputs of the data
    buffer. These contents are available to a computer or micro-
    processor on a "read-only" basis. That is, the computer or
    microprocessor cannot "write" new data into this address.
    Only the human programmer can do this. Since the human
    programmer can erase the current contents and write in new
    contents by resetting the switches, we can refer to this as an
    EROM or erasable read-only memory.

3. Let us increase the number of words in our EROM. Connect a new
    switch register (composed of SPDTs this time) to a new set of
    Tri-states and address decoders as shown in Figure III-4(b). Connect
    this circuitry to the correspondingly labeled inputs and outputs of
    Figure III-4(a). Notice that the "bus lines" (a defined collection of
    conductors used for carrying signals) connected to LEDs 3 through
    0 are now fed by more than one source (the circuitry of parts a and

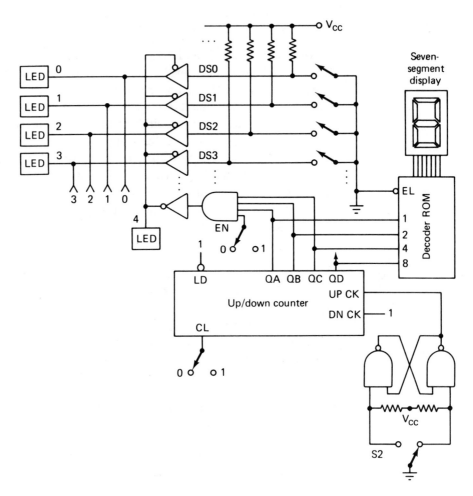

(a) Switch register EROM using SPSTs

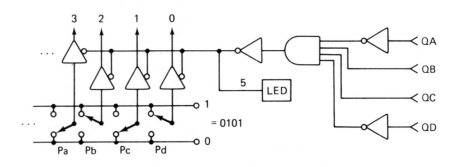

(b) Switch register EROM using SPDTs

FIGURE III-4 Switch registers as EROMs.

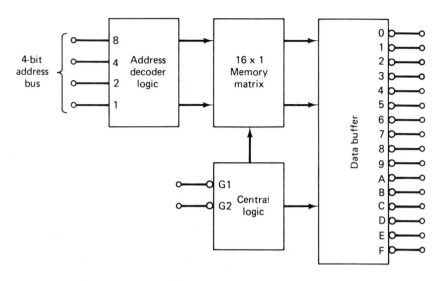

(c) 74154

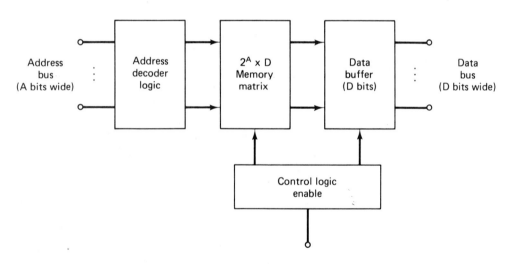

(d) ROM diagram

FIGURE III-4 (continued)

b). Whenever bus lines are fed by multiple sources, we can refer to this as "party-line" bus operations.

a. Set the SPDT register to (0101). Leave the SPST register set to (1010). Clear the counter to all 0's. The outputs at LEDs 4 and 5 are now _____. Both sets of Tri-state drivers are at the

_____ level and LEDs 3 through 0 read
(_____).

b. The output at LED 5 will be at the high level until the counter reaches (_____)R16. At this count, the LEDs 3 through 0 will read (_____), which is the same as the contents of the SP _____ register. Toggle S2 until the seven-segment display reaches (6)R16 and verify these predictions.

c. When S2 toggles the counter to (7)R16, LEDs 3 through 0 will read (_____), which is the same as the contents of the SP _____ register. Toggle S2 and verify this.

d. When the counter is advanced to (8)R16, LEDs 3 through 0 will read (_____), indicating that _____

_____

_____.

This bus reading will continue until the counter advances to (_____)R16, at which count the four LEDs on the bus will again read (_____). Use S2 to advance the counter and verify these predictions.

a. 1's, high-impedance level, (1111)
b. (6)R16, 0101, SPDT
c. 1010, SPST
d. 1111, both Tri-state buffers have returned to their high-impedance levels, (F)R16, 1010

Did you notice that the SPST register contents were presented to the LEDs on the data bus for two nonconsecutive N-tuples our of 16 possible N-tuples? When partial decoding is deliberately done so that the same contents are presented to the data bus for more than one N-tuple, we have a special form of ROM referred to as a programmable logic array (PLA). Let us examine an application for PLAs.

Suppose that we want to use a member of the ROM family to construct a multiplication table for multiplying a 4-bit multiplicand by a 4-bit multiplier to obtain an 8-bit product. We can use an 8-bit address bus with the upper 4 bits containing the multiplicand and the lower 4 bits containing the multiplier. Therefore, if we want to multiply (8)R16 by (2)R16, our address bus will read (1000, 0010)R2. Now, the product of (8)R16 times (2)R16 is (16)R10 = (10)R16, which, in 8 binary bits, should be indicated on the data bus lines as (0001,0000)R2.

Now if we consider that there are 16 possible N-tuples for our 4-bit multiplicand and that there are 16 possible n-tuples for our 4-bit multiplier, this means there are (256)R10 possible N-tuples that can occur on our address bus (16 times 16). Therefore, we could purchase a 256 × 8 PROM (256 addresses with each address having an 8-bit content) and "blast" or "burn" in our multiplication table. However, a little thought might convince us that so many of these 8-bit contents will be identical that a programmable logic array might be a more economical alternative. For instance, while it is true that (8)R16 times (2)R16 will appear on our address bus as (1000,0010)R2, causing (0001,0000)R2 = (16)R10 to appear on our data bus, it is also true that (2)R16 times (8)R16 should cause the same product to appear on our data bus. [That is, the address (0010,1000)R2 should also cause (0001,0000)R2 to appear on our data bus.] Also, (4)R16 times (4)R16 should produce the same product. [That is, the address (0100,0100)R2 should also cause the data bus to read (0001,0000)R2.]

Obviously, there are a number of other products that can be produced by more than one combination of multiplicand and multiplier. Therefore, by applying the laws of Boolean algebra to the combinations on the address bus that cause a given product to appear on the data bus, we can come up with an address decoder for each product that will enable the same contents to be presented for more than one address combination. [Much the same as our example in Figure III-4(a) where the same contents were presented to the data bus for both the address (7)R16 and (F)R16.] This means that we will not require a full 256 × 8 PROM but can instead use a smaller PLA.

4. For a PROM or EROM that may require different contents for each memory address in a sequence of consecutively arranged locations, a PLA with partial address decoding is not sufficient. Since complete decoding of all addresses in the sequence of locations is required, one technique of achieving this is to use a ROM. In other words, a ROM can be used for the address decoder logic as a part of a larger ROM, PROM, or EROM that accomplishes the function of presenting D data bits as the contents of an address that was ROM decoded from A address lines. To study this further, examine the use of the 74154 (1-of-16 decoder ROM) shown in Figure III-4(c). When the G1 and G2 inputs are tied to 0's, the control logic allows the 4 bits on the address bus to be decoded. Since 1 of 16 N-tuples can be present at any instant, the corresponding output line from the data buffer will go to a 0. The other 15 data lines will remain at the 1 level.

This same 74154 ROM can now be used as the "address decoder logic" shown in the ROM diagram of Figure III-4(a). Let us examine this.

a. Disconnect the NOT gate outputs from the Tri-state enable lines and from LEDs 4 and 5 in Figure III-4(b) and (a). Connect LED 4 and its Tri-state enable line to output line 7 of the 74154 at the lower right side of the power supply and logic circuitry. Connect LED 5 and its Tri-state enable to output line 6 of the 74154. Connect the control logic enable lines G1 and G2 to ground. Connect the counter output QA to input line 1 of the 74154. Similarly connect line QB to line 2, QC to line 4, and QD to line 8. Set the SPST register to (1010) and the SPDT register to (0101). Clear the counter.

b. The counter is cleared to (0)R16 and LEDs 3 through 0 should read _____. This reading should not change until the counter advances to (_____)R16, at which time LEDs 3 through 0 will read (_____). Advance the counter and verify this prediction.

c. The next reading as we advance the counter will be (_____) followed by (_____) as we advance the counter once again. Advance the counter and verify these predictions.

b. all 1's, (6)R16, 0101
c. 1010, 1111 since all Tri-state buffers have returned to their high-impedance level

5. We have now seen how a ROM decoder can be used in conjunction with switch registers and Tri-state buffers to form an EROM, but what is an application for such a circuit? One application is shown in Figure III-5. Here a computer or microprocessor is monitoring the flow of liquid and/or gas from up to 16 different pipelines as they feed into a blending tank. Suppose that on Tuesday, the process operator is asked to produce a chemical blend that will require pipe A to flow at 100% of its maximum possible rate. (Its maximum possible rate should be known by the process operator. It can be determined as a function of pressure at the pump, diameter of the pipe, viscosity of the fluid, etc.). Furthermore, this blend requires that the flow from pipe B be shut off, that the flow from pipe C be maintained at 50% of its maximum rate, that pipe D flow at 25% of its maximum rate, and so on.

Now, how can the process operator tell the computer or microprocessor what the desired rates (called "set points") are to be for today's operation? One way is to construct an EROM similar to our Figure III-4. Only this time we would use 16 different switch regis-

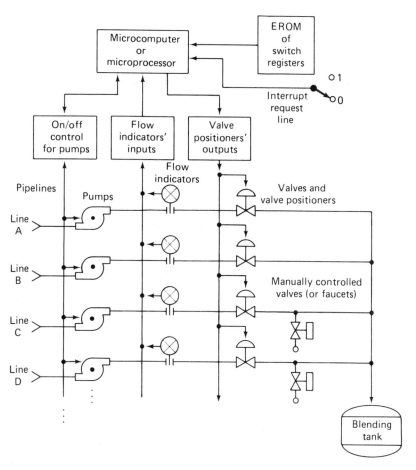

FIGURE III-5 Blending system.

ters. If we could control these flows with satisfactory accuracy using only 4 bits of resolution, we would require a 16 × 4 EROM. Since pipe A is to flow at 100%, the operator might set the first set of four switches to (1111)R2 (representing 100% as the largest possible value of a 4-bit number). Similarly, the operator might reset the second switch register to (0000)R2 to represent 0% flow. The third set of switches might be set to (1000)R2 to represent a 50% set point (desired flow rate) and the fourth set of switches to (0100)R2 to represent a 25% flow rate, and so on.

Now the operator starts this computer-controlled process by setting the switch registers and then by toggling his Interrupt Request line to signal the computer to read the new set points in the EROM. Then the pump on pipeline A will be turned on and the valve in the line will be completely opened. The pump on line B will be stopped and its valve will be closed. The pumps will be turned on at pipelines C and D and their valves will be partially open.

Suppose that there is an increase in the flow rate above the set point in pipeline C. That is, suppose that the flow transducer suddenly tells the computer that the flow rate has just increased to 60% of its maximum possible rate (perhaps the pressure was just increased by turning off a faucet and this resulted in a sudden increase in the flow rate at the flow indicator.) The computer will have to take steps to reduce this flow rate back to the desired set point of 50%. Since it knows that the rate has increased by an undesirable 10%, it will send the appropriate signals to the valve positioner on line C to close the valve a little more until the set-point value is again present at the flow indicator.

Similarly, if a faucet was opened on line D, the pressure and flow rate in that line would drop below the desired 25% rate. The computer would then subtract the indicated rate from line D's flow indicator from the desired flow rate. It would then know how much to open the valve on that line to increase the flow rate back to the set point of 25%.

6. The flowchart in Figure III-6 depicts a sequence for controlling a blending system such as the one shown in Figure III-5. In addition to the control and monitoring actions of the computer or microprocessor the flowchart also shows the procedural steps for writing a sequence of set points into the EROM studied in Figure III-4, and for requesting that the computer or microprocessor interrupt its current process and read in the set points for the new process.

Study this flowchart until you are sure you understand how each symbol in the flowchart relates to the operations you have performed in these experiments. While the circuitry consisting of your two switch registers, two Tri-state buffers, and decoder ROM is still connected, follow the flowchart symbols as you establish new set points and then advance your counter inputs to the decoder ROM to read each new set point in the sequence just as the computer or microprocessor would. Be sure that you practice until you can demonstrate and explain each step of the sequence.

7. Reread the objectives for these experiments. Study these experiments until you feel sure that you have mastered and can demonstrate each of the objectives. You will then be ready to take the exam on this unit. After passing the test, you will then be ready to study sequential access memories and memory registers.

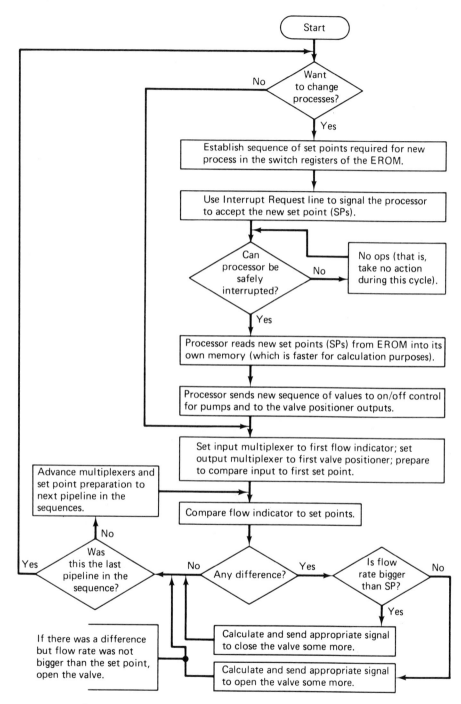

FIGURE III-6   Flowchart of control sequence for blending system.

SAMPLE TEST FOR UNIT III

(Closed book, closed notes. Use only writing materials, templates, and logic circuitry.)

1. Explain the meaning of each of the following terms. Give an example of an application for each term.
   a. ROM
   b. PROM
   c. EROM
   d. PLA
   e. Decoder ROM
   f. Decoder/driver ROM
   g. Switch register EROM
   h. Party-line operations

2. Draw and explain a functional block diagram for a ROM with 2^A addresses each containing D data bits and a single control line Enable. Label each block and show the flow of signals.

3. Explain the manipulation of the individual segments of a seven-segment common-cathode display to view the hexadecimal character set.

4. Explain the manipulation of the address lines and the construction of the PROM "program" to form a multiplication table for a 3-bit multiplier. Explain how and why a PLA might be used as an alternative.

5. Draw a flowchart that shows the procedural steps to continuously read the contents of a ROM which has been preprogrammed to perform a given code conversion. Using only your flowchart, a power supply, and logic circuitry, connect the circuitry and demonstrate the validity of your flowchart.

6. Explain the use of a switch register, Tri-state buffer chips, and AND and NOT gates to form an EROM. Draw a schematic, flowchart the procedural steps, and connect and demonstrate the necessary circuitry.

Sequential Access Memory:
memory registers

INTRODUCTION

Perhaps the best way to understand sequentially accessed memory is to contrast it to randomly accessed memory. Assume that we have data stored in four consecutive memory locations called LOC (X), LOC (X + 1), LOC (X + 2), and LOC (X + 3). Furthermore, suppose that we have just "accessed" LOC (X) (this means that we either read data from this location or we wrote new data into it) and suppose we now want to access the data in LOC (X + 3).

In randomly accessed memory we could go directly from accessing LOC (X) to accessing LOC (X + 3) without having to access the intermediate locations LOC (X + 1) and LOC (X + 2). In a sequentially accessed memory, we must "pass through" or "access" each location in the sequence until we reach the location we are seeking.

A shift register is a form of sequential access memory. For example, if a bit of data is strobed into the first flip-flop of a 4-bit shift register and if we are observing the output of the last flip-flop in the register, we must observe (or access) the contents from the last three flip-flops as we shift the data through the observation point before we can observe the bit that was initially strobed into the first flip-flop (see Figure IV-0).

Sequential access memory is available in other forms in addition to registers. Paper tape, magnetic tape, and disk are also forms of sequential access memory. However, because of the increasingly important role of registers in the arithmetic and control logic units of computers and microprocessors, this unit will concentrate exclusively on the major types of memory register operations.

There are four major types of register operations that can be classified by the manner in which data enters and leaves the register. If the data are "serial in–serial out," we say that the register is operating as a "SISO register." When there is no feedback from the output to the input, the SISO register is merely a shift register and, as such, can be used as a digital delay line or as a temporary storage register in a serial arithmetic logic unit. When, after serially loading the register, feedback is inserted between the output and the input, the register is functioning as a "ring counter" and the memory contents are said to be "recirculating." Banks of recirculating memory are often used to "refresh" the screen of a cathode ray tube used as a computer terminal. This refresh action is necessary to keep the alphanumeric data steadily displayed on

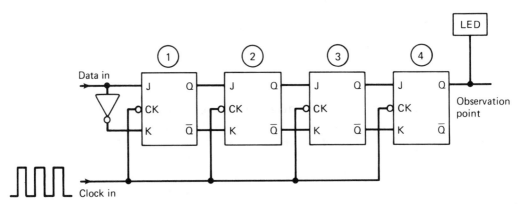

When a new bit of data, say x, is strobed by a clock pulse into flip-flop ①, the current contents of flip-flop ① will be shifted into flip-flop ②. Similarly, all other current flip-flop contents will be shifted one place to the right. As clock pulses are applied, the LED display at the observation point will show the contents of each flip-flop in sequence until the fourth clock pulse has shifted x into the fourth flip-flop.

FIGURE IV-0 Shift register as a form of sequential access memory.

the screen while the beam of the CRT's electron gun rapidly scans the screen.

Another type of sequential access memory operation is the "serial in–parallel out" (SIPO). This operation is also referred to as "serial-to-parallel" conversion, since the data that enter the register in serial form (one bit after the other) will leave the register in parallel form (all bits leave at the same time). Since many computer terminals such as Teletypes provide serial output data to computers that are designed to work with parallel data, SIPOs are extremely important.

Another type of register operation to be studied in this unit is the "parallel in–serial out" or PISO operation. Obviously, if a computer or microprocessor has parallel data to send to a serial device (such as the printer on a Teletype), a PISO operation is indicated. (Please note that the integrated circuit register used for the PISO may be designed specifically for PISO operations or may be a general-purpose register that can be used for PISO, SIPO, or other operations. In fact, this unit will use the same "7496" register to demonstrate all four of the major sequential access operations.)

The fourth type of operation is the "parallel in–parallel out" (PIPO). This operation is often used to provide temporary storage for parallel data. For example, a microprocessor capable of thousands of operations per second may be responsible for controlling several devices which are capable of performing only a few operations per minute. So that the microprocessor does not have to waste time waiting for a relatively slow device to respond to a command, the microprocessor may transmit the command to a PIPO located at the slow device. Then the processor can tend to other chores while the device slowly interprets and responds to the instruction stored in the PIPO register.

There are many possible combinations of these four basic register operations such as the SIPOSO, which provides both serial and parallel outputs. However, an understanding of the four basic operations should enable you to readily understand the combinations. With this in mind, there are five principal objectives for each of the four operations covered in this unit. By the end of the experiments in this unit, you should be able to correctly perform each of the following objectives using only a power supply, logic circuitry, and the notes and data obtained from running these experiments.

Objectives of Unit IV

For each of the following sequential access memory operations, PIPO, PISO, SIPO, SISO:

1. Explain the meaning of the operation and give an example of a typical application.

2. Name and explain the use of the control lines typically encountered in the operation.

3. Name the counters and explain the combined use of the counters and the control lines encountered in the operation. Draw the circuitry necessary to accomplish this.

4. Demonstrate the procedural steps and explain how any given unit of data is "input" into the register and is "output" from the register during the operation.

5. Without consulting any references, draw a flowchart that shows the procedural steps to load and then to transmit any unit of data. Using only your flowchart, the schematics in your book, a power supply, and logic circuitry, connect the circuitry and demonstrate the validity of your flowchart.

6. Pass a closed-book, closed-note, written/laboratory exam over the material of this unit with at least 80% accuracy.

7. Explain the relationship of each of the topics in this unit to the remote terminal unit of Figure II-0.

LIST OF EQUIPMENT AND COMPONENTS USED IN UNIT IV

Equipment:

Oscilloscope: dc-coupled, 10-MHz BW
Power supply: 5 V dc at 1 A

Commonly used logic circuits (see Appendix G):

4   bounceless input switches
6   LED indicators
6   SPDT input switches
2   seven-segment hex displays

Components:

1   7400   quad 2-input NAND
1   7404   hex NOT
1   7408   quad 2-input AND
1   7411   triple 3-input AND
1   7432   quad 2-input OR
1   7473   dual JK flip-flops

1 7486   quad XOR
1 7496   5-bit shift register
1 74193   4-bit up/down counter
2 74125   quad three-state drivers

PROBLEMS AND EXPERIMENTS

Parallel In–Parallel Out (PIPO) Operations

Objectives: By the end of these experiments and the associated problems, you should be able to correctly perform each of the following objectives using only a power supply, logic circuitry, and the notes and data obtained from running these experiments.

1. Explain the meaning of PIPO operations. Give an example of a typical application.
2. Explain the use of the two control lines (Preset Enable and Clear) typically encountered in PIPO operations.
3. Explain the use of a Gray code counter to control PIPO operations. Draw the circuitry for a 2-bit Gray code counter.
4. Demonstrate the procedural steps and explain how a (0010)R2 is loaded into the register and how subsequent loads are then disabled until another PIPO operation is desired.
5. Without consulting any references, draw a flowchart that shows the procedural steps to load any data into a PIPO circuit and then to disable subsequent loads until another PIPO operation is desired. Using only your flowchart, a power supply, and logic circuitry, connect the circuitry and demonstrate the validity of your flowchart.

Procedures:

1. After reading the narrative on registers and sequential access memories, you should be ready to learn how to load a (00101)R2 into a PIPO circuit and then to disable subsequent loads. Remember that a PIPO circuit is often used for temporary storage for parallel data. For example, a computer may want to order a motor to increase rpm's (revolutions per minute) by 20%. Since the computer works at much greater speed than the motor and since the computer probably has many other chores to perform the computer can write the instruction to increase rpm's by 20% into a

PIPO circuit. Then the computer can perform other chores while the PIPO patiently waits for the motor to read and obey the instruction which is now contained in the PIPO register. When the instruction has been obeyed, the PIPO can be reset to wait for the next instruction from the computer. Connect the circuit of Figure IV-1 and apply power.

2. There are two control lines, called Preset En. (preset enable) and CL (clear). There are five output lines (Q points) to be connected to the LED displays and five input lines to be connected to any five binary input switches. Set all switches to the 0 level.

a. The Q outputs from left to right read (_____)R2 as indicated by the LED displays.

b. Set the five input switches to (00101)R2. The Q outputs now read (_____)R2 as shown by the LEDs.

c. In other words, changing the binary levels of the input switches while Preset En. and CL are held low causes _____ at the Q points. In fact, the (00)R2 combination on the control lines where CL = 0 and Preset En. = 0, respectively, is used to clear the registers to all 0's.

a. (00000)R2
b. (00000)R2
c. no change

3. Change the control lines setting to (01)R2 (where CL = 0 and Preset En. = 1) while leaving the input switches set to (00101)R2.

a. The Q outputs now read (_____)R2. Change the input switches to (10111)R2 to observe the effects at the Q points.

b. The Q outputs now read (_____)R2. Change the input switches back to (00101)R2 to observe the effects at the Q points.

c. The Q outputs now read (_____)R2.

d. In other words, the Q outputs are at _____ levels as their respective input switches. In fact, the (01)R2 combination on the control lines (CL = 0 and Preset En. = 1) allow the Q points to follow their respective input lines to a 1 or to a 0. (In a moment you will observe a combination on the control lines that allow the Q points to follow the input lines to a 1 but not to a 0.)

a. (00101)R2

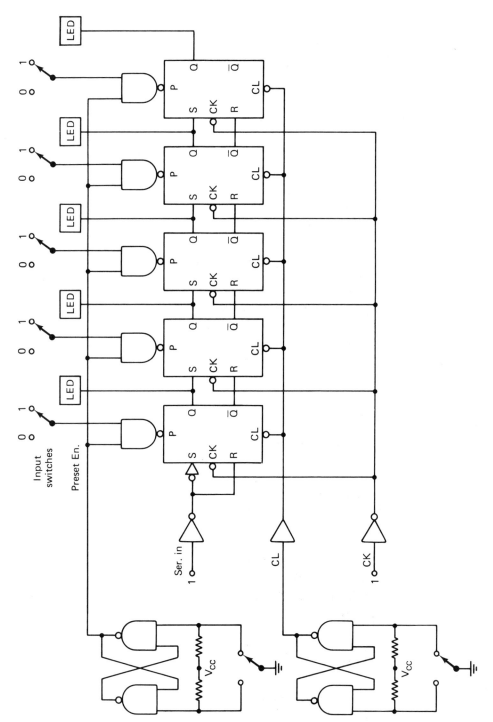

FIGURE IV-1 Circuit for PIPO operation.

93

    b. (10111)R2
    c. (00101)R2
    d. the same

4. Change the control lines setting to a (11)R2 (CL = 1 and Preset En. = 1) while leaving the input switches set to (00101)R2.
    a. The Q outputs now read (_____)R2. Change the input switches to (10111)R2 to observe the effects at the Q points.
    b. The Q outputs now read (_____)R2. Change the input switches back to (00101)R2 to observe the effects at the Q points.
    c. The Q outputs now read (_____)R2.
    d. Did you notice that the Q outputs will now follow their respective inputs to a _____ level but not to a _____ level?

This means that you will need to clear the register to all 0's (by placing a 00 on the control lines) if any flip-flop in the register is to contain a 0. Then you will need to raise to a 1 level only those input lines whose respective Q points are to be loaded with 1's. This is illustrated in the next step.

    a. (00101)R2
    b. (10111)R2
    c. (10111)R2
    d. 1 or high, 0 or low

5. With the input switches set to (00101) R2, set the control lines to (00)R2 (CL = 0 and Preset En. = 0).
    a. The Q outputs now read (_____)R2. Set the control lines to (11)R2.
    b. The Q outputs now read (_____)R2. Note that (00)R2 on the control lines cleared the register although some of the input lines were high. Also note that we are now back in the (11)R2 mode of operation, where an output can follow its corresponding input from a 0 to a 1 but not from a 1 to a 0.

    a. (00000)R2
    b. (00101)R2

6. Change the control lines from a (11)R2 to a (10)R2, where CL = 1 and Preset En. = 0.

a. The Q outputs now read (_____)R2. Change the input switches to (10110)R2.

b. The Q outputs now read (_____)R2. Note that the Q points are not changing value even though their respective inputs may change level.

c. In other words, subsequent parallel loads are _____ until another PIPO operation is desired.

a. (00101)R2
b. (00101)R2
c. disabled

7. Complete the table below. It is a summary of the effects of ma nipulating the CL and the Preset En. lines.

Binary Values of CL Preset En.	Effects of Binary Values on CL and Preset En.
a. _____	Clears the Q points to 0's
b. _____	Allows Q points to follow their respective inputs to a 1 or a 0.
c. _____	Allows Q points to follow their respective inputs from a 0 to a 1 but not from a 1 to a 0.
d. _____	Disables changes at the inputs from affecting the Q outputs.

a. 00
b. 01
c. 11
d. 10

8. Did you notice in step 7 that as you answered parts a through d, there was a change in only one binary digit as you progressed sequentially from one answer to the next? This is an example of a Gray code count and is shown below:

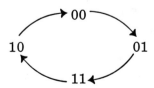

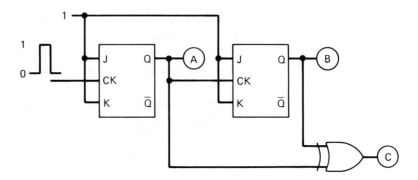

FIGURE IV-2 Two-bit Gray code counter.

Gray code counters may be used to sequence PIPO operations. Let us examine a circuit for a Gray code 2-bit (binary-digit) counter. Look at Figure IV-2.

Notice that the two JK flip-flops are connected as a straight-code, 2-bit counter. The outputs at A and B are shown in the truth table below. Remember that an Exclusive-OR has a 1 output if and only if one and only one of the two inputs are at the 1 level. Complete the truth table with your predictions for the output at C. You may want to connect the circuit and verify your predictions. Record your predictions for C in both tables.

	C	B A		B	C
a.		0 0		0	e.
b.		0 1		0	f.
c.		1 0		1	g.
d.		1 1		1	h.

i. By using B as the most significant bit and C as the least significant bit (B = MSB and C = LSB), have we established the Gray code sequence? _____

a. = 0 = e.
b. = 1 = f.
c. = 1 = g.
d. = 0 = h.
i. yes

9. Suppose that we want to replace the register contents with any

other value. The flowchart in Figure IV-3 depicts the necessary sequence. Study this flowchart. Then replace the (00101)R2 with (11000)R2 by using the flowchart as your operational guide. Be sure that you can correctly explain each symbol in the flowchart and how it relates to your PIPO operation.

10. Reread the objectives for these experiments. Study these experiments until you feel sure that you have mastered and can demonstrate each of the objectives. You will then be ready to study PISO operations.

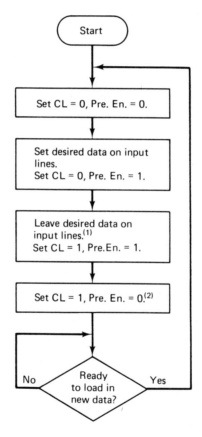

(1) The (11) condition is necessary to insert between the (01) and the (10) conditions to avoid having two different bits change at the same step. If, for example, the LSB changed states a few nanoseconds before the MSB, the register would have been cleared a second time.

(2) The data are now securely loaded into the register.

FIGURE IV-3   PIPO flowchart.

PROBLEMS AND EXPERIMENTS

Parallel In–Serial Out (PISO) Operations

Objectives: By the end of these experiments and the associated problems, you should be able to correctly perform each of the following objectives using only a power supply, logic circuitry, and the notes and data obtained from running these experiments.

1. Explain the meaning of PISO operations. Give an example of a typical application.
2. Explain the use of the three control lines (Preset Enable, Clear, and Clock) typically encountered in PISO operations.
3. Explain the combined use of a Gray code counter and a straight-code counter to control PISO operations. Draw the circuitry necessary to demonstrate this.
4. Demonstrate the procedural steps and explain how a (10011)R2 is parallel-loaded into the register, how subsequent parallel loads are disabled, and how serial output is accomplished.
5. Without consulting any references, draw a flowchart that shows the procedural steps to load any data into a PISO circuit in parallel form and then to transmit the data out in serial form. Using only your flowchart, the circuit of Figure IV-4, a power supply, and logic circuitry, connect the circuitry and demonstrate the validity of your flowchart.

Procedures:

1. After performing the experiments on PIPO operations, you should be ready to learn how PISO circuits work. Remember that PISO operations are also referred to as parallel-to-serial conversion. Connect the circuitry of Figure IV-4(b). The circuitry of Figure IV-4(a) will be added to this circuit later in this experiment. After connecting the circuitry of part b, you should have four unconnected leads labeled: "Preset Enable of Register," "Last Q of Register," "Clock of Register," and "Clear Register." These will later be used to interconnect circuit *a* to circuit *b*.
2. In this experiment we will be working with three control lines, including two (Preset Enable and Clear) that we studied in the PIPO experiments and one new one called "Clock of Register" or simply "CK." Before examining the CK control function, let us study the

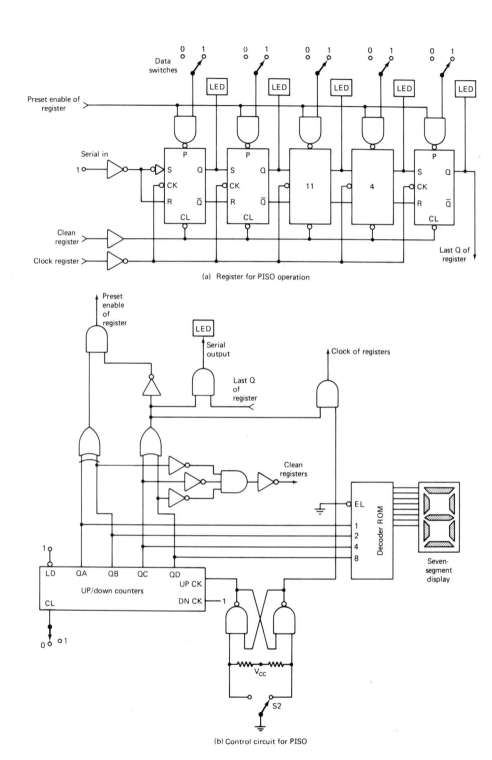

(a) Register for PISO operation

(b) Control circuit for PISO

FIGURE IV-4   Circuitry for PISO operation.

99

operation of the parallel loading of data into the register. Then we can study how the clock line is used to transmit the data out of the register in serial form.

Recall from the PIPO experiments that a Gray code is used to control the parallel load and then to disable subsequent parallel loads until they are desired. In question 7 of the PIPO experiment, we summarized the effects of each N-tuple of the code. There we stated that the (00)R2 N-tuple (CL = 0 and Preset En. = 0) clears the Q points of the register to 0's. The circuitry you have connected in Figure IV-4(b) contains a counter with a "Clear Counter" or "CL counter" line shown connected to a switch contact normally at the 0 level. Raise this switch level to a 1 and then return it to a 0. You have now reset the Q points of the counter to all 0's. This should be indicated by 0 displayed by the seven-segment display.

a. The counter outputs QA and QB are connected to the inputs of an Exclusive-OR. Since QA and QB are both 0's, the output of the Exclusive-OR will be _____ . Since this level is input to an AND gate, the output of the AND (labeled "Preset Enable of Register") will be at the _____ level.

b. Notice that the counter outputs QB, QC, and QD are each connected to NOT gates, which are in turn connected to an AND. Since QB, QC, and QD are presently at the 0 level, the outputs of the three NOTs are at the _____ level and the output of the AND is at the _____ level. Since the AND's output is tied to the input of another NOT, the output of this NOT (labeled "Clear Register") must be at the _____ level. Since the "Preset Enable" output and the "Clear Register" output are both at the 0 level, then if these lines were connected to the register for PISO operation in Figure IV-4(a), we could expect this (00)R2 N-tuple to clear the PISO register to all 0's.

c. By the way, it is worth noting at this point that the counter outputs QC and QD are also connected to an OR gate. Since QC and QD are both at the low level, the output of the OR is at the _____ level. Since the output of the OR is connected to the inputs of two AND gates, these two AND outputs (labeled "Serial Output" and "Clock of Register") will both be at the _____ level. In fact, these two outputs will remain at the low level as long as the output of the OR is at a low level. And since the output of the OR is dependent only upon QC and QD of the counter, the OR output cannot go high until a count of

(4)R10 or higher has been reached. [Remember that QD is the most significant bit of the counter, QA is the least significant bit, and (4)R10 is equivalent to (0100)R2, which will be the first high level on QC or QD during a straight-code up-count.]

While the counter is still reset to all 0's, measure and verify the levels you predicted in parts a, b, and c of this question.

a. 0, 0
b. 1, 1, 0
c. 0 or low, 0

3. Apply a pulse to the "Up Clock" input of the counter by raising and lowering the buffered switch. (The RS flip-flop is made from the two NANDs, two pull-up resistors, and the SPDT switch.) The seven-segment display should now read "1," indicating that the counter now contains the (0001)R2 N-tuple. (QD = QC = QB = 0, QA = 1).)

a. Since the counter outputs QA and QB now read QB = 0 and QA = 1, the output of the Exclusive-OR, which is a function of QA and QB, will be at the _____ level. Since this output becomes the input to an AND and since this is at a high level, the output of the AND will now be determined by its other input. That is, if the other input is also at a high level, all inputs to the AND are high and the output will be a _____. If the other input is a low, the output will be a _____. Let us examine this other input to the AND.

b. Since QC = 0 and QD = 0, the output of the OR will be a _____. The OR output is connected to the input of a NOT. Therefore, the output of this NOT will be a _____. But this NOT output is the "other input" to the AND we were just examining. Therefore, the output of this AND (labeled "Preset Enable of the Register") will be a _____.

c. Since QD = 0, QC = 0, and QB = 0 exist for the current N-tuple and since these three points are inputs to three NOTs, all three of the NOT outputs are _____. The output of the AND gate connected to these three NOTs is a _____ and the output of the NOT (labeled "Clear Register") is a _____. Therefore, if the two points labeled "Clear Register" (= 0) and "Preset Enable of Register" (currently = 1) were connected to the register for PISO operation of circuit b, this "01" combina-

tion would allow the Q points of the PISO register to follow
their respective data switches to a 1 or a 0 (as summarized in
question ·7 of the PIPO experiments).

d. In Figure IV-4(b) the current output of the OR connected to
QC and QD is a _____. Therefore, the outputs of the two
ANDs labeled "Serial Output" and "Clock of Register" will
both be _____ and will remain so until the counter contains
a number greater than or equal to (_____)R10.

a. 1 or high, 1, 0
b. 0, 1, 1
c. 1's, 1, 0
d. 0, 0, (4)R10

4. Raise and lower the buffered switch that drives the Up Clock input
of the counter. The seven-segment display should now read "2"
indicating that the counter contains the (0010)R2 N-tuple.
a. Since QB = 1 and QA = 0, the output of the Exclusive-OR will
be a _____. Since this point is one of two inputs to an
AND, the output of the AND (labeled "Preset Enable of Register") will now be determined by _____
_____. Let us investigate its status.
b. Since QC = 0 and QD = 0, the output of the connecting OR is a
_____. The output of the NOT connected to this OR will
be a _____ and therefore "Preset Enable of Register" will
equal a _____.
c. Since QD = 0, QC = 0, and QB = 1, the output "Clear Register"
will equal _____. (The output of the NOT connected to QB
would be a 0, which makes the AND output a 0, which makes
the final NOT output a 1.) Since a "11" combination would be
applied to the "Clear" and "Preset Enable" lines of the PISO
register, what would be the relationship between the data
switches and the Q points of the PISO register? _____
_____
_____
Note that these two lines are following the Gray code sequence
of 00, 01, 11, ... What should the next combination be?
_____
d. What are the current output levels of "Serial Output" and
"Clock of Register"? _____ and _____. Note that
these two outputs have been "disabled" by the output of the

OR since we started with the counter reset to (0000)R2. These two outputs will remain disabled until the counter reaches a value of (_____)R2.

a. 1, the other input to the AND
b. 0, 1, 1
c. 1, the Q points can follow their respective inputs from a 0 to a 1 but not from a 1 to a 0, (10)
d. 0 and 0, (0100)R2

5. Advance the counter so that the seven-segment display reads "3."
   a. The counter now contains the N-tuple (_____)R2. Since QB = 1 and QA = 1, the output of the Exclusive-OR will be a _____ and the output labeled "Preset Enable" will be a _____.

   b. Since QD = 0, QC = 0, and QB = 1, the "Clear Register" output = _____. Therefore, the PISO register would receive a 1 on its "Clear Register" input control line and a 0 on its "Preset Enable" control line. What relationship would exist between the data switches and the Q points of the PISO register?

   _____

   _____

   c. "Serial Output" and "Clock of Register" currently are at the _____ level because they are still disabled by the OR gate, which monitors QC and QD.

      Measure and verify your predictions for the questions of steps of 3, 4, and 5 if you have not already done so.

   a. (0011)R2, 0, 0
   b. 1, changes at the data switches would not affect the Q outputs
   c. 0

6. Let us examine the status of our two control lines "Preset Enable" and "Clear Register" for all counter values above (0011)R2.
   a. The largest value our 4-bit counter can contain is a (_____) R16 or (_____)R2. For all counts greater than (3)R16, either QC = 1 or QD = 1 or both equal 1. Therefore, the output of the OR will be a _____ for counts (4)R16 through (F)R16. The output of the NOT connected to this OR will be a _____ for all these counts and so will the output "_____ _____." Furthermore, the functions "Serial Output" and

"Clock of Register" are now _____ by this OR (i.e., able to go to a 1 or a 0, depending upon their other input line).

b. For all remaining counts up to (F)R16, either QB, QC, or QD or some combination of these three lines will be at the _____ level. This means that one of the three connecting NOTs must have a _____ output, which means the connecting AND must have a _____ output and the "Clear Register" output will remain at the _____ level. (Note that these four NOTs and the AND are performing the equivalent work of a three-input OR. This can be quickly verified by recalling your laws of Boolean algebra.)

c. Since "Clear Register" = 1 and "Preset Enable of Register" = 0 for all counter values above (3)R16, subsequent counts disable other parallel input loads from occurring. However, the contents of the last Q point of the PISO register are now enabled to pass through the AND gate with the output labeled "Serial Output" and be displayed by the LED indicator circuit. The output of this AND gate will equal the current contents of the last flip-flop in the PISO register for the remainder of the operation. However, the output of the AND gate labeled "Clock of Register" is now enabled to drive the five flip-flops of our PISO register in coordination with the drive of our counter. With each pulse from the "Clock of Register" line, the contents of each flip-flop are shifted one place to the right. It requires _____ pulses to completely shift out in serial form the information that was loaded in parallel form. (Note that the information at "Serial Output" is in Non Return to Zero (NRZ) format. Also note that a "shutdown circuit" would be useful to clear the counter after the fifth bit has been shifted out of the register.)

a. (F)R16 = (1111)R2, 1, 0, Preset Enable of Register, enabled
b. 1, 0, 0, 1
c. 5

7. The flowchart in Figure IV-5 depicts the necessary sequence for parallel-to-serial conversion (PISO) operation. Study it until you are sure you understand how each symbol in the flowchart relates to your PISO operation. Connect the circuitry of part (a) to part (b) of Figure IV-4. While following the operational steps on your flowchart, practice loading values such as (10011)R2 in parallel and then shifting the values out in serial NRZ format. Be sure that you

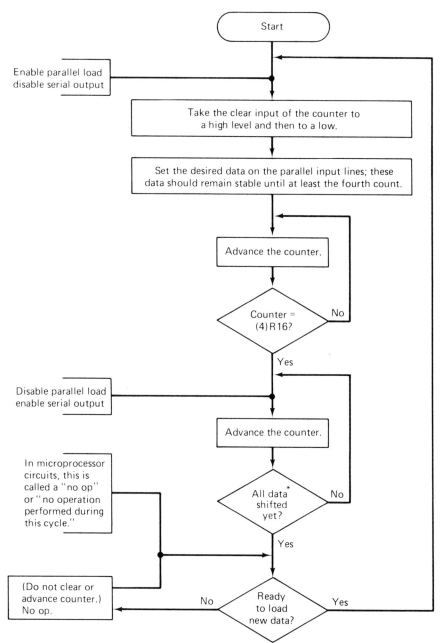

Start

Enable parallel load
disable serial output

Take the clear input of the counter to
a high level and then to a low.

Set the desired data on the parallel input lines; these
data should remain stable until at least the fourth count.

Advance the counter.

Counter =
(4)R16?

No

Yes

Disable parallel load
enable serial output

Advance the counter.

In microprocessor
circuits, this is
called a "no op"
or "no operation
performed during
this cycle."

All data*
shifted
yet?

No

Yes

(Do not clear or
advance counter.)
No op.

No

Ready
to load
new data?

Yes

*Note: A counter value is not specified in this flowchart for "data shifted yet" for two reasons. First, it allows the flowchart to remain valid for any number of flip-flops that we might care to add to our PISO register (at least one count per flip-flop will be necessary). Second, it is not uncommon in serial transmission to insert one or two "start bits" and one or two "stop bits" around each set of data to be transmitted. This signals the receiver of the data when to prepare for new information. Start and stop bits are explained more thoroughly in books on telecommunications and peripherals.

FIGURE IV–5 PISO flowchart.

practice until you can demonstrate the procedural steps and explain how the serial outputs are disabled while parallel loads are taking place and then how parallel loads are disabled while serial outputs are taking place.

8. Reread the objectives for these experiments. Study these experiments until you feel sure you have mastered and can demonstrate each of the objectives. You will then be ready to study SIPO operations.

PROBLEMS AND EXPERIMENTS

Serial In–Parallel Out (SIPO) Operations

Objectives: By the end of these experiments and the associated problems, you should be able to correctly perform each of the following objectives using only a power supply, logic circuitry, and the notes and data obtained from running these experiments.

1. Explain the meaning of SIPO operations. Give an example of a typical application.
2. Explain the use of the following lines as encountered in SIPO operations: Preset Enable, Clear, Clock, and Serial Input.
3. Explain the combined use of a straight-code counter and the Clear lines of the counter and the register to control SIPO operations. Draw the circuitry necessary to demonstrate this.
4. Demonstrate the procedural steps and explain how a (10011)R2 is serially loaded into the register, how subsequent serial loads are disabled, and how parallel output to a receiver is accomplished.
5. Without consulting any references, from memory draw a flowchart that shows the procedural steps to load any data into an SIPO circuit in serial form and then to transmit the data out in parallel form. Using only your flowchart, the circuit of Figure IV-6, a power supply, and logic circuitry, connect the circuitry and demonstrate the validity of your flowchart.

Procedures:

1. After performing the experiments on PIPO and PISO operations, you should be ready to learn how SIPO circuits work. Remember that SIPO operations are also referred to as serial-to-parallel conversion. Connect the circuitry of Figure IV-6(c) to the circuitry of

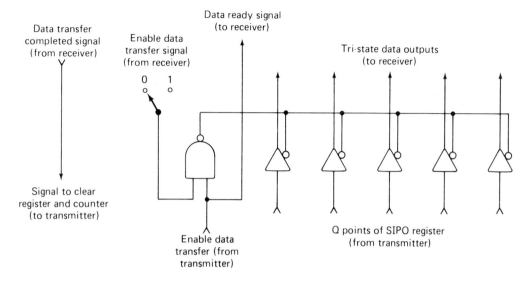

(a) Interface circuitry to receiver

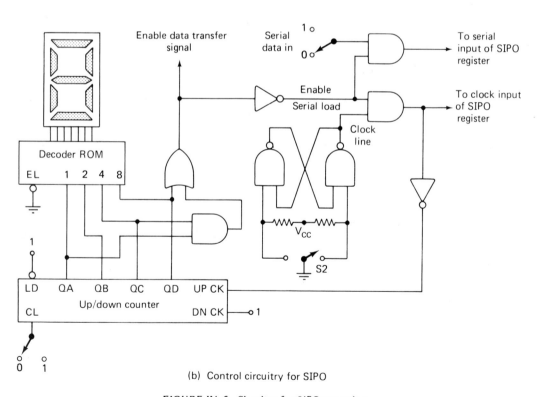

(b) Control circuitry for SIPO

FIGURE IV-6 Circuitry for SIPO operation.

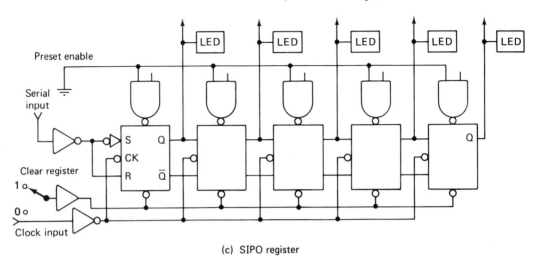

(c) SIPO register

FIGURE IV-6 (continued)

Figure IV-6(b). The circuitry of Figure IV-6(a) will be considered later in these experiments.

Note that there are two output control lines in part (b) (Serial Input and Clock Input) that are connected to two corresponding input control lines in part (c). Both of these output control lines in part (b) come from AND gates, which are enabled by a NOT gate output labeled "Enable Serial Load." Let us examine the control of these lines.

2. If, in the circuitry of part (c), Preset Enable = 0 and Clear Register = 1, then from the two previous sets of experiments we know that parallel loads are disabled. Therefore, we can turn our attention to the serial input and clock input lines which come from the circuitry in Figure IV-6(b). Note that both lines will be low unless Enable Serial Load = 1. By applying the laws of Boolean algebra we can derive the logic equation for this function to be

$$\text{Enable Serial Load} = \overline{(QD + QA \cdot QC)}$$

Since this is the logic equation for the output of the NOT gate, the equation for the input of the NOT gate (labeled "Enable Data Transfer Signal") is

$$\text{Enable Data Transfer} = QD + QA \cdot QC$$

a. The 4-bit counter counts from (0)R16 to (F)R16. QD = 1 for counts (_____)R16 = (_____)R2 through (_____) R16 = (_____)R2. Therefore, the output of the OR is at the _____ level for counter values $\geqslant$ (8)R16 because of the OR input coming from QD. This means that Enable Serial Load = _____ for these same counts, which _____ both the Serial Input and the Clock Input lines.

b. The OR gate will also have a high output whenever its input from the AND gate is high. This AND gate has inputs from QA and QC and will have a 1 output for four of the 16 N-tuples of the counter. In ascending order, these four N-tuples that will cause a high output from the AND (and hence a high output from the OR and a low output on the NOT which disables Serial Input and Clock Input) are (_____)R16 = (_____) R2, (_____)R16 = (_____)R2, (_____)R16 = (_____)R2, and (_____)R16 = (_____)R2.

c. Since Serial Input and Clock Input are disabled (held to a low level) whenever the OR gate has a 1 output, we can conclude that serial load operations would be disabled once the counter reaches a value $\geqslant$ (_____)R16 = (_____)R2. However, notice that the Clock Input of the SIPO Register also drives a NOT gate, which in turn drives the UP Clock input of the counter. Therefore, a 1 level is maintained on UP CK from the N-tuple (_____)R16 = (_____)R2 until the Clear line of the counter is taken to a low value to reset the counter to all 0's. [Although this CL line of the counter is shown connected to a SPDT switch in Figure IV-6(b), in actual practice it would more likely be a function of the Data Transfer Completed Signal from the interface circuitry in Figure IV-6(a). There will be more discussion about this later in this experiment.]

a. (8)R16 = (1000)R2 through (F)R16 = (1111)R2, 1, 0, disables
b. (5)R16 = (0101)R2, (7)R16 = (0111)R2, (D)R16 = (1101)R2, (F)R16 = (1111)R2
c. (5)R16 = (0101)R2, (5)R16 = (0101)R2

3. Raise to a 1 level and then return to a 0 level the Clear switch on the counter to reset the Q points to (0000)R2. The seven-segment display should read (0)R16.

   Lower to a 0 level and return to a 1 level the Clear Register switch. The LEDs attached to the Q points of the SIPO register should read (00000)R2 from left to right.

Set the Serial Data In switch to a 1. (Although this line is shown connected to a SPDT switch, in actual practice it would be connected to a source of serial data such as a teletype output. The combined functions of parts (a) through (c) of this figure might then be to accept the serial data from a Teletype, convert it to parallel form, notify a microprocessor or minicomputer that the register now contains new data and then to hold the parallel data until the processor has accepted it and issued a signal to clear the register and the counter so that the sequence may begin again.)

a. With the counter reset to 0's, Enable Serial Load = _____ and the Serial Input of the SIPO register = _____. Change the level of S2 and then return to the original level. This presents a "pulse" containing a trailing edge to both the counter and the register. This first pulse should have "strobed" the high level from the SPDT Serial Data In switch into the SIPO register. The LEDs attached to the register now read from left to right (_____)R2. The seven-segment display shows the counter contents to be (_____)R16 = (_____)R2. Enable Serial Load now is at the _____ level.

b. Leave the Serial Data In switch set to a 1 so that we can strobe a second 1 into the register. Pulse (change level and return) S2. The LEDs now read (_____)R2, the seven-segment display reads (_____)R16 and Enable Serial Load now is at the _____ level.

c. Reset the Serial Data In switch to the 0 level so that we can see a 0 strobed into the register after our two 1's. Pulse S2. The LEDs now read (_____)R2, the counter display reads (_____)R16, and Enable Serial Load is at the _____ level.

d. In our initial statement of objectives we were told that we would be converting a (10011)R2 from serial to parallel form. Note that the last 3 bits of this number (--011)R2 are presently in the first three flip-flops of our SIPO register and are moving one place to the right with each S2 pulse. Therefore, our next task is to shift in a _____. To accomplish this, the Serial Data In switch should be at the _____ level before we pulse S2. Pulse S2. The LEDs now read (————)R2, the counter display reads (_____)R16, and Enable Serial Load is at the _____ level.

e. Set the Serial Data In switch to a 1. Pulse S2. The LEDs now read (_____)R2, the counter display reads (_____)R16

and (be careful on this one!) Enable Serial Load is at the
_____ level. Let us be sure that this last level is what it
should be. The counter display of (5)R16 is equivalent to
(_____)R2 which means that QA and Q_____ are high.
Therefore, the AND attached to these outputs will cause the
OR output labeled Enagle Data Transfer to go to a _____
level. [We will return to this point in our conclusions in a
moment and follow this signal up to the circuitry in Figure
IV-6(c). For now, let us follow this signal to the right.] Since
the OR output presents a 1 to the input of the NOT, this means
that Enable Serial Load will now be a 0, thus forcing the
outputs of the two connecting ANDs to the _____ level.
Note that this disables further pulses from S2 from advancing
the counter or strobing the register. (Try pulsing S2 to change
the LEDs or the display and you can verify this.) The register
will hold this (10011)R2 until it and the counter are cleared.
They will normally be cleared by the receiver interface circuit
after the receiver (possibly a microprocessor or a computer) has
accepted the parallel data from the register.

a. 1, 1, (10000)R2, (1)R16 = (0001)R2, 1
b. (11000)R2, (2)R16, 1
c. (01100)R2, (3)R16, 1
d. 0, 0 or low, (00110)R2, (4)R16, 1
e. (10011)R2, (5)R16, 0, 0101, QC, 1, 0

4. Examine the circuitry in Figure IV-6(a). Note that this "interface"
   circuitry connects the SIPO register and control lines to the receiver. Note that the Enable Data Transfer signal from the OR
   output of part (b) is presenting a high level to the NAND and is also
   used to notify the receiver that the data are ready in the SIPO.
   a. When the receiver is ready to accept new data, it will place a
      high level on the Enable Data Transfer line. [This can be simu-
      lated by the SPDT switch as shown in part (a).] The output of
      the NAND now goes to a _____ level, which enables the
      outputs of the Tri-state drivers to come out of their high-
      impedance state and to present the output levels of the Q points
      of the SIPO register to the receiver. The Tri-state outputs should
      now read (_____)R2.
   b. When the receiver has "read" or accepted the parallel data from
      the Tri-state outputs, it will return the level of its Enable Data

Transfer line to a low (simulated by returning the pole contact of the SPDT switch to the 0 level). The Tri-state outputs will then return to _____. Next the receiver will pulse its output line labeled "Data Transfer Completed." [This can be simulated by manipulating the SPDT switch in part (c) to clear the register and then by manipulating the SPDT switch in part (b) which clears the counter.] After both of these switches have been returned to their normal level as shown in the figure, the SIPO is now ready to accept 5 new bits of serial data which can now be strobed in by the clock line. (This is simulated by the S2 circuit.) Connect this circuitry and verify your predictions.

   a. 0, (10011)R2
   b. the high-impedance state

5. Suppose that we want to convert the serial data (00101)R2 (or any other 5-bit value) into parallel form and deliver it to a receiver. The flowchart in Figure IV-7 depicts the necessary sequence. Study this flowchart and then convert the (00101)R2 by using the flowchart as your operational guide. Be sure you can correctly explain each symbol in the flowchart and how it relates to your SIPO operation.

6. Reread the objectives for these experiments. Study these experiments until you feel sure you have mastered and can demonstrate each of the objectives. You will then be ready to study SISO operations.

PROBLEMS AND EXPERIMENTS

Serial In–Serial Out (SISO) Operations

Objectives: By the end of these experiments and the associated problems, you should be able to correctly perform each of the following objectives using only a power supply, logic circuitry, and the notes and data obtained from running these experiments.

1. Explain the meaning of SISO operations. Give an example of a typical application.

2. Explain the use of the following lines as encountered in SISO operations: Preset Enable, Clear, Clock, and Serial Input.

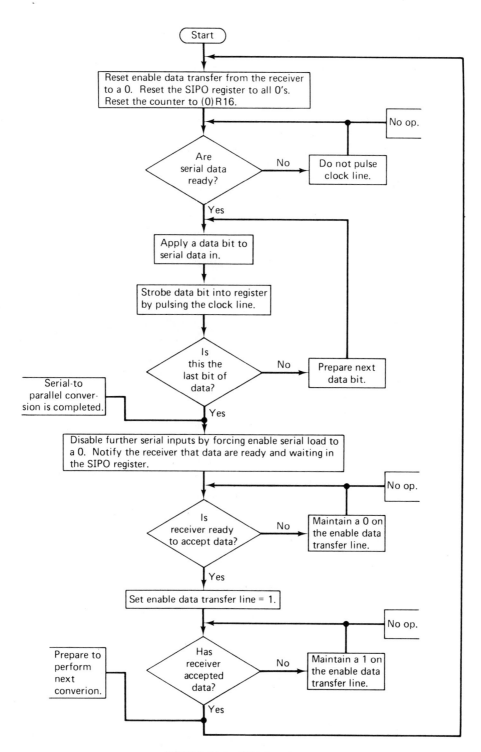

FIGURE IV-7 SIPO flowchart.

113

3. Explain the combined use of a straight-code counter and the Clear lines of the counter and the register to control SISO operations. Draw the circuitry necessary to demonstrate this.

4. Demonstrate the procedural steps and explain how a (1001)R2 is serially loaded into the register, how these data are recirculated along with a "sync" pulse, and how subsequent serial loads are disabled during this recirculation until it is desired to load new data.

5. Without consulting any references, from memory draw a flowchart that shows the procedural steps to load any data into a SISO circuit, recirculate, and "sync" it as many times as desired and then to load in new data. Using only your flowchart, the circuit of Figure IV-8, a power supply, and logic circuitry, connect the circuitry and demonstrate the validity of your flowchart.

Procedures:

1. After performing the experiments on PIPO, PISO, and SIPO operations, you should be ready to learn how SISO circuits work. Remember that SISO operations with end-around feedback are also referred to as recirculating memory. When a number of SISO circuits (often referred to as banks of SISOs) are used together in a recirculating manner, they are sometimes referred to as "refresh" memory. (This term probably originated with the need to refresh the alphanumeric contents shown on computer terminals using a cathode ray tube display. For example, to display a message on the CRT screen such as "PLEASE SIGN IN" would require refreshing the screen as it is repetitively scanned by the electron beam.)

   Connect the circuitry of Figure IV-8(a) to the circuitry of Figure IV-8(b). Note that there are two output lines (Serial Input and Clock Input) in part (a) that are to be connected to part (b). Note that there is one output line in part (b) (bit 4 of Register) that is to be connected to part (a). Let us examine the control of these lines.

2. If in the circuitry of part (b), Preset Enable = 0 and Clear Register = 0, we know from previous experiments that the register is cleared to all 0s. If we leave Preset Enable = 0 and set Clear Register = 1, we disable parallel loads. Perform this procedure on your connected circuitry.

   If in the circuitry of part (a), LD = 1, DN CK = 1, and CL = 1, we know from previous experiments that the counter is cleared to all 0's. If we leave LD = 1 and DN CK = 1 and reset CL = 0, we

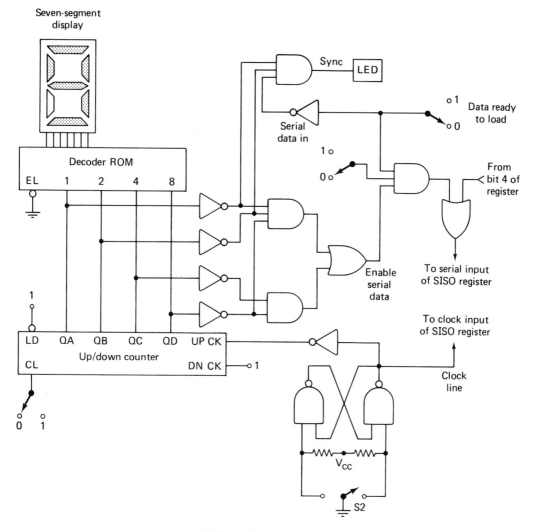

(a) Control circuitry for SISO

FIGURE IV-8 Circuitry for SISO operation.

allow the counter to count up from (0)R16. Perform this procedure on your connected circuitry.

Note the OR output labeled Enable Serial Data. By applying the laws of Boolean algebra, we can derive the logic equation to be

$$\text{Enable Serial Data} = \overline{QD} \cdot \overline{QC} + \overline{QD} \cdot \overline{QB} \cdot \overline{QA}$$

Since the register has been cleared to all 0's, this means that the first four signals from bit 4 of Register will be 0's. Therefore,

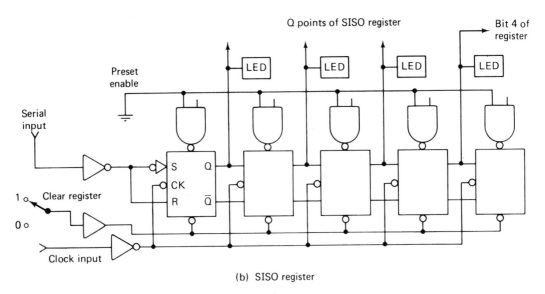

(b) SISO register

FIGURE IV-8 (continued)

the OR output labeled to Serial Input of SISO Register will, for the first 4-bits of data, depend solely upon the output of the AND which is enabled by the Data Ready to Load and the Enable Serial Data lines. Let us examine this.

a. The output of the AND gate whose inputs are $\overline{QC}$ and $\overline{QD}$ will be at a high level for four of the 16 N-tuples. In ascending order, these four are (_____)R16 = (_____)R2, (_____) R16 = (_____)R2, (_____)R16 = (_____)R2, and R16 = (_____)R2. Since this AND is connected to an OR, the output of the OR must be a 1 for these same N-tuples.

b. The output of the AND gate whose inputs are $\overline{QD}$, $\overline{QB}$, and $\overline{QA}$ will be at a high level for two of the 16 N-tuples. In ascending order, these are (_____)R16 = (_____)R2 and (_____)R16 = (_____)R2. Since this output is connected to an OR, the output of the OR must be a 1 for these same N-tuples.

c. Since the OR with the output labeled Enable Serial Data receives inputs from these two ANDs, we can conclude that the level on the SPDT switch labeled Serial Data In will be passed through the connecting AND gate only during the N-tuples: (_____)R16, (_____)R16, (_____)R16, (_____) R16, and (_____)R16 provided that the SPDT switch Data Ready to Load is set to 1. (In actual practice these SPDT switches would be replaced with circuitry that had received new data to be loaded into the "recirculating" or "refresh" memory. When new data became ready, the counter and the register would be cleared to all 0's, then Data Ready to Load would go high and remain high while the data at Serial Data In would be clocked in. After the data had been loaded, Data Ready to Load would go low and the register contents would recirculate.)

d. Examine the AND gate with the output labeled Sync. This output is intended to provide a signal that is "synchronized" with the start of the message in the SISO register each time the message is recirculated. If the Data Ready to Load switch is at the 0 level, the Sync output is dependent upon the two inputs $\overline{QA}$ and $\overline{QB}$. These two inputs are both high for four of the 16 N-tuples: (_____)R16, (_____)R16, (_____)R16, and (_____)R16. Therefore, the Sync output is high once every 4 bits (at the start of the 4-bit message).

e. Let us load and recirculate a (1001)R2. With the register cleared to 0's and Clear Register = 1 and with the counter cleared to all 0's and CL = 0, set Data Ready to Load = 1 and Serial Data In = 1. "Pulse" (change level and return to original level) S2. The register LEDs now read from left to right (_____)R2 and the counter display reads (_____)R16. Reset Serial Data In = 0. Pulse S2. The register LEDs now read (_____)R2 and the counter display reads (_____)R16. Leave Serial Data In = 0 and pulse S2. The register LEDs now read (_____)R2 and the counter display reads (_____)R16. Set Serial Data In = 1 and pulse S2. The register LEDs now read (_____)R2 and the counter display reads (_____)R16. Reset Data Ready to Load = 0.

f. The Sync LED now reads (_____)R2. Pulse S2. Register LEDs = (_____)R2, Counter Display = (_____)R16, Sync = (_____)2. Pulse S2. Register LEDs = (_____) R2, Counter Display = (_____)R16, Sync = (_____)R2. Pulse S2. Register LEDs = (_____)R2, Counter Display = (_____)R16, Sync = (_____)R2. Pulse S2. Register LEDs = (_____)R2, Counter Display = (_____)R16, Sync = (_____)R2. Pulse S2 four more times and Counter Display = (_____)R16 and Register LEDs = (_____)R2. A Sync pulse is being generated every _____ clock pulse.

a. (0)R16 = (0000)R2, (1)R16 = (0001)R2, (2)R16 = (0010)R2, (3)R16 = (0011)R2

b. (0)R16 = (0000)R2, (4)R16 = (0100)R2
c. (0)R16, (1)R16, (2)R16, (3)R16, (4)R16
d. (0)R16, (4)R16, (8)R16, (C)R16
e. (1000)R2, (1)R16; (0100)R2, (2)R16; (0010)R2, (3)R16;
    (1001)R2, (4)R16
f. 1; (1100)R2, (5)R16, (0)R2; (0110)R2, (6)R16, (0)R2;
    (0011)R2, (7)R16, (0)R2; (1001)R2, (8)R16, (1)R2, (C)R16,
    (1001)R2, fourth

3. Suppose that we want to load and recirculate the serial data (0111)
    R2 (or any other 4-bit value). The flowchart in Figure IV-9 depicts
    the necessary sequence. Study this flowchart and then load and re-
    circulate (0111)R2 by using the flowchart as your operational
    guide. Be sure that you can correctly explain each symbol in the
    flowchart and how it relates to your SISO operation.

4. Reread the objectives for these experiments. Study these experi-
    ments until you feel sure you have mastered and can demonstrate
    each of the objectives. You will then be ready to take the exam on
    this unit. After passing the test, you will then be ready to study
    random access memories.

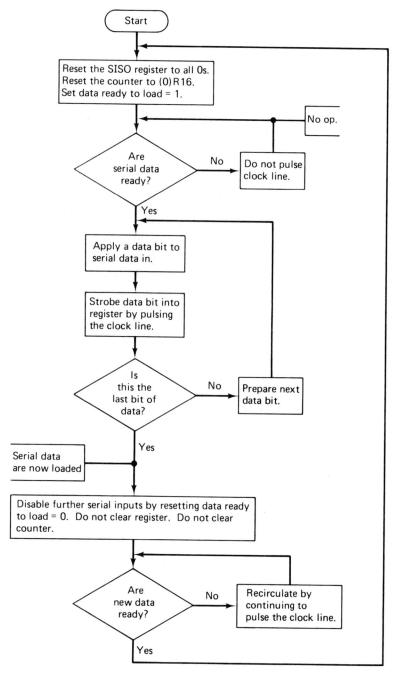

FIGURE IV-9 SISO flowchart.

SAMPLE TEST FOR UNIT IV

(Closed book. Closed notes. Use only writing materials, templates, and logic circuitry.)

1. Explain the meaning of each of the following terms. Give an example of an application for each.
   a. Sequential access memory
   b. PIPO operations
   c. PISO operations
   d. SIPO operations
   e. SISO operations
2. Explain the use of a Gray code counter to control PIPO operations. Draw the circuitry for a 2-bit Gray code counter.
3. Draw a flowchart that shows the procedural steps to load any data into a PISO circuit and then transmit it out.
4. For a SIPO circuit, explain the combined use of a straight-code counter and the Clear lines of the register and counter to control SIPO operations. Draw the schematics, connect the circuitry, and demonstrate the procedural steps in a SIPO operation.
5. Draw a flowchart that shows the procedural steps to load any data into a SISO circuit, recirculate, and "Sync" it as many times as desired and then load in new data.

unit

Random Access Read/Write Memory:
the static RAM family

INTRODUCTION

A memory location is the smallest subdivision of memory that can be used for the storage and retrieval of data. A read-only memory has data written into its locations (usually data are inserted off-line away from the system where the ROM is to be used) and once the ROM is placed on-line, the data contents of each location can be read but not altered (written). By contrast, a read/write memory can be used in an on-line environment such that appropriate elements in the system (such as a microprocessor) can read data from a location or write new data into the location.

A sequential access memory requires data to be read from or written into a series of memory locations such that each location must be accessed in sequence until the location we are seeking is reached. By contrast a random access read/write memory permits access for reading or writing data to any of its address locations in any desired sequence with similar access time for each location. These read/write random access memories are usually referred to a RAMs. There are two types of RAMs in current use. Both are based on semiconductor storage principles: the dynamic RAM and the static RAM. Although memory technologies are still evolving, your author believes the static RAM will continue to emerge as the best choice for most RAM applications. Therefore, this unit will concentrate on the static RAMs. Cores, bubbles, and dynamic RAMs are discussed in the appendices.

Before examining the objectives for this unit, look at Figure II-0 and locate the RAM module in our RTU block diagram. Let us consider for a moment some of the possible uses of the RAM module and its relationship to other modules in the diagram. Suppose, for instance, that this RTU is one of many RTUs in a large plant that manufactures windows and doors. Suppose further that this particular RTU receives large sheets of glass in various thicknesses as its input of raw materials. Depending upon the production goals of the day, the RTU will be responsible for cutting the sheets of glass into the desired number of small diamond-shaped pieces of glass (for decorative windows for the home), into small rectangular panes of glass (perhaps for storm doors), into larger rectangular panes of glass (for picture windows possibly), and so on. In addition to receiving the glass and making the desired cuts, the RTU must inspect its work (to maintain quality control) and must communicate with the host computer. That is, it must periodically receive instructions from the host computer as to how much raw materials it is to receive, what to do to the raw materials, and where the finished materials are to be sent. The RTU must also report back to the host computer periodically to tell it how the work is progressing, what problems have been encountered, whether its running low on raw materials, and so on. Let us go through a possible sequence of activities.

People work with the host computer to tabulate the numbers of orders for each type of door and window in their product line. These orders may come in from all over the country. Certain commitments have been made as to delivery dates and prices. As a result of considering the orders placed, the projections for orders not yet received, the materials on hand, schedules of manufacturing costs and associated time requirements, and other factors, the host computer works with the people to evolve production goals, strategies, and assignments. Beginning at the top of Figure II-0, the host computer will communicate to each RTU in the plant what that particular RTU is expected to receive and to produce during the forthcoming production period. This information is stored in parallel form in the host computer system. It is converted to serial form to be sent from the host computer's transmitter to the RTU's receiver, since serial form is the most practical, cost-effective way to send digital information over any distance of more than a few yards. The information is converted back to parallel form at the RTU and is written into the RAM module. Once the information is stored in the RAM, the microprocessor reads the RAM data to see what needs to be done. The microprocessor takes the RAM data on how many panes and shapes of each size are needed and feeds the data as inputs to control programs stored in the ROM module. The ROM module may contain, for example, a number of frequently used programs that looks at the size of the glass sheets used as input materials, looks at the outputs to be produced, and tells the microprocessor how to calculate the optimum cutting patterns for the glass sheets. If a nonstandard series of shapes and sizes are to be cut by this RTU during the next several days, the host computer may decide to prepare some new control programs in an EROM module. Someone will then be sent to install this EROM for this production run. The microprocessor uses these patterns to calculate the values to be sent to the output data registers. These output data registers are used in conjunction with the timing and sequencing controls of the counter module to control the machinery that positions the glass sheets, positions the cutting device, controls the speed of operation, and so on. To make certain the patterns are being cut to the desired specifications, the microprocessor looks at values actually measured during the cutting process in the input data registers module. Discrepancies between the desired values and the measured values can be analyzed and compensated for by sending the error data through a calculation process based upon a set of control algorithms. Much of the calculation work is done by the extended arithmetic logic unit. A log of accomplishments, problems, and corrective actions will be written into the RAM. Later in the day the real-time clock module may interrupt the microprocessor to remind it that the time has come to send a progress report to the host computer. The activities log is then sent from the RAM to the parallel-to-serial converters at the RTUs transmitter. This information is then transmitted to the appropriate host computer for analysis while the process continues.

Did you notice that the RAM module(s) plays one of the most important roles in the RTU? Many digital systems designers believe that the key to a good system is the design and utilization of its memory components. Let us look at the parts of a typical RAM.

Note to the reader: The RAM is the most important of the three categories of memory functions. If we had to, we could write our computer programs to make the RAM behave just like a fixed program memory (ROM) or a sequential access memory (registers). The results might not be as cost-effective or as time-effective, but they would work. In fact, this is often how we verify our "software" before we turn it into "firmware." That is, we use the RAM to make sure there are no bugs in the data or instructions which we want to permanently place in a ROM. (Remember that we can correct errors easily and quickly in RAM.) We are also now using RAMs to cost-effectively replace registers in many applications (especially low-speed ones) which were done almost exclusively with registers only 5 years ago. Because of this importance, the introductory material of this unit is somewhat longer than that of previous units. To derive the most benefit from this material, please turn to the objectives at the end of this introduction and study them carefully before returning to this point to resume your reading.

The architecture (the arrangement of functional parts) of a typical static RAM is shown in Figure V-0(a). As indicated in this figure there are four functional blocks to consider. First there is the address decoder logic. This block accepts signals from an address bus which, for a X $*$ Y (read as "X by Y") memory matrix, will contain address lines A0, A1, . . . , AN, where typically $2^{N+1} = X$. The number of bits in almost all types of memory chips is usually a power of 2. Thus an Intel 2102 which is organized as a 1024 $*$ 1 memory matrix (meaning 1024 locations containing 1 bit each) will have a 10-line address bus ranging from A0 through A9, since substituting values into $2^{N+1} = X$ gives $2^{10} = 1024$. (The current literature often abbreviates 1024 by referring to it as 1K.) This RAM is shown in Figure V-0(b). Similarly, the Motorola 6810, which is organized as a 128 $*$ 8 memory matrix (128 locations containing 8 bits each), will have a seven-line address bus ($2^7 = 128$) and an Intersil 7114 chip (a 1024 $*$ 4 organization) will have a 10-line address bus. Both the 6810 and the 7114 are shown in Figure V-0. For all static RAMs it is important that the address bus be completely stable both before and after reading or writing data to or from a location. If the address bus is allowed to change during this R/W (read/write) time, we may read or write multiple locations during what was intended to be a single operation.

A second functional block of the static RAM is the data buffer. The data buffer contains data bus lines over which information can be written into a previously selected memory location or read from a previously selected memory location. If the data buffer supports unidirectional bus lines (signals flow in one way only), there will be an input data bus and an output data bus. The 2102 has unidirectional bus lines. Since we may need to interface this 16-pin chip to one of the many microprocessors or minicomputers that feature bidirectional bus lines (signals can go either way but only one way at a time), we may need to add a circuit similar to Figure V-0(e). Note that a Read (R/W = 1) signal disables the tri-state gate connected to D in of the data buffer, but it enables the tri-state gate connected to D out. Similarly, a Write signal (R/W = 0) allows data to be written into the RAM but prevents

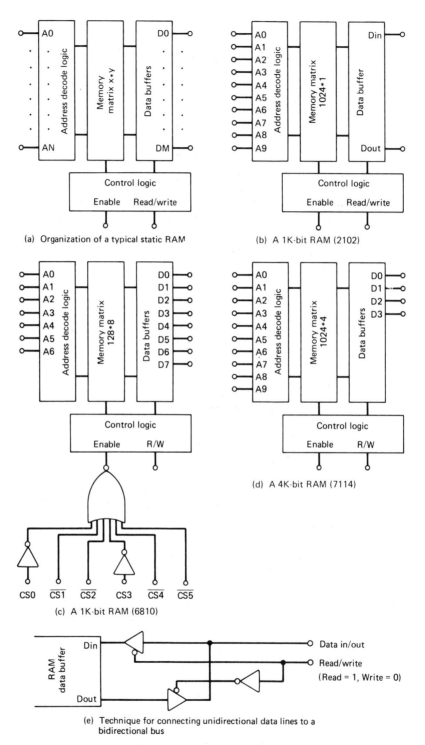

(a) Organization of a typical static RAM

(b) A 1K-bit RAM (2102)

(c) A 1K-bit RAM (6810)

(d) A 4K-bit RAM (7114)

(e) Technique for connecting unidirectional data lines to a bidirectional bus

FIGURE V-0 The RAM family.

output signals from the RAM from reaching the common bus connection "Data In/Out." Many static RAMs are manufactured with a bidirectional data bus such as the 6810 and the 7114.

The width of the RAM data bus (input or output) is equal to the number of bits at each location in memory. Thus a 2102 has a 1-bit data bus width, a 6810 has an 8-bit data bus width, and a 7114 has a 4-bit data bus width. Since the data bus width of the RAM is not necessarily equal to the data bus width of the microprocessor or minicomputer we wish to use it with, we sometimes need to parallel data lines without shorting them out. For example, suppose that we want to construct a 4K word memory for a Z80 microprocessor out of 7114s. Since the Z80 has an 8-bit data bus and since the 7114 has a 4-bit data bus, we can parallel the control lines and address lines of two of the RAMs (i.e., R/W to R/W, EN to EN, A0 to A0, . . ., A9 to A9) and let the 4-bit bus of the first RAM be connected to D0, D1, D2, and D3 of the Z80 bus. Similarly, the 4-bit bus of the second RAM will be connected to D4, D5, D6, and D7 of the Z80 bus. Now both RAMs respond to the same addresses and they jointly appear as an 8-bit data bus to the Z80. These two 7114s have formed a 1K∗8 memory. To make our 4K ∗ 8 memory we will simply parallel four sets of these two chips. There will be more about this in the experiments section.

These parallel bus line connections can be made without shorting the chips out if the chips have open collector outputs (as discussed in Unit II) or Tri-state buffering. Like most MOS chips, the 18-pin 7114 uses Tri-state data buffers. Also, like most MOS chips, these data buffers are referred to as "TTL-compatible," which means that they can drive approximately one unit of TTL fan-in load or about six to seven units of load in the same MOS family. For large digital systems this lack of driving power often requires external buffering. For example, two inverters of a 7404 (a TTL hex inverter chip) can be connected in series to a MOS output line. The input of the first NOT imposes a fan-in of one unit of load on the MOS driver. The output of the second NOT has a fan-out of 10 units of load and should (with the exception of a slight propagation delay) be identical to the MOS output. Still another technique is to use external Tri-state buffers such as shown in Figure V-0(e) with a higher drive capability than the internal Tri-state buffers of the MOS RAM.

The third functional block to be considered is the memory matrix. It is within this matrix that data are to be stored and retrieved. This is therefore the block that contains the most circuitry and has the biggest impact on cost and performance.

In a memory matrix each bit is said to be stored in a "cell." When the memory is a static Ram, this "cell" is a flip-flop. Groups of these flip-flops are arranged to form a multiple-bit unit of memory. Each of these multiple-bit units are regarded as data storage locations with known, unique addresses. When a location is addressed via the address bus, all bistables in the group at that location will be read (or written) at the same time. Thus a memory matrix that is organized as an X ∗ Y will contain X locations with Y bits (flip-flops) at each location. The computers of today typically regard the group of characters coming from or going to a single location in memory as a "word." A word length for a large-scale computer may be as much as 60 bits long (the Cyber 70, for example). A word length for a minicomputer may be as much as 32 bits long (such as the SEL 32). A word length for a microprocessor may be as much as 16 bits long (such as Texas Instrument's SBP9900). The more common word lengths for the large scales, minis, and micros are 32 bits (IBM 360), 16 bits (PDP11), and 8 bits (M6800), respectively.[1] Often "words" will be subdivided into "bytes" and "bytes" will be subdivided into "nibbles." For example, a computer may have a 16-bit word length with the ability to manipulate all 16 bits at once or to manipulate just one of the two 8-bit bytes in the word or to manipulate just one of the word's four 4-bit nibbles. You should remember that the system designer is the one who actually defines the number of bits in that system's word, byte, or nibble. The trend seems to be toward 4 bits per nibble and 8 bits per byte. For microcomputer systems, the terms "word" and "byte" are often used interchangably for an 8-bit memory location. This will probably change in the future to be consistent with the terminology of the minis. That is, a word will consist of a certain number of bytes.

A comparison of the memory matrix of today's static RAMs to the memory matrix of "core" memories shows an increasingly impressive cost/performance ratio in favor of the static RAM, with one possible exception — applications that require all random access memory contents to be retained if power is lost. The core memory is inherently nonvolatile (retains contents if power is removed), whereas a static RAM is inherently volatile. To compensate for this deficiency in those applications that require nonvolatile storage, we have the following choices. First, we can place all data and instructions that do not change in ROMs since they are nonvolatile. Second, we can use a power-down system that detects ac power loss and switches to battery backup without power interruption. This is especially easy to do with CMOS memories, since they require a very small amount of standby

---

[1] Obviously, the large machines operate simultaneously on many more bits than the micros can. Therefore, they can typically "crunch" more numbers in a shorter period of time than can the micros. However, the costs of a large-scale computer system are often over $3,000,000.00, whereas the cost of a microcomputer system is often close to $3000.00. Obviously, considerations of needs, resources, and cost effectiveness should govern the selection of a computer system.

power to retain data intact. Third, we can use a power-down system that detects power loss, switches to battery backup, and copies the RAM contents to a digital cassette or floppy disk. With this technique, even if ac line power is not restored before the battery is drained, the nonvolatile cassette or floppy can be used to restore the RAM contents once power is made available. These techniques are referred to as volatile memory protection.

A final point to consider in our study of the memory matrix block is the type of construction used. Bipolar memories are faster than MOS memories and they require no special handling precautions. However, each bit of bipolar memory tends to cost more to manufacture, occupies more "real estate" on the chip (which results in a smaller density of bits per chip), and consumes more power than the MOS memories. The degree to which each of these three relative disadvantages holds true depends upon which of the bipolar types (TTL, Schottky, ECL, or I^2L) you are comparing to which of the MOS types (PMOS, NMOS, CMOS, or SOS). At the moment, NMOS is the most popular choice for large-scale, general-purpose memories. The I^2L family appears to hold the best chance of taking over the lead from NMOS if certain manufacturing costs can be lowered sufficiently.

The fourth functional block of the static RAM to be considered is the control logic block. Two inputs which must be present are the read/write line and the chip enable line (sometimes called "chip select line"). The read/write (R/W) line is used to determine whether data are to be read from the memory (typically R/W = 1) or data are to be written into the memory (R/W = 0). The enable line (EN) is used to enable the data buffer for the input or output transfer. For example, the 2102 in Figure V-0(b) will float its Tri-state data buffer at the high-impedance state as long as EN = 1. When the appropriate address is on the address bus and EN = 0, then either an input or output data transfer will occur depending upon the input state of the R/W line. The 6810, on the other hand [Figure V-0(c)], provides the user with a number of optional conditions that must be satisfied to enable the IOT (input–output transfer). That is, if CS0 = CS3 = 1 and the other four chip select lines are at the 0 level, the chip will be enabled. The user desiring a single control line to enable a 6810 can simply tie the other chip select lines to a 0 or a 1 as appropriate. Note that the 2102 is a 1K-bit chip in a 16-pin package (10 address lines, two data lines, two control lines, and two lines for the power supply). Note that the 6810 is also a 1K-bit chip (128 * 8 = 1024), but this chip requires a 24-pin package (seven address lines, eight data lines, seven control lines, and two lines for the power supply). The 7114, which is a 4K chip, can be seen to require an 18-pin package.

Now that we have discussed the four functional blocks of a single

static RAM, the next question we might address is the overall performance of a memory module (such as a 1K $*$ 8 or a 16K $*$ 8) made from several static RAM chips. A key factor here is the cycle time. In the days of core memory, cycle time had to refer to the time to read data from a location and then write the same or different data back into the location. This was because we had to perform a destructive read operation to see what a location contained. (Details are given in Appendix A.) Then we would reinsert a copy of the contents we had just destroyed (called "restoration") or we would modify the contents. Since static RAMs use bistables to store data, there is no need to do a destructive read operation to see what is contained in a memory location. We simply read from it or write to it, but a memory cycle no longer requires a restoration step. Therefore, we now have two separate kinds of cycle times: a read cycle time and a write cycle time. The read cycle time (or write cycle time) is the total time interval between the time you start and the time you finish the cycle. For today's solid-state memories, the cycle times vary from faster than 15 ns for ECL (emitter-coupled logic) to almost 2 μs for the older MOS RAMs. The widely used NMOS static RAMs typically range from 200 to 450 ns. It is not uncommon to find that the write cycle time is a few nanoseconds longer than the read cycle time.

Power consumption is the second major factor that affects overall performance of a memory module made from several static RAM chips. A 4K-bit chip can be purchased today with a power dissipation rating of 710 mW maximum and a cycle time of 450 ns. For a little more money, a pin-for-pin compatible 4K-bit replacement chip is available that operates at 200 ns with a maximum power dissipation of 265 mW. Generally, the selection of a memory chip is made by comparing the chip manufacturer's specifications for speed and power to the cycle time requirements imposed by the microprocessor or minicomputer that will use the memory module and also by considering the load to be imposed by the memory module on the system's power supply. Once the "possible" chips have been identified, other factors, such as costs and delivery dates, help to make the best selection. Hopefully, this selection will be a chip that is "second-sourced" (made by more than one manufacturer), since this improves the probability of future availability and lower costs. Let us look at some more of these practical considerations of configureing memory modules.

Because of the handling precautions for using MOS memories and the need for replacement from time to time, we have the best chance of removing one or two defective chips without damaging the other chips on the board if we have used IC sockets. Since sockets sometimes cost as much or more than the ICs and since socket prices rise sharply with an increase in pin numbers, be sure to examine a comparison of the combined costs of sockets and chips before selecting the RAMs to be used in your memory modules.

Another tip is to make certain that all bus lines are TTL-compatible if you are going to connect to a totally TTL-compatible bus. Some RAMs have all lines compatible with TTL except for the chip enable line.

Also watch temperature ranges. The commercial-trade plastic package that performs well in an air-conditioned environment with good air circulation over the chip may be destroyed if operated in rough field conditions (for example, in the fuel control system of an automobile during a hot summer). The military-grade ceramics may be a better choice for remote installations with widely varying ambient conditions.

Another rule is to consistently be sure to take all the precautions necessary when handling MOS logic (as discussed in the first unit). You may forget to ground yourself or your tools and still be lucky enough to avoid damaging the MOS chips the first few times you handle them. The manufacturers are getting better with their on-chip protection circuits. However, this lulls you into false confidence. The next time you touch the chip without being grounded just may be the time that blows it. Keep your ground strap handy and use it!

You also want to remember our discussion in Unit II on noise-reduction techniques. A liberal usage of filter capacitors on the power supply lines can eliminate a lot of noise and grief. For example, a 0.1-μF capacitor could be located immediately adjacent to each 1K RAM chip on the module.

Before proceeding to the experiments, study your objectives for this unit carefully. You may find it helpful to reread this introductory material before going on. Experiments are always more meaningful if you know what to look for.

By the end of the experiments in this unit you whould be able to correctly perform each of the following objectives using only a power supply, logic circuitry, and the notes and data obtained from running these experiments.

Objectives of Unit V

For each of the following concepts in random access read/write memory.

1. Explain the meaning of each of the following terms. Give an example of an application for each term.
   a. Static RAM vs fixed program memory vs. sequential access memory
   b. Volatile RAM protection

c. Read operations vs. write operations

d. LIFO stacks, stack pointers, and stack pointer operations

e. Interrupt requests, priority interrupt levels, interrupt masks, main program vs. interrupt service routines

f. Main program vs. subroutines, subroutine arguments, subroutine jumps vs. other jumps and branches

g. Memory pages and locations within pages

h. Current page operations vs. zero page operations

i. Paged write protection and fence registers

j. Direct vs. indirect vs. indexed addressing

k. LSI memory chips vs. memory modules vs. memory system

2. Compare bipolar RAMs to MOS RAMs. Discuss the major considerations (speed, power, second sourcing, etc.) for selecting RAM chips to be used in memory modules. Discuss the practical aspects of module construction (sockets, noise reduction, handling, etc.)

3. Draw and explain the function of each block of a functional block diagram for a static RAM organized as an A $*$ D. Explain how to calculate the number of bits in the memory matrix, the number of address lines, the number of data lines, and, assuming a single enable input, the number of pins required on the chip. Apply this to a specific example such as a 64 $*$ 4 organization. Name the two control line functions common to all static RAMs. Explain the function of each line, the data bus, and the address bus during a write operation. Explain the function of each line, the data bus, and the address bus during a read operation.

4. For a 128 $*$ 8 static RAM, explain how to write the following data into the indicated locations: $[(34)R16 \rightarrow (04)R16, (F3)R16 \rightarrow (16)R16, (29)R16 \rightarrow (0E)R16]$. Explain how to read the data from these locations. Draw the schematic, flowchart the procedural steps, connect the circuitry, and demonstrate the operations.

5. Explain how a microprocessor with an internal stack pointer and access to a static RAM maintains stack records of nested interrupt routines in progress and of nested subroutines in progress.

6. With the use of the flowchart in Figure V-1(c), explain how the bit-slice microcomputer system in Figure V-1(d) uses the stack pointer circuitry shown in Figure V-1(e) to handle subroutine jumps and returns such as those encountered in the example of Figure V-4(b). Connect the circuitry and demonstrate the accuracy of your explanation.

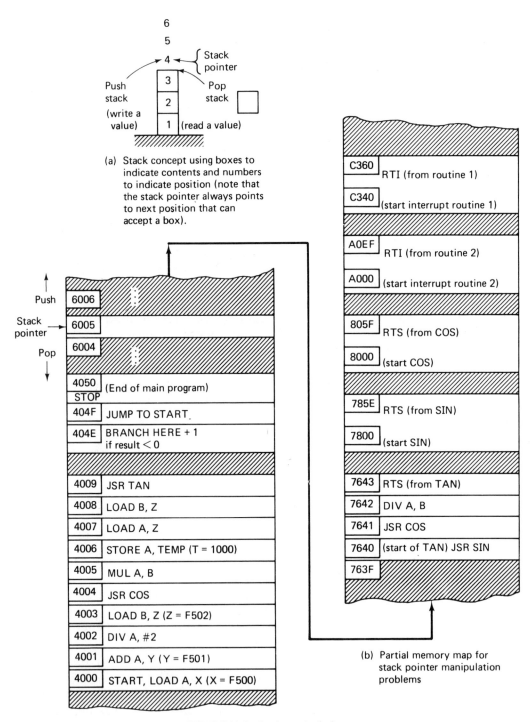

(a) Stack concept using boxes to indicate contents and numbers to indicate position (note that the stack pointer always points to next position that can accept a box).

(b) Partial memory map for stack pointer manipulation problems

FIGURE V-1 Stack manipulation.

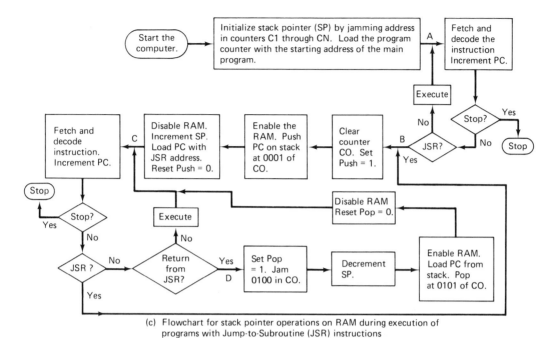

(c) Flowchart for stack pointer operations on RAM during execution of
programs with Jump-to-Subroutine (JSR) instructions

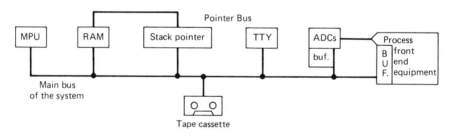

(d) Block diagram of microcomputer with external stack pointer

FIGURE V-1   (continued)

7. Draw and explain the organization of 128 * 8 LSI memory
   chips into a memory module consisting of 16 pages of 256
   addresses per page with 16 bits per location. Explain how
   decoding can be accomplished so that up to 15 of these
   modules could be used for contiguous memory for a 16-bit
   address bus.

8. Use the op codes of Figure V-2. Assume the PC = 1200 and
   the XR = B800. Write a short program (code it in hexadecimal) to begin in 1200. Show the hex code for each location
   and its contents if the program is to:

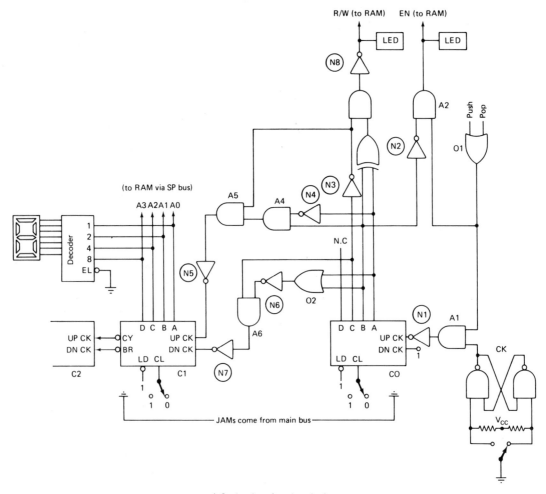

(e) Stack pointer for subroutine jumps

FIGURE V-1 (continued)

a. Load A directly from T on the current page.
b. Add to A directly from T on the zero page.
c. Store A via the index register in B804.
d. Load A indirectly from S on the current page.
e. Add to A indirectly from S on the zero page.
f. Store A via the index register in B805.
g. Load A indirectly from W on the current page.
h. Add to A via the index register from W.
i. Store A via the index register in B806.
j. Stop the program.

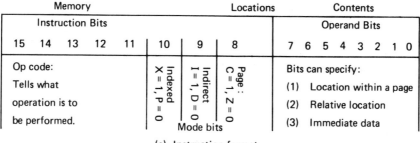

(a) Instruction format

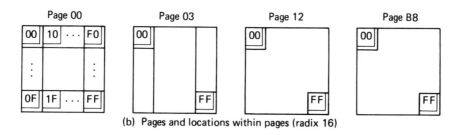

(b) Pages and locations within pages (radix 16)

Program counter | 15 — PC page bits — 8 | | 7 — PC loc. bits — 0 |

Index register | 15 — XR page bits — 8 | | 7 — XR loc. bits — 0 |

(c) Addressing registers

Binary Op codes					Coding	Operations: A = Accumulator A = contents of effective address	Addresses	Contents
Bits: 15	14	13	12	11	Mnemonics			
0	1	1	0	0	ADD A,	$A + \square \rightarrow A$	008E	B8FF
0	1	1	1	0	SUB A,	$A - \square \rightarrow A$	008F	00FF
1	0	0	0	0	MUL A,	$A * \square \rightarrow A$	00FF	0001
1	0	0	1	0	DIV A,	$A / \square \rightarrow A$	038E	B800
1	0	1	0	0	LOD A,	Load A from memory	038F	1100
1	0	1	1	0	STR A,	store A in memory	03FF	5555
1	1	1	1	1	STP	stop execution	128E	03FF
							128F	038F
							12FF	B88E
							B88E	0110
							B88F	008E
							B8FF	4444

Location Labels	Bits	Addressing Mode
W = 8E	8	Page: C = 1 (current), Z = 0 (zero)
S = 8F	9	Indirect: I = 1 (indirect), D = 0 (direct)
T = FF	10	Indexed: X = 1 (indexed), P = 0 (PC)

(d) Op codes, addresses, contents

FIGURE V-2 Programming concepts.

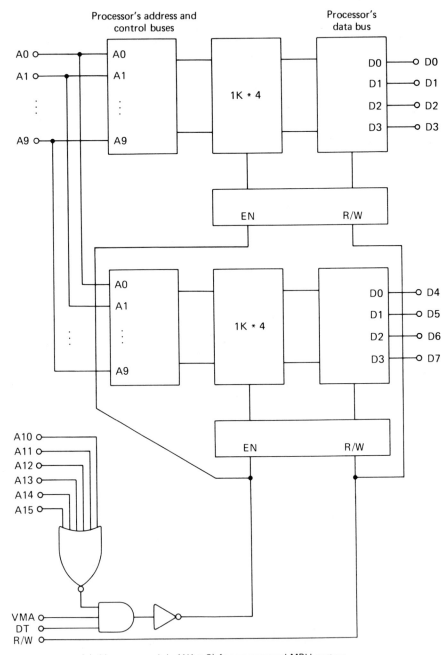

(a) Memory module (1K * 8) for an unpaged MPU system

FIGURE V-3 Modular memory system.

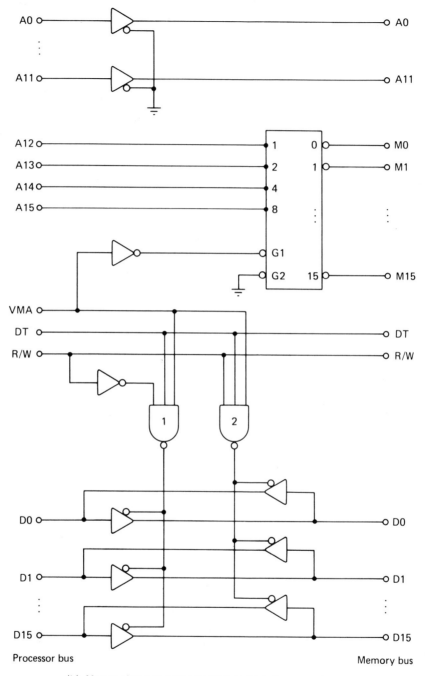

(b) Memory bus extender and module driver for a paged memory
system

FIGURE V-3 (continued)

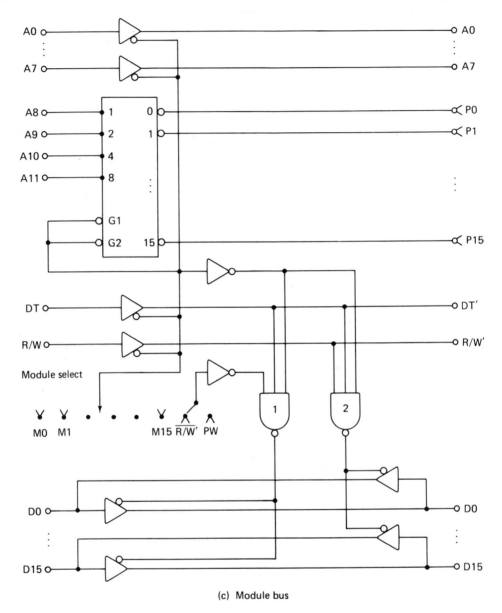

(c) Module bus

FIGURE V-3   (continued)

Record the contents of B804, B805, and B806 after the program is executed.

9. By referring to the circuitry in Figure V-3, explain:
    a. Why bus line buffering is needed and how it can be accomplished.

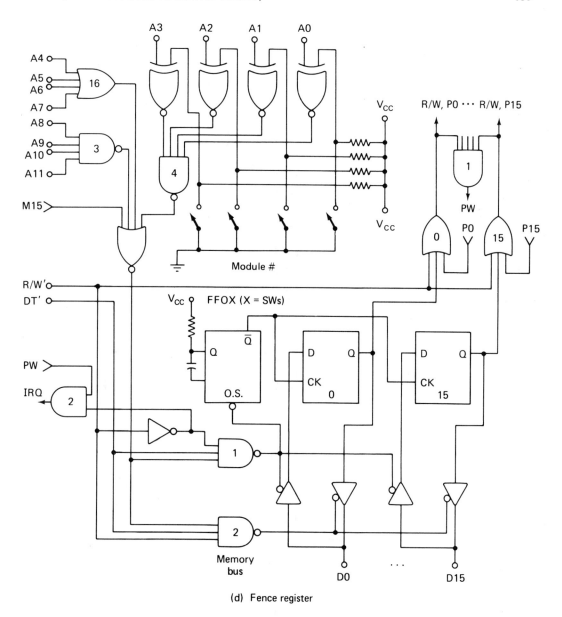

(d) Fence register

FIGURE V-3 (continued)

b. Why the data bus should be "free" whenever the processor is not using it for a read or write operation. Connect the circuitry and demonstrate how this can be accomplished.

c. Why a magnitude comparator is useful for address selection. Connect the circuitry and demonstrate.

d. How the fence registers establish paged write protection.

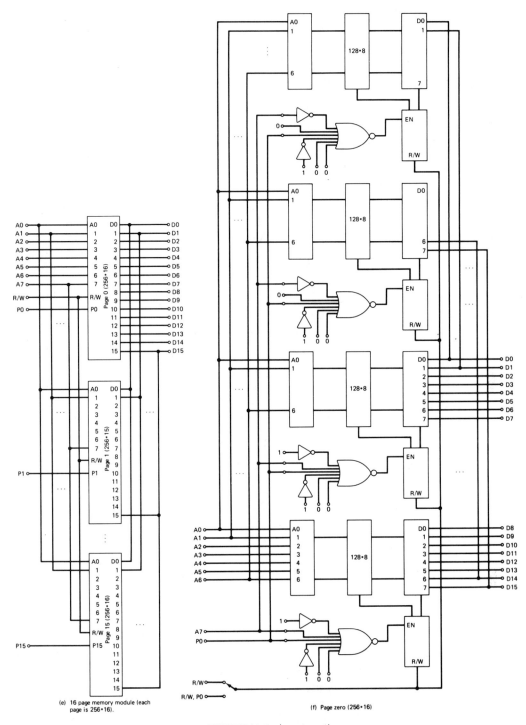

(e) 16 page memory module (each page is 256•16).

(f) Page zero (256•16)

FIGURE V-3 (continued)

10. Pass a closed-book, closed-note, written/laboratory exam over the material of this unit with at least 80% accuracy.

11. Explain the relationship of each of the topics in this unit to the remote terminal unit of Figure II-0.

LIST OF EQUIPMENT AND COMPONENTS
USED IN UNIT V

Equipment:

Oscilloscope: dc-coupled, 10-MHz BW
Power supply: 5 V dc at 1 A

Common used logic circuits (see Appendix G):

4   bounceless input switches
6   LED indicators
6   SPDT input switches
8   mini-DIP SPST switches
2   seven-segment hex displays

Components:

3   7404   hex NOT
2   7408   quad 2-input AND
1   7410   triple 3-input NAND
1   7411   triple 3-input AND
1   7420   dual 4-input NAND
1   7421   dual 4-input AND
3   7427   triple 3-input NOR
1   7432   quad 2-input OR
1   7475   quad D flip-flops
1   7486   quad XOR
1   74121   one-shot
3   74125   quad three-state drivers
2   74154   4-to-16 line decoder/demultiplexer
1   6810   1024-bit RAM
1   0.001-μF   capacitor
1   series resistance combination (1-kΩ fixed resistance plus 20-kΩ variable resistance)

Note that R and C above are used to set the time constant of the 74121 one-shot. Required power is less than $\frac{1}{8}$ W at 5 V.

PROBLEMS AND EXPERIMENTS

Read/Write Operations

Objectives: By the end of these experiments and the associated problems you should be able to corectly perform each of the following objectives using only a power supply, logic circuitry, and the notes and data obtained from running these experiments.

1. Draw and explain the function of each block of a functional block diagram for static RAM organized as an A * D. Explain how to calculate the number of bits in the memory matrix, the number of address lines, the number of data lines, and, assuming a single enable input, the number of pins required on the chip. Apply this to a specific example such as a 64 * 4 organization. Name the two control line functions common to all static RAMs. Explain the function of each line, the data bus, and the address bus during a write operation. Explain the function of each line, the data bus, and the address bus during a read operation.

2. For a 128 * 8 static RAM, explain how to write the following data into the indicated locations: [(34)R16 → (04)R16, (F3)R16 → (06)R16, (29)R16 → (0E)R16]. Explain how to read the data from these locations. Draw the schematic, flowchart the procedural steps, connect the circuitry, and demonstrate the operations.

Procedures:

1. After reading the narrative on random access read/write memories, you should be ready to learn how to write an (AB)R16 into location (08)R16 [an abbreviated notation is (AB)R16 → (08)R16], how to write (BC)R16 into location (0C)R16 [(BC)R16 → (0C)R16], how to write (CD)R16 → (4E)R16, and then how to return to each location and read the contents that were deposited there. Examine Figure V-4(a). Connect the circuit and apply power. (Remember that you are working with NMOS. Put on your ground strap.)

2. The memory chip is a M6810 with chip select leads connected so that the remaining EN control line will enable the chip for a read or

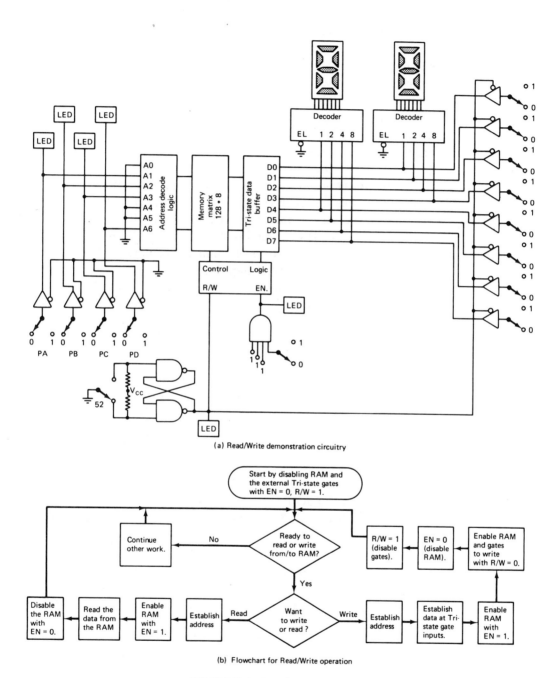

(a) Read/Write demonstration circuitry

(b) Flowchart for Read/Write operation

FIGURE V-4 Read/write operations.

write operation when EN = 1. The other control line is connected so that R/W = 1 causes the seven-segment displays to show the data being read from the RAM. The tri-state gates are at their high-impedance· level when R/W = 1. These same Tri-states are enabled when R/W = 0. Also, the RAM is prepared to have data written to the selected location when R/W = 0. The seven-segment displays should show the data being written. Note that the address lines are only partially connected to binary inputs. (A0, A4, and A5 are grounded. The input switches to the Tri-state drivers can be taken from the preset inputs of one of the up/down counters. Set the address switches to (08)R16 (PA = B = D = 0, PE = 1), set R/W = 1, set EN = 0, and set the data bus switches to (AB)R16.

a. The address (08)R16 implies that the only address line which is high is _____ . The seven-segment displays read _____ , indicating that the RAM data buffer is _____ and the ex-ternal tri-state gates are _____ . When you raise EN to a high level, what is your prediction for the reading of the seven-segment displays? _____

_____

_____

Raise EN = 1. Lower R/W to a 0. [The displays should now read (AB)R16 if your data switches are set correctly.] Lower EN = 0. The display now reads _____ . Raise R/W = 1. The display now reads _____ since _____

_____

Set the address to (0C)R16 (PA = PD = 0, PB = PC = 1). Set the data switch to (BC)R16.

b. The address (0C)R16 implies that the only address lines which are high are _____ and _____ .   The seven-segment displays read _____ because the data bus is _____ . Raise EN = 1. Lower R/W = 0. Lower EN = 0. The displays now read _____ . Raise R/W = 1. The display reads _____ , since the data bus is _____ . Set the address to (4E)R16 (PA = PB = PC = PD = 1). Set the data switches to (CD)R16.

c. The address (4E)R16 implies that the only address lines which are high are _____ . The seven-segment displays read _____ because the data bus is _____ . Raise EN = 1. Lower R/W = 0. Lower EN = 0. The displays now read _____ because the _____ are enabled. Raise R/W = 1. The displays read _____ because _____ is disabled. Set the address to (08)R16. Set the data switches to (CC)R16.

d. With R/W left high, when EN is raised to a 1, the display should read the _____ we previously wrote into this location. Raise EN = 1 to verify this. Lower EN = 0 and set the address to (0C)R16.

e. With R/W left high, when EN = 1 the display should read _____. Verify this. Then return EN = 0 and set the address to (4E)R16.

f. When EN = 1 the display should read _____. Verify this and return EN = 0. Study the flowchart in Figure V-4(b) to see if it explains the operating sequence you just demonstrated. Practice drawing this flowchart from memory a couple of times. Then use the flowchart and the circuitry of Figure V-4(a) to deposit data as follows: (11)R16 → (00)R16, (33)R16 → (02)R16, (77)R16 → (06)R16. Then use the flowchart to read and verify the contents of the three locations that were written to.

a. A3, (FF)R16, disabled (high-impedance state), disabled (high-impedance state), (we cannot predict, since there is no way of knowing what value flip-flops will assume when power is applied), (AB)R16, (FF)R16, the data buffer and the Tri-state gates are both disabled

b. A3 and A2, (FF)R16, disabled, (BC)R16, (FF)R16, disabled

c. A6, A3, A2, A1; FF; disabled; CD; external Tri-state gates; FF; data bus

d. AB

e. BC

f. CD

PROBLEMS AND EXPERIMENTS

Stacks, Stack Pointer Operations, Interrupts, Nested Interrupt Routines, Subroutines, and Nested Subroutines

Objectives: By the end of these experiments and the associated problems, you should be able to correctly perform each of the following objectives using only a power supply, logic circuitry, and the notes and data obtained from running these experiments.

1. Explain the meaning of each of the following terms. Give an example of an application for each term.
   a. LIFO stacks, stack pointers, and stack pointer operations
   b. Interrupt requests, priority interrupt levels, interrupt masks, main program vs. interrupt service routines
   c. Main program vs. subroutines, arguments, subroutine jumps vs. other jumps and branches
2. Explain how a microprocessor with an internal stack pointer and access to a static RAM maintains stack records of nested interrupt routines in progress and of nested subroutines in progress.
3. With the use of the flowchart in Figure V-1(c), explain how the bit-slice microcomputer system in Figure V-1(d) uses the stack pointer circuitry shown in Figure V-1(e) to handle subroutine jumps and returns such as those encountered in the example of Figure V-1(b). Connect the circuitry and demonstrate the accuracy of your explanation.

Procedures:

1. After reading the narrative on random access read/write memories and performing the experiments on read/write operations, you should be ready to learn about the theory and application of stacks and stack pointers.

   Stacks and stack manipulations are playing a major role in today's digital systems. In fact, the fixed-word-length microprocessors (those capable of manipulating only a fixed number of bits per operation) typically have the stack manipulation circuitry built right into the microprocessor (MPU) chip. The bit-slice microprocessors (those capable of being expanded to provide parallel processing of any number of bits per operation) are often connected to external stack manipulation circuitry to increase their computing power in three vital areas:
   a. To maintain stack records of nested subroutines in progress.
   b. To maintain stack records of nested interrupt routines in progress.
   c. To provide stack processing of arithmetic and logic operations.
   In this section we examine the first two applications. The third application will be explored in the next unit.

   Although there are different types of stacks, the most common one in use today is called the LIFO (last in, first out). Although some calculators and MPUs (microprocessors) still use sequential access memory (that is, a small number of registers) for their LIFOs, the trend is to use a RAM with a stack pointer to manipulate the RAM contents to produce the same results that the registers would. However, the RAM can be much more cost-effective if the stacks are to be of any size plus the RAM can serve other purposes as well. (A LIFO stack consisting of only 10 registers costs about as much as a RAM with 128 locations that can be manipulated by a stack pointer to appear as though it is a LIFO stack with 128 registers.)

Figure V-1(a) shows a pictorial representation of a LIFO stack which is to be simulated by a RAM and a stack pointer. The numbers represent locations on a vertical column where boxes (data) can be stacked. The drawing shows that data have been stored (i.e., "pushed" onto the stack) in locations 1, 2, and 3. The stack pointer is always used to point to the next location, where data may be stored on the stack. In this case, location 4 is the next available address. If we push another box of data on top of the other three, location 4 will be referred to as the "top of the stack"and the stack pointer will increment to point to the next available location for storage, which is 5. If we decide to retrieve the data we stored in position 4, we "pop" it off the top of the stack and the stack pointer decrements to 4 to indicate that this is once again the first available stack location for storage. Now the top of the stack is location 3. Do you see why it is called a LIFO? [Or at least it is behaving ("simulating") as a LIFO would.] The last data pushed onto the stack will have to be the first data to be popped off the stack if we which to start reading our previously stored data.

To appreciate how helpful this can be, let us examine the block diagram in Figure V-1(d). Assume that a microprocessor has been formed by paralleling several high-speed bit-slice chips to produce an 18-bit word length. The microprocessor is to be devoted to processing acoustic signals in a sonar research laboratory. (An 18-bit word length is not uncommon in this type of signal processing.) The signals come in through the process front-end equipment. This equipment contains receivers, filters, demultiplexers, and several types of hardware that aid in extracting useful signals out of the noise. Some of the information is extracted in digital form and goes directly into high-speed buffer memory, where the MPU can access it for further processing. Some of the information is in analog form and must be passed through the analog-to-digital converters (ADCs) before being stored in high-speed buffer memory for the MPU to access. Normally, the MPU executes instructions out of the main control program with its associated subroutines which are stored in the RAM. The MPU uses the stack pointer to facilitate jumping back and forth between the main program and the subroutines. However, from time to time the process front-end equipment will detect an out-of-limits alarm condition such as the sudden intrusion of an overpowering signal source that threatens to totally wash out the signal we want to monitor. (Perhaps a convoy of tugboats and barges are passing over the transducers.) The front-end alarm circuitry generates a very high priority request to interrupt the MPU's normal program execution sequence. The MPU uses the stack pointer to record exactly what it was doing when the request for service came in. It then jumps to a special diagnostic routine stored elsewhere in the RAM and begins to execute a sequence of instructions that will aid the front-end equipment in identifying the characteristics of the offensive signal so that jointly the MPU and the front-end circuitry can minimize its effects and return their attention to the signals originally being analyzed. When this minimization has been accomplished, the MPU uses the stack pointer to return to exactly the same conditions that prevailed when the request for interrupt service arrived. It resumes processing as though nothing has interrupted it.

From time to time a human operator may request a statistical report on some phase of the process from the Teletype (TTY). If the MPU is not in the middle of a critical calculation and if the front-end equipment has no alarm conditions, the MPU may choose to grant this request for service. If so, it will again use the stack pointer to facilitate the transition from its regular program to the TTY interrupt routine and back again. (The MPU could have ignored the TTY until all critical tasks were resolved. This is called "interrupt masking.")

Let's see how the stack manipulations are performed with subroutine jumps.

2. When a microprocessor is to be dedicated to performing a task such as signal processing, someone who understands the task must "program" the computer system. That is, someone must tell the machine what to do, how to do it, when to do it (called an "instruction"), and what to do it to. (This is called an "operand." An operand usually refers to the location whose contents are to be operated upon by the instruction. For example, "Load A · X" could stand for "load the accumulator A with the contents of location X." Here X is the operand.) Therefore, the program will normally have a sequence of "instruction" followed by the "operand" the instruction is to manipulate.

In order to fetch each instruction (and operand) to be executed, the program must be placed where the processor can access it. In this example, the memory "map" in Figure V-1(b) shows that the first instruction of this program has been stored in location 4000 of the RAM. Before the processor can fetch this instruction to be deciphered and executed, we have to tell a special processor register called the program counter where this starting instruction is located in the RAM. After we have fetched this first instruction from location 4000 and copied it into the processor's instruction register (which has the responsibility of deciphering it and seeing that it is executed), the program counter (PC) will look for the location containing the next instruction. (The program counter is always responsible for finding the next instruction to be placed in the instruction register (IR), so that as quickly as the IR has finished executing one instruction, the PC has the next one ready. Unless specifically told otherwise, the program counter will increment sequentially to the next instruction. Thus, when the IR is executing the instruction in location 4000, the PC has located the next instruction in location 4001. When the IR has finished executing the instruction in 4000 (loading the accumulator with the contents of "X," where X is a symbol for location F500), the PC will see that the IR is loaded with the instruction in location 4001. The PC will then increment to the next instruction (which it will find in 4002), while the IR deciphers and executes the instruction to "add the accumulator A to the contents of location F501 (affectionately referred to by the human programmer as location "Y". Why? Well, would you rather remember the letter "Y" or the location number "F501"? Especially if your computer can remember for you that whenever you refer to the operand "Y," the computer is to substitute "F501.")

As the programmer was working out the details of the "main computer program" to analyze the incoming signals, there were, in this example, 10 times when the processor had to calculate the trigonometric sine of a measured phase angle. Since computers do not have a single instruction that calculates the sine of an angle, the programer had to program a sequence of about 96 instructions to enable the computer to calculate the sine function. Now the programmer had a choice. This sequence of 96 instructions could be inserted in the main program at each of the 10 places where it is needed (for a total of 960 instructions working on the sine function), or the 96 instructions could be inserted just once somewhere outside the main program as a "subroutine." Then for each of the 10 places in the main program where we need to calculate the sine

of an angle, we will just Jump to the Subroutine (JSR) located at
the beginning address which we refer to as SIN (JSR SIN), which
causes the program counter to find the next instruction in location
7800. (Check the memory map for the beginning location of the
sine calculation routine.) After completing the 96 instructions that
produce the sine of the measured angle, we need to return from the
subroutine back to the main program by loading the program
counter with the address of the next instruction in the main program immediately following the JSR SIN which was just completed.
The question is: How do we know where to return to? The answer
is provided by the stack manipulations. Let us see how.

a.   Before we begin to execute the program, we need to "initialize"
     the program counter with the address containing the first in-
     struction. We also need to initialize the stack pointer (SP) with
     the RAM address where the programmer decided to begin the
     simulated stack. From the memory map record the address
     values for PC ← (_____), SP ← (_____).

          The instruction register (IR) relies on the PC to tell it
     where the next instruction is to be fetched from. The IR
     fetches the contents of 4000, deciphers it to mean "load
     accumulator · A from location F500." (F500 is a front-end
     address containing the peak signal amplitude measured on the
     first reading.) While the IR is busy executing this instruction
     (i.e., transferring a copy of peak reading 1 to accumulator A),
     the PC increments to the next instruction.

b.   The PC now reads (_____). When the IR has finished trans-
     ferring the data from location X to accumulator A (abbreviated
     $X \rightarrow A$), it looks at the PC to see where it is to fetch the next
     instruction from. This instruction is deciphered to mean "add
     the contents of location Y to accumulator A and store the sum
     in A" (abbreviated $A + Y \rightarrow A$). Since F501 is a location in the
     front-end equipment where the second peak signal reading is
     stored, A will contain the sum of the _____
     _____ after this instruction is executed. In the meantime, the
     PC has _____ to _____. (Remember that the PC
     always assumes that the next instruction can be found by in-
     crementing in a sequential fashion. Only if an interrupt request
     is received from an acceptable source or if the instruction
     register tells it to do otherwise can the PC "jump" or "branch"
     out of this incrementation sequence.)

c.   After the sum is stored in A, the IR consults with the _____ to find out _____.

The IR fetches the contents of _____ , which tells it to see that the contents of A are divided by 2 and the quotient is to be stored in A (A/2 → A). Note that the "#" tells the IR that the operand "2" is to be treated as a number rather than as an address whose contents are to be manipulated. [Also note that shifting a straight-code binary number one to the right is the same as dividing by 2. For example, (0100)R2 = (4)R10. Shift right one bit and (0010)R2 = (2)R10, and so on.]

After this instruction is executed, the PC will be waiting with a _____ and A will contain the _____ of the two peak signal measurements. This value is to be multiplied by the cosine of the phase angle. Let us see how this is to be done.

d. The IR is loaded next from _____ , which tells it to load accumulator B with the contents of location Z. Z is a location (F502) in the front-end equipment which contains the measured phase angle of the signal being processed. The programmer has chosen to use accumulator B to carry the angle into the subroutine that is to calculate the cosine. (This is sometimes referred to as "passing the arguments" or "passing the parameters" from the main program to the subroutine.) In other words, the programmer has constructed the COS subroutine so that it always looks in accumulator B for the angle, calculates the cosine of the angle, and stores the result back in accumulator B (replacing the angle with its cosine) to be returned to the main program. While B is being loaded with the phase angle, the PC has incremented to the next instruction in _____ .

e. After the IR has supervised the Z → B transfer, it looks to the PC for the location of the next instruction. After the IR fetches the instruction from _____ , the PC increments to _____ . However, the IR deciphers the instruction ————, which tells it that control of the program is to be "jumped" out of its present sequence. In fact, an examination of the memory map reveals that the next instruction is to be fetched from location _____ (Remember that "COS" is the operand of the instruction to "jump to subroutine." Therefore, "COS" is a symbol or label for the location containing the first instruction in this particular subroutine.)

f. Since the IR has deciphered a "jump" instruction, it notifies the PC to alter its normal incrementation process. The PC presently contains _____ , which is the location containing

the first instruction to be processed *after* we return from the
COS subroutine. Since the COS subroutine never knows where
it is being called from (it only knows to obtain the angle from
B and calculate the cosine), it does not know where to return
program control to after it is finished. Somehow this return
address, which is now in the PC, has to be saved.

The PC looks to the stack pointer for help. The SP was
initialized to _____. A copy of the PC's contents (4005) is
pushed into this stack location. The stack pointer _____ to
the next available location for storage on the stack.

The PC can now turn its attention to looking up the
address where the first instruction in COS is contained. The PC
is then loaded with _____. It signals the IR that everything
is now ready for the next instruction to be fetched. The IR
fetches the instruction from 8000 and the PC _____ to
_____ to point to the next instruction to be fetched.

g. The PC and the IR continue this sequence of "fetch and execute" from succeeding locations until the IR encounters the
RTS instruction in location _____. At the time this RTS is
deciphered by the IR as a "return from subroutine" instruction, the PC is pointing to location _____. (We will not
need to retain this location since it is outside of our subroutine.)

The IR notifies the PC that it needs to receive its next
instruction from back in the main program. The PC requests
the SP to _____ the stack. This causes the contents of
location _____ to be copied into the PC. The PC now
reads _____ and the SP has decremented to _____
since this is once again available to store another return address
if another subroutine is encountered.

The PC notifies the IR that the next instruction is to be
fetched from 4005. This is deciphered to mean multiply A (containing the average value of the measured peak signals) by B
(containing the cosine of the phase angle) and to store the result
in A. While the IR supervises the execution of this instruction,
the PC has advanced to _____.

h. When the next instruction is fetched, it tells the IR to supervise
the copying of the contents of accumulator A into a temporary
storage location (1000). This value can be retrieved later in the
program, but right now the programmer has to free A for the
next instruction. The next instruction will _____ A with
the _____. The instruction in 4008 will cause

_____ to be loaded with _____.
Since the instruction in 4009 is a JSR, we can guess that the
programmer has just loaded A and B with the _____
_____ to be carried from the main program into the
TAN subroutine. Why load both registers with the same value?
Because of the way this particular programmer designed the
subroutines. You see, one of the easiest ways for a computer to
calculate the tangent of an angle is to first find its sine, then
find its cosine, and then divide the sine by the cosine. This programmer decided to pass the angle (the argument) into the COS
routine through register B. The final result (the cosine) would
be passed back to the calling program in the same register
(accumulator B). Similarly, the programmer decided to pass the
angle into the SIN routine through accumulator A. After the
sine of the angle has been calculated, this result is written into
A (destroying its copy of the measured angle) to be passed
back to the calling program. Let us see what the jump to TAN
does to the stack pointer.

i.   After the JSR TAN instruction has been fetched from _____
     the PC _____ to point to _____. When the IR de-
     ciphers this instruction to jump out of the main program, it
     quickly notifies the program counter. The PC at the time con-
     tains the _____ for the subroutine. That is, once the tan-
     gent of the angle is found, the PC should return to this location
     to find the next instruction to be fetched by the IR.
         To save this return address the PC calls upon the _____
     to _____ a copy of this 400A on the _____. The
     _____ now increments to _____, which is the next
     available location for storage on the _____. The PC is then
     free to point to _____ as the location containing the first
     instruction in the TAN subroutine. The PC signals the IR to
     fetch this instruction.

j.   After the instruction "_____" is fetched by the IR, the PC
     increments to _____. But the IR deciphers the jump in-
     struction and signals the PC. The address now contained in the
     PC is the _____ address for this latest JSR. That is, the
     programmer wants to jump to the SIN routine, calculate the
     value, and then come back to the next instruction in the TAN
     routine.
         Therefore, the PC calls upon the _____ to _____
     a copy of this 7641 on the _____. The _____ incre-

ments to _____ to point to the next available stack location. The stack now contains two subroutine return addresses. When subroutines begin jumping us to other subroutines in this manner, we say we are "nesting" them.

After the return address is pushed on the stack, the PC is loaded to point to _____ . The instruction register fetches the instruction from this address and the calculation of the sine of the angle in A begins. The PC and IR continue their sequential processing until the IR fetches and deciphers the contents of _____ . At that time the PC is pointing to _____ . Does this need to be saved as a return address? _____

k. The contents of the IR are deciphered as "RTS," meaning "return from subroutine." The IR notifies the PC. The PC calls upon the _____ to _____ the _____ , that is, to copy the return address _____ back into the PC. The IR is notified and fetches the contents of the address pointed to by the PC. The PC then increments to _____ .

The IR deciphers the instruction "_____" and notifies the PC. The PC calls upon the _____ to _____ the _____ address on the _____ . The PC is then loaded with _____ , the beginning location of the COS routine. Once again we have _____ our subroutines since one has called another.

The IR fetches and executes the routine of instructions beginning at 8000 and ending with an _____ instruction in _____ . At the end of this routine the value of the angle stored in B has been replaced with the cosine of the angle.

l. The IR notifies the PC it has found another RTS. The PC calls upon the _____ to _____ the return address. This leaves only one value (400A) on the stack. The PC now points to _____ . The IR fetches the instruction from this location. The indicated operation is A/B → A. In other words, the sine is to be divided by the cosine to produce the tangent which is to be stored in A.

When this instruction is executed, the IR fetches the contents of _____ while the PC increments. When the IR deciphers the RTS, it notifies the PC, which in turn calls upon the _____ to _____ the last _____ address off the stack. This value is copied into the PC and the next instruction to be fetched by the IR will come from location _____ in the main program.

m. Processing of the signal values will continue until the IR fetches
the contents of 404E. At this time the PC points to _____ .
When the "BRANCH HERE + 1 if result negative" instruction
is deciphered, the processor must make a decision. If the result
of the last operation (whatever it was) was negative, the program counter should branch-control one place further than
where it is now pointing (HERE = 404F, 404F + 1 = 4050). In
other words, if a negative result occurred, the PC should be
branched up one extra location (where the STOP statement is
contained). Once the IR fetches and deciphers the "STOP"
command, the processor will end the execution of the program.

On the other hand, if the result of the last operation was
not negative, the PC should be left alone. This means the next
instruction will come from the location presently pointed to by
the PC, which is 404F. After this instruction is fetched, the PC
increments to _____ . The IR decodes the instruction as
"Jump to Start." Start is the label for location 4000 at the
beginning of our program. Since this is an "unconditional
jump" rather than a jump to subroutine, no return address is
needed. Therefore, the PC is loaded with location 4000 and our
program control returns to the beginning instruction. Hopefully, the front-end equipment has gathered a new set of
readings for us to analyze.

Before we examine some of the hardware that makes this
possible, let us examine the flowchart in Figure V-1(c) to see
how it agrees with our analysis of the preceding program.

n. Note that we start the computer by initializing both the stack
pointer (to 6005) and the program counter (to 4000). Also
note that a reference is made to the SP consisting of counters
C1 through CN. These counters are up/down (push/pop)
counters that provide us with as many bits as the number of
lines in the address bus. (This machine must have at least 16
address lines, since it addresses locations with a four-digit hexadecimal label. We already know that each address contains 18
data bits. Note that the circuit of Figure V-1(e) only shows C1
and part of C2 of the stack pointer. The C0 counter and the
logic gates are used to sequence the push-and-pop operations.)

As we go into the flowchart block, we fetch and decode
the instruction from 4000. We increment the PC. Since this
instruction is not a STOP or a JSR, we execute it and reenter
the block at A. We will continue looping through point A until

we fetch and decode the instruction in location _____.
This takes us out of the loop to point B.

The next block tells us to clear C0 and to raise the Push
input to the stack pointer. [We will always clear C0 to push
and jam (parallel load) 0100 into the counter to pop. Note that
the signal to Push comes in at the upper right-hand corner of
the drawing.]

Next we enable the RAM and push the PC onto the stack
at 6005. Note that the EN (enable input of the RAM) is done
by the output of the AND gate labeled _____. This AND
gate has a 1 output because the OR gate 01 went high when the
_____ signal arrived. While 01 enables the clock pulses to
advance the C0 counter, the A2 output will remain high as long
as a _____ is present on the B output of C0. In other
words, the RAM is enabled to read the SP address contained in
C1 through CN for the C0 counts of 0000 and 0001. (The next
C0 count of 0010 will place a high on the input of N2 and
disable the RAM.)

o. Let us examine the R/W output since the second flowchart
block past point B says that we should write the PC contents
onto the stack at count 0001 of C0. Note that on count 0000
the Exclusive-OR connected to counter outputs A and B will
present a _____ output level to the input of the A3 AND
gate. Therefore, the R/W output from N8 must be high for this
count. However, when C0 counts up to 0001, both the
Exclusive-OR and N3 present a _____ to the inputs of A3.
Therefore, the R/W input to the RAM goes to a _____
level of the enabled chip, which allows us to write the PC
contents into location 6005 of the stack (a Push operation).
The counter advances to 0010, causing the output of A2 to go
to a _____, which _____ the RAM from subsequent
data transfers. Notice that this corresponds to the description
in the third flowchart box past point B. Notice also in this box
that we are now ready to increment the stack pointer (C1
through CN) to 6006. Let us see how this is done.

p. The C0 count 0010 that disabled the stack RAM caused the
output of the A5 AND gate to go to a _____ level, which
in turn caused the UpCk input of C1 to go to a _____.
Since the counters we are using change state on a leading edge
only, no change occurs in C1. However the Push input to the
01 OR gate is still high, which allows the next clock pulse

(again we are using the SR flip-flop to simulate an astable) to advance C0 to 0011. This count causes the A5 output to go to a _____ (thanks to N4 and A4) and the N5 output goes to a _____, presenting a _____ edge to advance the C1 counter. The stack pointer is now pointing to the next available stack location at _____. We now reset the Push input to 01, which prevents C0 from advancing further. Also, the PC is now free to be loaded with the first JSR address, which is _____. On our flowchart we have just exited the block at point C.

q. The instruction register fetches and decodes the first instruction in the COS subroutine. It is not a STOP or another JSR or a RTS. Therefore, it is executed and we are back to point C on our flowchart. We continue in this loop until the instruction in location _____ is fetched and decoded. This RTS is deciphered by the IR and causes us to proceed to point D on the flowchart.

The C0 counter is parallel-loaded with a 0100, as it always will be on a pop operation. By the way, the counter already contained 0100 left over from the last push operation, but this would not have been true if we had been popping out of nested subroutines. Hence the jam transfer to preset the counter is necessary. Note also in this block that the Pop input to the 01 OR gate is set so that C0 can now advance with the clock.

The 0100 value in C0 causes the output of the A6 AND gate to go to a _____ level. This causes the DnCk input to go to a _____ level, thus presenting a _____ edge to C1. (The UpCk input is at the 1 level while this is taking place.) C1 ignores this trailing edge.

r. The next clock pulse advances C0 to 0101, which causes the output of N6 to go to a _____ level (thanks to the A output of C0), which in turn causes the output of N7 to go to a _____ level, thus presenting a _____ edge to DnCk, which _____ the stack pointer (C1 through CN). We are now at the second flowchart block past point D.

The 0101 in C0 and the Pop = 1 signal causes the output of A2 to go to a _____, which _____ the RAM stack. The 0101 also causes the output of N3 to go to _____, which causes the output of N8 to go to a _____ level. (Actually, it was already at a 1 level. We just made sure it stayed there so we could provide a _____ signal to the enabled RAM.) We are now enabled to read the contents of the RAM pointed to by the decremented stack pointer as location _____ . These contents were sent into the Program Counter.

What has happened is that the MPU has addressed the stack pointer via the main address bus with a request for the PC (inside the MPU) to be loaded with the appropriate return address. The stack pointer uses its own private address bus to the RAM to cause the contents to be read from the top of the stack to the main data bus and back to the MPU, which loads it into the PC. In other words, the MPU addresses the stack pointer with a request for data, and the stack pointer in turn addresses the RAM (note there are two addresses concurrently present on two different address buses; we will see how this is done in the next unit) and causes the RAM contents to be put on the main data bus going back to the MPU, thus completing the hardware loop of MPU to SP to RAM to MPU.

s.   When C0 advances to 0110 the output of A2 goes to _____, which _____ the RAM from subsequent data transfers. The pop signal to 01 is reset to stop the counter from advancing and we are back to point C on our flowchart.

The next instruction to be fetched and decoded by the IR will come from location _____ . We resume normal processing in this inner loop (STOP?-JSR?-RTS?-Execute-Fetch, etc.) until the instruction in location _____ is decoded.

See if you can follow through the rest of the program control sequence on the flowchart. In particular, study the way nesting and unnesting is handled. Then connect the circuitry shown in Figure V-1(e) and verify your predictions.

a.   PC ← 4000, SP ← 6005
b.   4001, two peak signal readings, incremented to 4002
c.   PC, where the next instruction is to come from, 4002, 4003, average [(peak 1 + peak 2)/2]
d.   4003, 4004
e.   4004, 4005, JSR COS, 8000
f.   4005, 6005, increments, 8000, increments, 8001
g.   805F, 8060, pop, 6005, 4005, 6005, 4006
h.   load, contents of Z (i.e., the phase angle), B, loaded with the phase angle, arguments or parameters
i.   4009, increments, 400A, return, SP, push, stack, SP, 6005, stack, 7640
j.   JSR SIN, 7641, return, SP, push, stack, SP, 6007, 7800, 785E, 785F, no

k. SP, pop, stack, 7641, 7642, JSR Cos, SP, push, return, stack, 8000, nested, RTS, 805F
l. SP, pop, 7642, 7643, SP, pop, return, 400A
m. 404F, 4050
n. 4004, A2, Push, 0
o. 0, 1, 0, 0, disables
p. 1, 0, 0, 1, leading, 6006, 8000
q. 805F, 1, 0, trailing
r. 0, 1, leading, decrements, 1, enables, 0, 1, read = 1, 6005
s. 0, disables, 4005, 4009

3. Let us see how interrupt requests from the teletype and the front-end processing equipment are handled.

To begin with, the MPU chips may be in the middle of an important calculation that the programmer does not want to have interrupted when a request for service is generated. If the programmer anticipates this, an instruction is placed in the program just before the critical instruction sequence is entered. This instruction addresses (and sets $Q = 1$) the flip-flop in Figure V-5. This is intended to set the "interrupt mask." That is, $\overline{Q} = 0$ disables the AND gates shown in this figure so that even if the TTY or the front-end equipment ask for service, the requests do not make it through the AND gates to reach the bus lines going into the MPU. In fact, the only interrupt line still connected to the processor is the one referred to as the "nonmaskable interrupt" (NMI), which we will discuss in a minute.

At the conclusion of the critical instruction sequence, the programmer inserts an instruction that resets the interrupt mask flip-flop. Now that $Q = 1$, the mask will not block interrupt requests below the NMI priority level. Suppose that the mask is not set and the program counter has just incremented to 4002 when someone at the Teletype requests a report on the processing for the day.

Since the mask is not set and there is no NMI signal or first-priority-level signal from the front-end equipment, a high level on the interrupt request line feeding into AND gate 2 will be passed into the MPU on its priority 2 line. [Note from the figure that a request on level 2 disables requests from the level 3 AND, which in turn disables all lower levels so that lower-level requests cannot make it into the MPU until all higher-level requests are resolved. (This is because the AND outputs are fed into the inputs of lower-level ANDs.)]

As soon as the processor has finished executing its current

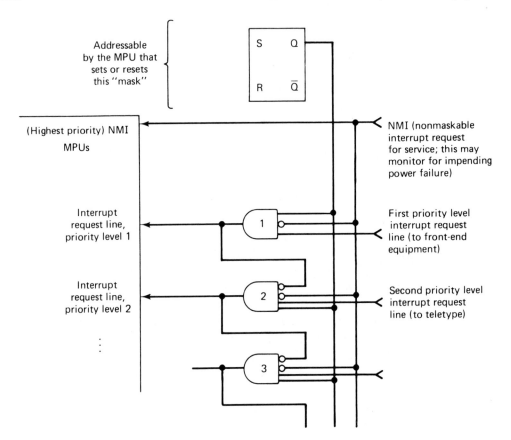

FIGURE V-5 Interrupt structures.

instruction (add A to Y and store in A), the processor will push all MPU registers on the stack, including accumulators A and B, and the PC, which is currently pointing to 4002. The PC will then be loaded with the location of the first instruction of the routine to service the Teletype interrupt. Note that no arguments are passed to this routine, since it is a nonscheduled request and we could not predict when it would occur. Also, the routine may not need access to the current MPU contents.

Now the IR begins to process the TTY service routine by sending the printer a report on processing for the day. If the service routine is completed before a higher-level request arrives, the RTI (return from interrupt routine) instruction causes the stack pointer to begin popping the stack. The contents of the accumulators and the program counter are restored just as they were when the request for service arrived and the IR proceeds to fetch and decipher the instruction in 4002 just as if an interrupt had never occurred.

Suppose, however, that in the middle of the TTY printout, a request for service came in from the front-end equipment on priority level 1. Once again, the MPU would complete its current instruction before taking further action. Then once again, the contents of all key MPU registers, including A, B, and PC, would be pushed on the stack. Then the PC would be loaded with the location of the first instruction in the service routine for level 1 interrupts. (Note that we have now nested our interrupt service routines. That is, we are calling one service routine while inside another service routine.)

When the level 1 routine is completed, the RTI in C360 [Fig.V-2(b)] will cause the stack pointer to pop values off the stack which will be used to restore all MPU registers to the exact values they contained when the level 2 routine was interrupted by the level 1 request. The MPU continues processing the sequence of instructions in this routine (that is, outputting to the TTY) until the RTI in location AOEF is decoded. Once again, all MPU register values are popped off the stack so that the processor and its registers are back to exactly the same status as they were when the original request came in from level 2. Normal processing is then resumed.

Most of the better MPUs have a nonmaskable interrupt level. It causes the same effects as the other interrupt lines, but things associated with this level are so important they are given the right to interrupt all other instruction sequences for all other priority interrupt levels. One of the most popular uses for NMI is to monitor the ac power line. If an impending power failure is detected (usually such a failure produces a damped oscillation that lasts for a few milliseconds, more than enough time for most MPUs to execute an NMI service routine), the MPU jumps to the service routine, which can be used to provide volatile memory protection by switching to battery backup and dumping the RAM contents to a nonvolatile storage device such as a cassette. After ac power is restored, the cassette can dump the contents back into the RAM.

PROBLEMS AND EXPERIMENTS

Memory Structures in Digital Computer Systems; RAM Modules for Primary Memory

Objectives: By the end of these experiments and the associated problems, you should be able to correctly perform each of the following objectives using only a power supply, logic circuitry, and the notes and data obtained from running these experiments.

1. Explain the meaning of each of the following terms. Give an example of an application for each term.
   a. Memory pages and locations within pages
   b. Current page and zero page operations
   c. Paged write protection and fence registers
2. Draw and explain the organization of 128 * 8 LSI memory chips into a memory module consisting of 16 pages of 256 addresses per page with 16 bits per location. Explain how decoding can be accomplished so that up to 15 of these modules could be used for contiguous memory for a 16-bit address bus. Draw and explain how "fence registers" can be used in the upper page locations to provide paged write protection.
3. Use the op codes of Figure V-2. Assume that PC = 1200 and the XR = B800. Write a short program (code it in hexadecimal) to begin in 1200. Show the hex code for each location and its contents if the program is to:
   a. Load A directly from T on the current page
   b. Add to A directly from T on the zero page
   c. Store A via the index register in B804
   d. Load A indirectly from S on the current page
   e. Add to A indirectly from S on the zero page
   f. Store A via the index register in B805
   g. Load A indirectly from W on the current page
   h. Add to A via the index register from W
   i. Store A via the index register in B806
   j. Stop the program
   Record the contents of B804, B805, and B806 after the program is executed.
4. By referring to the circuitry in Figure V-3, explain:
   a. Why bus line buffering is needed and how it can be accomplished.
   b. Why the data bus should be "free" whenever the processor is not using it for a read or write operation. Connect the circuitry and demonstrate how this can be accomplished.
   c. Why a magnitude comparator is useful for address selection. Connect the circuitry and demonstrate.
   d. How the fence registers establish paged write protection.

Procedures:

1. After reading the narrative on random access read/write memories and performing the experiments on read/write operations and on stack operations, you should be ready to learn about the theory and

techniques of organizing LSI RAM chips into modules that provide the memory structures for digital computer systems.

Consider the problem of a microprocessor or a minicomputer with a 12- or a 16-bit word length. (Remember that a processor's "word length" always refers to the number of data bits in each address. The address bus determines how many physical locations can be addressed and it can contain more or fewer lines than the data bus.) If an entire location is devoted to just containing the instruction and a subsequent location is devoted to just containing the operand that the instruction is to operate upon, how many different instruction codes could the instruction register be asked to decipher? Well, if an instruction occupies an entire location which is between 12 and 16 bits long, the IR might potentially be asked to decipher between 2^{11} and 2^{15} different instruction codes. In other words, there could be between 4K and 65K different instruction codes.

This is a waste! Today's smallest microprocessors only have about eight different codes, and today's largest minicomputers only have about 800 different instruction codes. The majority of the micros and the minis have closer to 100 different instruction codes and it only takes 7 bits in a memory location to safely represent all the possibilities that the IR will be asked to decipher and supervise the execution of.

A 16-bit word length leaves a lot of available space that ought to be gainfully utilized. [After all, next to the peripherals (disks, CRTs, cassettes, etc.), a full complement of memory modules for a typical processor will probably cost more than the processor does. So let's not waste memory space if we can help it.]

The temptation is obvious (and has been to computer designers since the 1950s). That is, let us try to fit the operand into the remaining bits. However, if the width of our address bus is greater than the remaining number of bits, we are going to have to do some clever memory organizing. For example, if our address bus is to be 16 lines wide (the same width as our data bus), how can we squeeze a 16-bit address into the 8 or 9 remaining bits of our location after the instruction has been inserted? One approach is to use paging.

2. Examine Figure V-2(b). Note that we are going to reserve the last 8 bits of our 16-bit word for the operand. The first 8 bits will be used for the instruction and its "modifiers" (to be explained in a minute). Let us examine the function of the operand bits.

   a. Notice that the operand bits can be used to specify any location within a "page." Since there are 8 bits to address these locations, a page can contain (_____)R10 or (_____)R16 locations. Since the address bus contains 16 lines and since 8 of the 16 are used to specify the desired location within a page, there are only 8 lines left to select the appropriate page. Therefore, we could have as many as (_____)R10 pages or (_____)R16 pages, each of which contains (256)R10 locations. (From now on, all locations and pages will be specified in hexadecimal, as is common in today's systems.) Four of these possible pages with a few labeled locations are shown in Figure V-2(b).

b. Note in the description of the operand bits in Figure V-2(a) that these bits can specify "Immediate Data." Note also in Figure V-2(c) that bits 8 through 15 of the program counter are designated as the page bits. Suppose that we have an instruction code that the IR deciphers to mean "load PC Page Register with the data immediately following in the operand bits." The instruction might look like this on the programmer's coding sheet: "LD PR, #12," meaning "jam a (12)R16 into the upper 8 bits (called the page register) of the program counter."

Suppose that this is followed by "LD LR, #00" meaning "jam a (00)R16 into the lower 8 bits (called the location register) of the program counter." The program counter now points to 1200 (page 12, location 00) as the address containing the next instruction to be fetched by the instruction register. If this happens to be the first instruction of our main program, let us study the effects on the registers.

Let the instruction contained in 1200 be "ADD A, W//P,D,C," meaning "add accumulator A to the contents of location W and store the sum in A." The two slashes indicate that a comment (which the processor does not use) has been added by the programmer to remind anyone using this program what the status of bits 10, 9, and 8 of the instruction bits are. The P says that bit 10 = 0, indicating that W is to be located through the use of the "program" counter. The D says that bit 9 = 0, indicating that the 16 bits of data are to be taken "directly" from location W. The C (bit 8 = 1) says that the current page of the program counter contains W. Since the operand bits are 0 through 7, W must be a 8-bit label for a location, say 8E. Then this instruction would add to accumulator A the contents taken "directly" from location 8E (= W) on page 12. (We used the "current" page bits of the program counter.)

Let us try another one. Suppose that the IR is loaded from location 1201, which contains as contents a 718F. Now the upper 8 bits are jammed into the IR. The lower 8 bits refer to a location, say S. The operation to be performed is deciphered by the IR as A – S → A. On the programmer's coding sheet this was written as "SUB A, S//P,D,C," meaning "subtract from accumulator A the contents of S and store the difference back in A." Furthermore the P,D,C refers to the way we go about finding S. This "mode" of locating S is specified in bits 10, 9, and 8 of the instruction bits. Since the upper 8 bits were (71)R16, a conversion to binary shows that bit 10 = _____, bit 9 = _____, and bit 8 = _____ (since the "1" of "71" is 0001 in binary).

Look at the instruction format under bit 10 of Figure V-2(a). A 0 in this bit means that the program counter will be used to find S: hence the programmer's comment of a "P" following the "//." Look under bit 9 in the same figure. A 0 in this bit means that the data to be manipulated will come "directly" out of S: hence the programmer's comment of a "D" after the "//P,."

Look under bit 8. A 1 in this bit means that the "current" contents of the upper 8 bits of the program counter contain the page number where location S (= 8F) is to be found. In other words, subtract the contents of page 12 location 8F from accumulator A and store the answer in A.

Did you notice that we are extracting data from locations that have a 16-bit address and yet all we are placing in the words of the program are the location bits (0 through 7) and the information that the data are to be taken directly from the page that the program counter is currently pointing to.

c. Try to analyze the next couple of words as we sequence through our program. Address 1202 contains a 818E. What memory location do you think is to be involved in this operation? (Do not give the page yet, just the location within the page.) _____ The 8-bit instruction register will be decoding a _____. The second hexadecimal digit indicates the values of bits 10, 9, and 8 are _____, _____, and _____, respectively, which will cause the programmer to comment // _____, _____, _____. The P (bit 10 = 0) says that we will find W through the help of the _____. The D (bit 9 = 0) says that the data will come directly out of W. The C (bit 8 = 1) says to use the current page of the program counter to find W. The operation performed is A * W → A (multiply the contents of A by the contents of W and store the product in A). What do you think this looked like on the programmer's coding sheet? _____

d. After executing the instruction in 1202, we proceed to 1203, which contains a 918F. What location do you think will be involved in this operation? _____ What is fetched into the 8-bit instruction register to be deciphered? _____ Bits 10, 9, and 8 are therefore _____, _____, and _____. The operation performed is A/S → A. The programmer probably coded this as _____

e. So far, all of our example codings ended in //P,D,C. One problem with this can be the fact that there are only FF locations within a page. A large program may occupy several pages. What if the data to be operated upon cannot be placed in the current page containing the instructions we are executing? Well, one partial solution is to allow a choice of taking data from the indicated location of the current page of the program counter or to allow the data to be taken from the indicated location of page 00. Thus by decoding one bit (bit 8) in the instruction register the processor can tell whether to take data from the location (indicated in bits 0 through 7) in page "zero" or in the current page pointed to by bits 8 to 15 of the program counter. To see how this works, refer to Figure V-2(d). The instruction to load A "directly" with the contents of location W using the "current" page of the "program counter" is stored in address 1204. What was coded on the programmer's reference sheet? _____ From Figure V-2(d), what will be the contents of 1204? _____ What are the binary contents of the instruction register? _____ (In other words, the 5-bit operation code was supplemented by bits 10, 9, and 8 to produce //P,D,C.)

   Big question: What is contained in accumulator A after this instruction has been executed? _____ [In other words, the contents of page 12 (the "current" page of the "PC"), location 8E within the page, were loaded "directly" into accumulator A and our table of addresses and contents tells us what these contents are. Compare this coding and the results with the next question.)

f. The instruction to load A "directly" with the contents of location W using the "zero" page (00) of the "program counter" is fetched from address 1205. From Figure V-2(d) what are the binary contents of the instruction register? _____ Therefore, what are the hexadecimal contents of 1205? _____. What will be the contents of accumulator A after this instruction has been executed? _____

Location 1206 contains a 618E. What will this cause to happen to the accumulator? _____

Location 1207 contains a 608E. What will this cause to happen to the accumulator? _____

g. What should be the contents of 1208 if we want to subtract the contents of 128F from A? _____

What should be the contents of 1208 if we want to subtract the contents of 008F from A? _____

Thus far we have studied ways of "directly" accessing (512)R10 locations. [(256)R10 locations on the "zero" page and (256)R10 locations on the "current" page.] What if we want to access locations that are not on either of these pages? One technique is to use "indirect addressing." This should give us access to any of (65,536)R10 addresses that are available on a 16-line address bus.

The "trick" is to decode bit 9 in the instruction register to see if this is a direct (bit 9 = 0) or an indirect (bit 9 = 1) addressing mode. If it is indirect, the location obtained through the deciphering of the page bit (bit 8) and the operand bits (0 through 7) does "not" contain the data to be operated upon! Instead, it contains 16 bits which are the address of the location that "does" contain the data to be operated upon. (In other words, the page and the operand bits tell the processor where a "pointer" can be found which will show it which one of all the possible memory locations actually contains the data to be operated upon.)

Let us see how this works with an example.

h. Location 1209 contains A18E. When executed, this will cause accumulator A to be _____ "directly" (bit 9 = 0) from page _____, location _____, which will result in a _____ being copied into A.

Location 1210 contains a A38E. When executed this will cause accumulator A to be loaded "_____" (bit 9 = 1) from page _____, location _____, which contains a _____. This is the 16-bit address of the location that contains the data the processor is to operate upon. Therefore, A is loaded with a copy of the contents of page 03, location FF within the page. From the table in Figure V-2(d), this location contains a 5555, which will be copied into accumulator A.

i. Location 1211 contains a A28E. When executed, this will cause accumulator A to be loaded "_____" (bit 9 = 1) from page _____ (bit 8 = 0), location _____, which contains a _____. Therefore, A is loaded with a copy of the contents of page _____, location _____ within the page. This means that a _____ is copied into accumulator A.

j. There remains one other major addressing mode which we have not discussed. It is called "indexed" and was first needed in Unit III when we discussed the use of fixed program memory to form "tables" of values. By "looking up" a value in the table (such as a logarithm or a trigonometric function) we may be able to save the time and effort required to program and execute a sequence of instructions which will calculate the desired value. For example, in the memory map of Figure V-1(b) we did a jump to subroutine to calculate the cosine of an angle. The processor executed (96)R10 instructions between locations 8000 and 805F (the beginning and end of the subroutine). This sequence of 96 instructions takes time and a lot of processing. (The programmer had to code a mathematical equation: "$\cos P = 1 - P^2 /2! + P^4 /4! - P^6 /6! + ...,$" where P is the phase angle in radians, in order to calculate the cosine function.) Suppose that the front-end equipment was only accurate to within 1° when measuring the phase angle. If this is so, then the complete ROM look-up table for all 90° of the cosine function could be placed in memory so that the cosine of 0° is located in address 8000, the cosine of 1° is located in 8001, and so on. Not only would this occupy six fewer memory locations than the calculation routine, but the cosine could be found by executing one instruction rather than 96, provided that the processor has an index register and an indexing address mode similar to the one shown in Figure V-2.

The idea is to initialize the index register to a "base address" before the first instruction is fetched which needs to use the indexed mode relative to this base address. In this case we would perform an immediate loading of the index register with 8000 just as we did with the initialization of the program counter. Then whenever the instruction register decodes a 1 in bit 10, the operand bits (0 through 7) will be added to the contents of the index register to compute the effective address whose data are to be operated upon.

For example, if the 90° cosine ROM table is installed beginning at 8000 and if the index register has been initialized to this base address, then if A400 is fetched from location 1212, the accumulator A will be loaded from the effective address obtained from adding the index register contents (8000) to the contents of the operand bits (00), which means the ROM value from 8000 representing the cosine of 0° will be loaded into the accumulator. Similarly, if A407 is fetched from location 1213 for execution, the accumulator A will be loaded from the index register plus the operand bits (or 8000 + 07 = 8007), which should copy the ROM contents representing the cosine of 7° into A. Note that this was done with one instruction rather than 96. Note also that bit 8 is ignored as having no meaning for an indexed instruction.

There are several uses for index registers other than table-look-up techniques. In particular, they are useful in establishing "counters." However, now that the programming theory has been developed to show the uses of paged memory, let us examine some of the hardware that will be required.

a. (256)R10 = (00-FF)R16, (256)R10, (00-FF)R16
b. 0, 0, 1
c. 8E; 81; 0,0,1; //P,D,C; PC; MUL A, W//P,D,C
d. 8F; 91; 0,0,1; DIV A, S//P,D,C
e. LOD A, W//P,D,C; A18E; 1010,0001; 03FF
f. 1010,0000; A08E; B8FF; a 03FF will be added to it; a B8FF will be added to it
g. 718F; 708F
h. loaded, 12, 8E, 03FF, indirectly, 12, 8E, 03FF
i. indirectly, 00, 8E, B8FF, B8, FF, 4444

3. Examine Figure V-3(a). The interconnections are shown for making a 1K * 8 memory module from two 1K * 4 LSI memory chips, such as the 7114 shown in Figure V-0. Note that the address lines A0 through A9 on the upper chip are tied to their respective counterparts on the lower chip. These 10 lines are then connected to the lower 10 address lines of a processor's 16-bit address bus. Note that the upper six lines of the processor's address bus (A10 through A15) are connected to a NOR. Since the output of this NOR is one

of three lines (along with VMA and DT) that determine when the
two chips are to be enabled, we can see that this 1K * 8 module can
be used to read or write data from/to any location that the processor selects with 0's on A10 through A15 and any one of 1024
possible location addresses on A0 through A9.

The three lines VMA, DT, and R/W are standard control bus
lines for most minicomputers and microprocessors. The VMA
(valid memory address) line is necessary because all address lines on
a processor's bus cannot change levels at precisely the same time.
For example, suppose that our processor is currently fetching data
from location (0000, 0000, 1111, 1100). In the next instruction
the processor is to be told to store data in location (0000, 0000,
1100, 1111). Note that two address lines must be raised to a high
level (A0, A1) and two lines must be dropped to a low level (A4,
A5) as we change from the first to the second instruction. Well,
if A0 and A4 change just a little bit faster than A1 and A5, then
for a brief instant the address lines will contain a false (i.e., unintended) address of (0000, 0000, 1110, 1101). To avoid trying to
read or write this unintended address which accidentally appeared
during the transition from one instruction to another, the processor gives all address lines plenty of time to "settle" to the
correct address and then sends a signal (high level usually) on
VMA to tell all devices on the bus that the address lines can now
be trusted. This line will go low at the end of each instruction.

Just because the address lines are valid does not necessarily
mean the processor is ready to begin a data transfer at that instant.
Often it is still preparing to execute the instruction that has just
been decoded. As soon as it is ready for the transfer of data to
begin, it signals by raising the DT (Data Transfer) line to a high
level. This signal, too, must go low at the end of each instruction.
Obviously, this DT signal should never precede the VMA signal.

The Read/Write (R/W) signal has the same function as we
discussed at the beginning of this unit. Note that the R/W inputs
of both chips have been tied together and then brought out to the
R/W line of the processor's control bus. Note also that the EN
inputs of both chips (remember that a 7114 requires a low to
enable) have been tied together. Therefore, both chips will be
enabled at the same time whenever A10 though A15 = 0's, VMA
= 1, and DT = 1.

Since a 7114 is organized as a 1K * 4, an 8-bit data bus will
require the low "nibble" (D0 through D3) to be stored in one chip

and the high nibble (D4 through D7) to be stored in the other. Observe in the figure that an 8-bit "byte" would be read from the memory chips to the processor's data bus, with the low-order nibble coming from the top 7114 and the high-order nibble from the bottom 7114.

This module illustrates some techniques for interconnecting memory chips that can be used for forming our paged memory system, as discussed in the programming concepts section of this unit. Let us see how the 6810 chip (Figure V-0) can be used to form a paged memory module containing 16 pages of 256 locations per page with 16 data bits per location. Let us then see how as many as 15 of these modules could be used in a 61K-word paged memory system complete with program-selectable paged write protection.

a. Study Figure V-3(f). Note that if P0 (page zero) is low and if A7 (address line from the processor's address bus) is also low, then the lower two 6810 chips are both enabled and the location addressed by A0 through A6 of the processor's address bus can be read from or written to depending on the level of R/W! (The use of the switch contact labeled "R/W, P0" will not be apparent until we study paged write protection a little later in this section.) In other words, the lower two chips provide storage for the lower and upper 8-bit bytes of a 16-bit word that resides in the first 128 locations of page zero.

But page zero is supposed to contain 256 locations. So where are the upper 128 locations? In the upper two 6810s. From the interconnections shown in the figure, these two chips are enabled whenever P0 = _____ and A7 = _____. (Note the NOTs on the A7 connections of these two chips.) Therefore, if R/W = 1 (Read signal) and P0 = 0, then the 16-bit data bus will be loaded from one of the lower 128 locations if _____ and from one of the upper 128 locations if _____. The specific location in either of the page halves is selected by the _____ lines from the processor's address bus.

This 256 * 16 memory page drawing has been simplified into a single rectangle (labeled Page Zero) in the upper portion of Figure V-3(e).

b. Figure V-3(e) shows the interconnection scheme used for forming a 16-page memory module. Observe that each of the 16 pages shares the common 16-bit data bus, the R/W line, and the lower eight address lines. In fact, there is only one unique line going to each page. This line is referred to as the _____ select line (such as P0, P1, . . ., P15) and only one of these 16 lines can be selected to a low level, depending upon the upper 8 _____ of the processor's bus.

To see how the pages are selected, study Figure V-3(c). Note that the 1-of-16 demultiplexer/decoder chip (such as the 74154 we studied in Unit II) is connected to address bus lines _____ through _____. This is because the third nibble of the 16-bit address is all that is needed to select the correct page on the module. Therefore, the fourth nibble of the address bus (A12 through A15) is available to select which _____ of the memory system is to be read from or written to. (Remember that each module contains about 4K words organized as 16 pages of 256 locations per page and that more than one module may be used to form the memory system.)

In Figure V-3(c) the 1-of-16 decoder used to select the appropriate page within the module is enabled by 0's on G1 and G2. The single control line that enables this 1-of-16 (as well as a number of other gates) is labeled _____. This line can be viewed as a single-pole, multiposition (or rotary) switch which has 16 contacts, connected to the M0 through M15 lines of Figure V-3(b). Notice in this figure that these lines also come from a 1-of-16 decoder. Only this one will select which one of its 16 outputs is to go low according to the levels on the _____ through _____ lines.

Therefore, returning our attention to Figure V-3(c), the first module of our memory system should have its Module Select line connected to _____. The second module to be "plugged in" to our memory system should have its Module Select line connected to _____; and so on.

c. In Figure V-3(c), if the Module Select line goes low, it does a good deal more than just enable the decoder chip. It also enables the Tri-state gates connected to lines A0 through A7 of the processor's address bus. This is for very practical reasons. Since it requires four 6810s to form a single page of memory and since it requires sixty-four 6810s to form a 16-page memory module and since lines A0 through A7 are connected to each of the 64 chips, there is a big "fan-in" presented to each of the lower 8 address lines. Furthermore, since there can be more than one module in the memory system, we would be asking the processor's address bus to drive a very unreasonable fan-in load unless we "buffer" these lines on each module.

Therefore the purpose of the eight Tri-state gates in Figure V-3(c) is to present only _____ unit of load to the processor bus, and in turn to drive _____ units of load as presented by the 64 NMOS memory chips on each module. This "buffering" (that is, inserting a circuit between other circuit elements to match impedances and drive capabilities) is also used on the processor bus as an extender to make sure that the processor can successfully drive each of the possible memory modules that might be added to our memory system [see Figure V-6(b)].

d. While our attention is directed to the processor's bus extender in Figure V-6(b), let us consider the memory bus side of the extender, including lines A0 through A11 and D0 through D15. When the processor is doing calculations that do not involve data transfers to and from memory, we want the data bus from the processor to be at a high-impedance state. This would allow peripherals such as a disk or cassette to "steal" time during these "cycles" when the processor is not using the memory modules to "directly access" the "memory" to insert new data or copy existing data. (Techniques of "cycle stealing" and "direct memory access" are covered in Unit VI.) If we are to allow other devices besides the processor to exchange data with the memory, each device should have circuitry similar to that connected to NAND1 and NAND2 to ensure that the bus is free (i.e., open-circuit impedance) when a transfer is not taking place.

NAND2 has three inputs, which are tied to _____, _____, and _____ of the processor's control bus. In other words, when a Valid Memory Address is present and a start Data Transfer signal is given while the Read/Write line requests the data to be read from memory into the processor $(R/W = 1)$, the output of NAND2 will go low, _____ the 16 Tri-state gates, which allow data to be transferred into the processor as a _____ operation.

On the other hand, if $VMA = 1$, $DT = 1$, and $R/W = 0$, the output of _____ will go low, enabling the 16 Tri-state gates, which allow data to be transferred out of the processor as a _____ operation.

Whenever $VMA = 0$ or $DT = 0$, the memory bus side of the data bus extender is at its _____ state, allowing other devices to exchange data with the memory system. This extender circuit is shown in Figure V-6(b) as an experimental

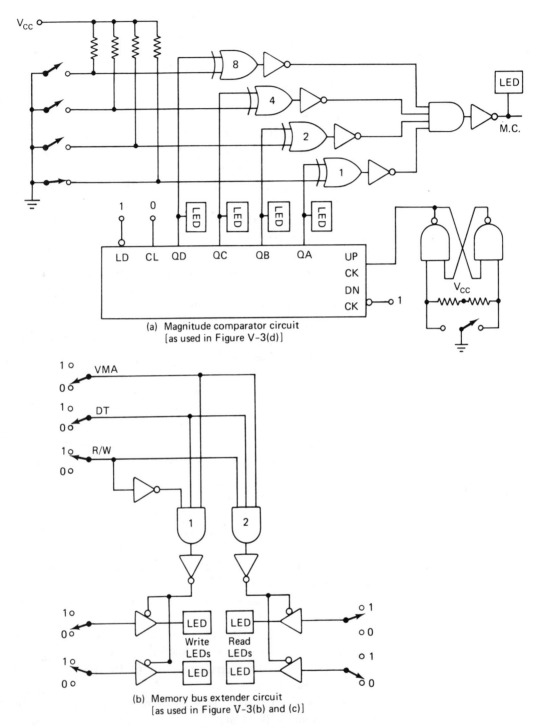

(a) Magnitude comparator circuit
[as used in Figure V-3(d)]

(b) Memory bus extender circuit
[as used in Figure V-3(b) and (c)]

FIGURE V-6 Circuits for modular memory system.

circuit for verification. Connect the circuit with VMA = 1, R/W = 1, and DT = 0. Place a 10 on the inputs of one set of Tri-states and a 01 on the inputs of the other set.

While DT = 0, both sets of LEDs are lighted, indicating that all Tri-state gates are at their _____ state. Raise DT = 1 and the LEDs on the "read" side should indicate the switch settings going into the gates. Drop VMA = 0 and DT = 0 (just as they would be dropped by the processor at the end of the read operation). Reset R/W = 0. Raise VMA = 1 and then raise DT = 1 (just as they would be raised in sequence by the processor at the start of another operation involving memory). Now the "_____" LEDs indicate the switch settings that are simulating output signals from the processor. Return VMA and DT to a low level and both sets of LEDs again indicate that the data bus is free for use by other devices.

a. 0, 1, A7 = 0, A7 = 1, A0 through A6
b. address, lines (A8 through A15); A8, A11; module; Module Select; A12, A15; M0; M1
c. 1, 64
d. VMA, DT, R/W, enabling, read; NAND2, write; high inpedance; high impedance; "write"

Let us review what we have accomplished thus far in our study of this memory module. First, we have learned how to organize four 128 * 8 LSI memory chips into pages of memory that are 256 * 16 [Figure V-3(f)]. Second, we have learned how to arrange these pages into a 16-page memory module [Figure V-3(e)]. Third, we have learned how module selection for a memory operation takes place [Figure V-3(b)]. Fourth, we have learned how page selection within the selected module takes place [Figure V-3(c)]. Fifth, we have seen how bus line buffering for the modules and the pages is accomplished, and why. Sixth, we have learned how to free the data bus so that devices other than the processor might use it whenever the processor is not involved in a data transfer with memory. Previously in this section we examined the relationship of programming concepts to memory organization. From this discussion we can conclude that the typical function of the upper byte of the program counter is to keep track of the module and the page within the module where the program segment is located that is presently being executed. This leads to our next topic of study, "paged write protection."

In process monitoring and control applications the microcomputers and the minicomputers are often "dedicated" to a special use.

For example, a microcomputer may be dedicated to monitoring and controlling the pattern weaving at a certain loom in a carpet factory that makes simulated "Oriental" rugs. Obviously, the programming effort and time are not trivial considerations in such an undertaking. There are several tasks that need to be under way more-or-less concurrently, such as selection of the fibers, positioning of the fibers, cutting and binding, and so on. Such applications profit by the use of "multiprogramming," where a number of program segments have been written (one segment to handle fiber selection, one segment to handle fiber positioning, etc.) that are to concurrently be in some phase of execution on the same microcomputer system. This means that the program segment associated with one task might be assigned to pages 1, 2, 3, and 4 of memory, where the instructions and data in the program segment that do not change are located in pages 1, 2, and 3. Page 4 is used for storage of values that do change, such as the last measured values from the process or the intermediate results of a calculation in progress.

Similarly, the program segment associated with a second task may occupy a four-page "partition" of memory, where the instructions and data that do not change are located in pages 5 and 6. This segment's "scratch pad" space for values that do change is designated as pages 7 and 8. Other task-associated program segments that should also be in some phase of execution can be assigned to other memory partitions with, once again, certain pages designated to hold the nonchanging control program.

Now, in an ideal environment we could simply load these program segments into memory via a cassette, floppy disk, or other peripheral, and there they would stay forever. There would be no component failures, no glitches on the power line to destroy certain memory contents, and no human beings or ac machines to insert noise into the system which is wrongly interpreted as valid information. Unfortunately, such an ideal environment is more a myth than a reality. The problems just described do occur, and what used to happen in the early days of "multiprogramming" is that the misinformation resulting from one of these problems caused one program segment to "run away" and write data into another program segment. Thus a "nonchanging" instruction was replaced with who knows what, and when the poor processor tried to fetch, decode, and execute, anything could happen and usually did. Pretty soon there were no valid program segments, a product run was a disaster, and our only solution was to load the program back into memory and try, try again.

A solution that became popular during the 1960s is to load memory with the program segments, check to see if they are loaded properly, and then to set certain flip-flops or memory locations in a register that "fence" off the pages containing nonchanging instructions and data from their associated scratch pad areas. In other words, certain pages of RAM memory are treated just like ROM and can be read from but not written to during normal operations. Furthermore, any attempt by a runaway program segment to write into a "write protected page" is not only prevented but also generates an interrupt signal back to the processor to let it and the human operators know that a problem just occurred that caused an attempted runaway. Then the processor and the operator can decide what action, if any, is indicated.

Later, if the operator wants to modify one or more program segments (perhaps to change the colors in a certain pattern), an instruction is sent to the fence registers to unprotect the appropriate memory pages. Now these page locations can be modified as we would modify any RAM pages. After the modifications have been made and verified, the operator sends out an instruction to the fence registers to "fence" these pages off from the rest of RAM as "write protected pages." Figure V-3(d) shows circuitry to accomplish these functions.

e. The scheme used in Figure V-3(d) is to provide the customer with an "extra cost" option that can be installed on each memory module purchased to provide paged write protection capability for each page on the module. For the customer who selects this option, the manufacturer will change the switch setting in Figure V-3(c) at the input of NAND1 from $\overline{R/W}$ to PW and install the fence register circuitry.

The customer will set the Module # switches shown in Figure V-3(d) to the number of the module. That is, the first module is set to 0000, the second module to 0001, and the last permissible module would be set to 1110. Note that the high-order nibble value of 1111 is reserved for addressing the fence registers on the individual modules. In a moment we will return to see how the "magnitude comparator" circuitry (the four inverted Exclusive-ORs and the NAND they feed) compares the incoming address against the number set in the module switches but for now, let us turn our attention to the NOR in this circuit.

The NOR has a high output if and only if the processor places an address of FFOX on the bus, where X represents any 4-bit value of the low-order address nibble which equals the Module # switch settings. When the NOR output is high and a Data Transfer signal is present, the processor may read or write the type D flip-flops in the fence register. A Q = 0 will permit subsequent writing into the selected page and a Q = 1 will inhibit subsequent writing into the page.

   When a write operation is addressed to the fence register at
FFOX the output of NAND1 not only enables the "write"
Tri-state gates but it also triggers a one shot. The $\overline{Q}$ output falls
from a 1 to a 0 and then quickly returns from a 0 to a 1, presenting a leading edge to the clock inputs of the type D's to
strobe in the levels on D0 through D15. Assume that page 0 of
the module is to be protected from subsequent write operations,
whereas page 15 of the module is to remain as a scratch pad for
reading or writing. Since page 1 is to be protected, a 1 is stored
in Q0. When this page is selected in a future operation the P0
(page zero selected) signal from the 1-of-16 decoder in Figure
V-3(c) goes low. Thus the OR (OR0) receives a low from P0, a
_____ from Q0, and anther input signal from R/W. If the
attempt is made to write data to this page, then R/W = 0.
However, the output of OR0 goes to the Read/Write inputs of
the four 6810s that form page zero as a _____ thanks to
the value from _____ at the input to OR0, and therefore
no "write" takes place.

f. There are other implications of this input combination. For
    example, look at AND1. Since page zero was selected for the
    attempted write operation, only the P0 output from the 1-of-16
    page selector was low. The levels on P1 through P15 were high,
    which means that the outputs on OR1 through OR15 are also
    high. Since all 16 OR gates therefore have high outputs, AND1
    has a _____ output at PW. This signal is connected through
    a NOT to the input of NAND1 in Figure V-3(c), which means
    that not only was a write operation disabled at the memory
    chips of page zero but the data the processor wanted to send
    into memory were disabled at the inputs to the module bus.
    (This keeps the data read from the page from having to fight the
    data from the processor.) Also, note in Figure V-3(d) that PW is
    fed as an input to AND2 along with R/W. Since both inputs
    are _____, the AND2 output goes to a _____ level,
    which signals the processor via the interrupt request line (IRQ)
    that an attempt was just made to write into a write protected
    page.

g. Now let us see how a write operation could be accomplished in
    a nonprotected page like page 15. When page 15 is selected, the
    P15 output of the 1-of-16 page selector goes to a _____.
    Since we want to write data from the processor to memory,
    R/W = _____. The third input to OR 15 is from _____,
    which is at the _____ level. Therefore, the output of OR15

goes to a _____, which prepares the 6810s in page 15 for a write operation.

The output of AND1 (PW) goes to a _____ because of the signal from _____. In Figure V-3(c) this is connected through a NOT to the input of NAND1, which enables data to flow from the processor into the selected memory location in page 15. Also note in Figure V-3(d) that the PW signal causes the output of AND2 to remain at a _____ level, thereby generating no interrupt signal to the processor.

To summarize, each module has a 16-bit register of type D flip-flops, which can be read from or written to via address FFOX, where X is equal to the 4-bit switch settings that contain the number of the particular modules. Setting a 1 into a type D will inhibit writing into its associated page. A 0 in the type D will allow writing into its associated page. An attempted write operation into a protected page will be blocked at the R/W inputs of the memory chips in the page. Also, the data from the processor will be blocked at the entrance to the module bus and an interrupt signal will be sent to the processor to notify it of the attempted violation.

h. Now let us return our attention to the circuitry which decodes the FFOX in Figure V-3(d). The NOR will have a 1 output if and only if all of its inputs are at the 0 level. The M15 input comes from the 1-of-16 module selector in Figure V-3(d). It will go to a low level when the high-order nibble equals _____. The output of NAND3 will be low only when the next nibble (A8 through A11) equals _____. The output of OR16 will be low only when the third nibble (A4 through A7) equals _____. Therefore, the NOR output will be high, provided that the three upper address nibbles equal FFO and the levels on A0 through A3 match the switch settings. This comparison of two sets of binary values is shown as an experimental circuit in Figure V-6(a). Connect the circuit, clear the counter, and set an "A" into the switches.

With the counter reset to 0000 and the switches set to 1010, the Exclusive-ORs with a 1 output are _____. These values are inverted before being fed into the AND, and therefore the LED at the output of the magnitude comparator indicates a _____ level, which would prevent the NOR in Figure V-3(d) from indicating that the address of its fence register had been recognized.

Advance the counter. Note that the high is maintained at

MC. When should MC = 0? _____ Advance the counter and
verify your prediction.

e. 1; 1, Q0
f. 1; 1, 1
g. 0; 0; Q15, 0; 0; 0, OR15; 0
h. F; F; 0; 8 and 2; 1; count A

Congratulations. You have just completed the longest and most
difficult unit in the book. Since it is also the most important unit in the
book, you should take particular care in reviewing the objectives and
the material before taking your sample exam.

SAMPLE TEST FOR UNIT V

(Closed book. Closed notes. Use only writing materials, templates, and logic circuitry.)

1. Explain the meaning of each of the following terms. Give an example of an application for each term.
   a. Read operations vs. write operations
   b. LIFO stacks, stack pointers, and stack pointer operations
   c. Interrupt requests, priority interrupt levels, interrupt masks, main program vs. interrupt service routines
   d. Main program vs. subroutines, subroutine arguments, subroutine jumps vs. other jumps and branches
   e. Current page operations vs. zero page operations
   f. Indirect vs. indexed addressing
   g. Paged write protection and fence registers
2. For a 128 * 8 static RAM, explain how to write the following data into the indicated locations: [(27)R16 → (04)R16, (F3)R16 → (06)R16, (C2)R16 → (0E)R16]. Explain how to read the data from these locations. Draw the schematic, flowchart the procedural steps, connect the circuitry, and demonstrate the operations.
3. Explain how a microprocessor with an internal stack pointer and access to a static RAM maintains stack records of nested interrupt routines in progress and of nested subroutines in progress.
4. Draw and explain the organization of 128 * 8 LSI memory chips into a memory module consisting of 16 pages of 256 addresses per page with 8 bits per location. Explain how de-decoding can be accomplished so that up to 16 of these modules could be used for contiguous memory for a 16-bit address bus.

VI

Memory Operations in Digital Systems

INTRODUCTION

In the last four units we have studied memory interfacing, fixed program memory, sequential access memory, random access read/write memory, and several of their applications. We have examined hardware and software techniques used with modular memory systems. Two common denominators were used throughout these units. First, a remote terminal unit was used as an example of a digital system employing each of the three types of memories. This gave us a common end goal for each unit: to understand how the unit material relates to this increasingly common digital system. Second, flowcharts were given to depict the sequence of operations necessary to implement and utilize these memories. By this time you should be able to explain each of the memory-related functions in the RTU block diagram. In fact, with the exception of the processors, the digital communications links, and the computer peripherals, you should feel very comfortable with your understanding of the RTU.

In this unit, we will not use the RTU for our introduction to the material to be covered. Instead, we shall study memory transfers to and from analog devices, multiported memories and direct memory access operations, and device controller circuits.

One application of memory transfers to and from analog devices is found in electronic test equipment such as storage oscilloscopes, signal generators, and other devices we examine in the first section of experiments and problems in this unit. In this section we also learn how to sequence the read and write operations with a timing chain made from counters. In the early days of core memories, timing chains were typically made from "one-shots." However, these were much more sensitive to noise triggering than are counter-based timing chains. Sometimes, more than one processor or device needs access to a particular memory module found in the primary memory of a computer system. When there is more than one path to a memory module, we say that we have a "multiported" module. When we allow a transfer of information to flow directly between a device (such as a disk or magnetic tape unit) and a memory module without going through the processor(s) we are allowing a "direct memory access" (DMA) operation to take place. Although we shall examine these functions in some detail in the second section of this unit, a quick glance at Figure VI-0 should give us a better idea of what to expect. Note that only one set of buses is to be connected to the memory module at any time. Of the four ports (paths) the master processor probably has the highest priority in gaining access to the memory module. However, if it allows the module to be available, then the slave processor has priority. If both processors are busy elsewhere and allow the module to be available, then disk may use it. If the processors and the disk are allowing it, the mag tape unit is free to use the module. Whenever the disk or the tape unit communicates directly with the module, a direct memory access is taking place between primary storage (data are directly accessible to the processor and are stored in electronic form) and secondary storage (the disk and the tape store the data in magnetic form).

Note in the figure that direct memory access operations between primary and secondary storage are dependent upon a device controller. This device controller receives instructions from the processor as to when such an operation is to take place and what storage locations are to be involved. Then the processors proceed to work on other tasks involving other memory modules and/or peripherals while the device controller supervises the transfer of information between the memory module and its peripheral device. This saves the processors from having

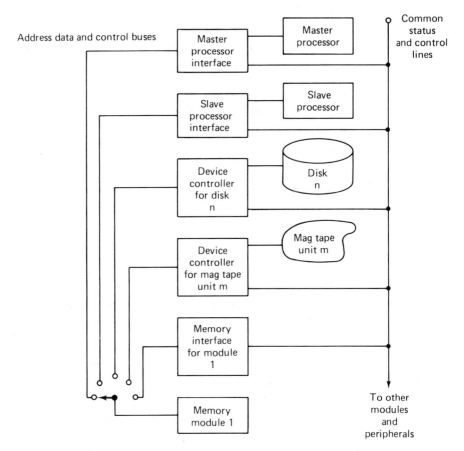

FIGURE VI-0 Conceptual diagram of switched memory transfers between different components of a computer system.

to idly wait for new program segments to be loaded from the disk or for a set of output data to be copied to a slow-speed magnetic tape unit, and so on. These device controllers will be studied in more detail in the latter part of this unit.

There will be one final difference between the objectives for this unit and the objectives for the other units. In previous units the operations were flowcharted for you and then were explained with frequent references to the flowcharts. In the real world we often start a new system by taking a few concepts and ideas to someone for discussion. The operational descriptions that result from these discussions often lead to flowcharts to make certain that all relationships are properly defined. These flowcharts often lead to the design and implementation of the system. In case you have not already guessed it, the author feels that you are ready to try a higher level of responsibility (i.e., higher than having to rely on others providing you with comprehensive, tutorial documentation). Therefore, in this unit, you are going to encounter instances where only the circuitry and a brief description of its operation is provided. (This is unfortunately very typical of the "real world.") To make sure you comprehend the operations involved, you will be asked to develop, explain, and demonstrate some of your own flowcharts. By the end of this unit, you should be able to correctly perform each of the following objectives using only a power supply, logic circuitry, an oscilloscope, and the notes and data obtained from running these experiments and working the associated problems.

Objectives for Unit VI

1. Explain the meaning of each of the following terms and how it relates to RAM applications.
    a. Hybrid environment vs. digital environment
    b. Sampling oscilloscope vs. traditional oscilloscope
    c. Timing chain based on counters vs. timing chain based on "one-shots"
    d. MTOS vs. memory partition vs. time slice vs. round-robin schedule vs. dispatcher
    e. Processor vs. device controller
    f. Two-ported memory module vs. DMA vs. IOTs
    g. Fence register for paged write protection (from Unit V) vs. Allow DMA flip-flop for a memory module (from this unit)
    h. Time-out-and-abort task vs. checkpoint restart
    i. Logical records vs. file vs. disk file directory
    j. Primary memory vs. secondary memory vs. device controller for a disk
    k. Generation and use of parity bits vs. generation and use of checksums in a device controller
    l. File address register vs. word count register in a device controller
    m. Soft errors vs. hard errors in copying a disk file back into primary memory

2. Using the sampling scope schematic and block diagrams in Figure VI-1, develop and explain a flowchart that depicts how input probe values are tracked, stored, and displayed when the OR2 input is set to "write from probe." The flowchart should also depict how the probe is isolated from the RAM while stored values are recalled from memory for display when the OR2 input is set to "display storage."

    Explain how each of the four timing chain outputs are related to the flowchart.

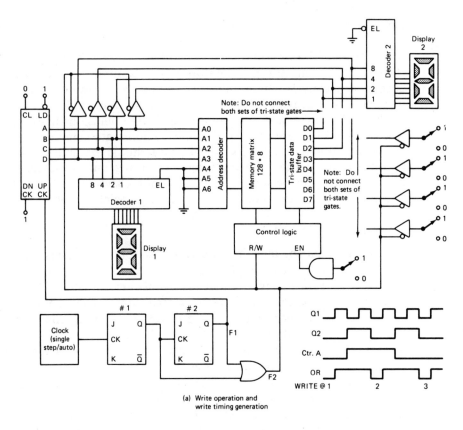

(a) Write operation and
write timing generation

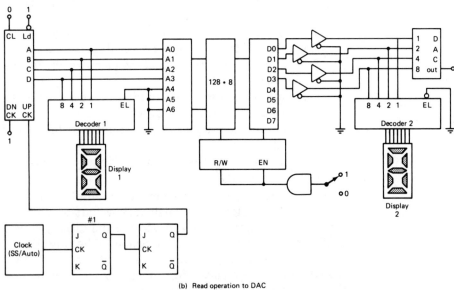

(b) Read operation to DAC

FIGURE VI-1 Memory transfers and analog devices.

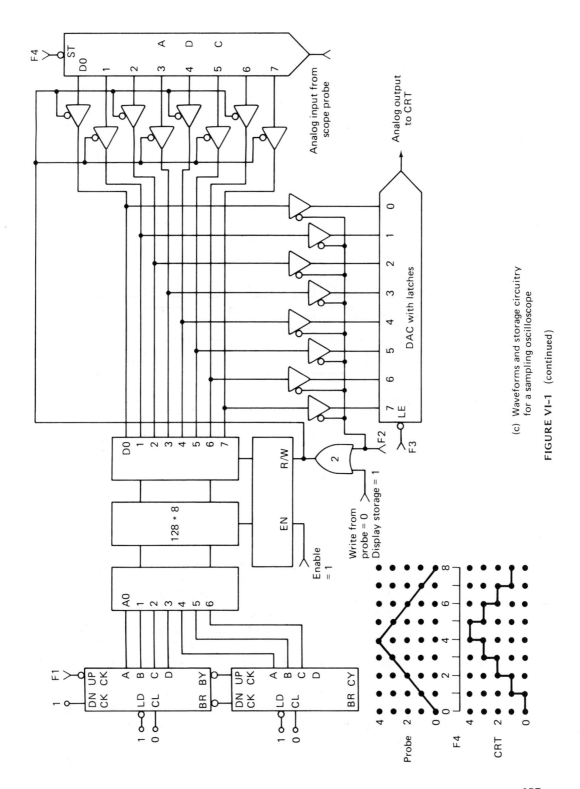

(c) Waveforms and storage circuitry for a sampling oscilloscope

FIGURE VI-1 (continued)

187

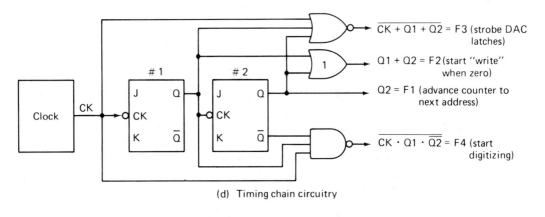

$\overline{CK + Q1 + Q2}$ = F3 (strobe DAC latches)

Q1 + Q2 = F2 (start "write" when zero)

Q2 = F1 (advance counter to next address)

$\overline{CK \cdot Q1 \cdot \overline{\overline{Q2}}}$ = F4 (start digitizing)

(d) Timing chain circuitry

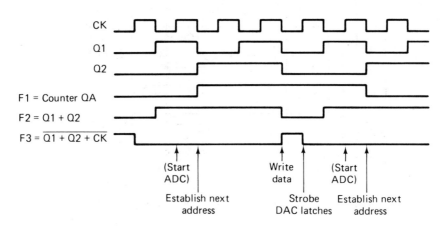

CK

Q1

Q2

F1 = Counter QA

F2 = Q1 + Q2

F3 = $\overline{Q1 + Q2 + CK}$

(Start ADC)

Establish next address

Write data

Strobe DAC latches

(Start ADC)

Establish next address

(e) Timing chain waveforms

FIGURE VI-1   (continued)

3. A periodic waveform is to be generated that can be thought of as having eight equal divisions of time in each waveform. During the first division of time the output amplitude is to be 0. During the second time slice a pulse is to be output with an amplitude of 25% of maximum DAC output. For the third slice, output = 0. Fourth slice, output = 50% of maximum amplitude. Fifth slice, output = 0. Sixth slice, 75% amplitude. Seventh slice, 0. Eighth slice, 100% amplitude. Explain how the circuit of Figure VI-1(a) and (b) can be used to implement this function. Explain what test pattern would be used. Connect the circuitry and demonstrate the accuracy of your predicted test pattern.

4. To avoid having the processor idly waiting around for a lengthy

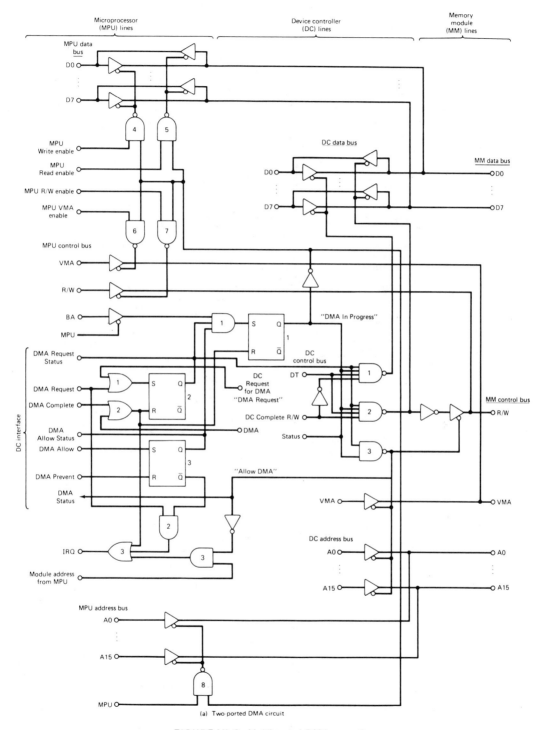

FIGURE VI-2 Multiported DMA operations.

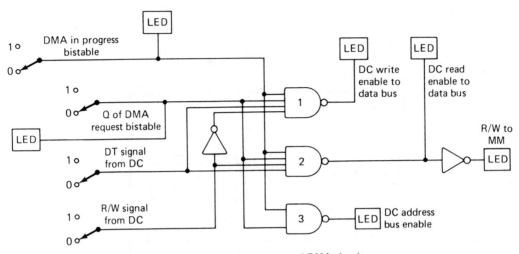

(b) Control logic for two-ported DMA circuit

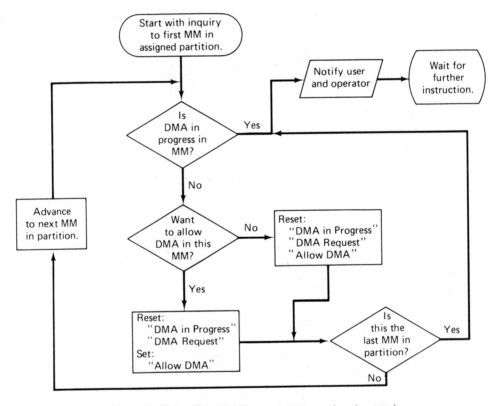

(c) Initialization of memory modules in a partition assigned to a task

FIGURE VI-2 (continued)

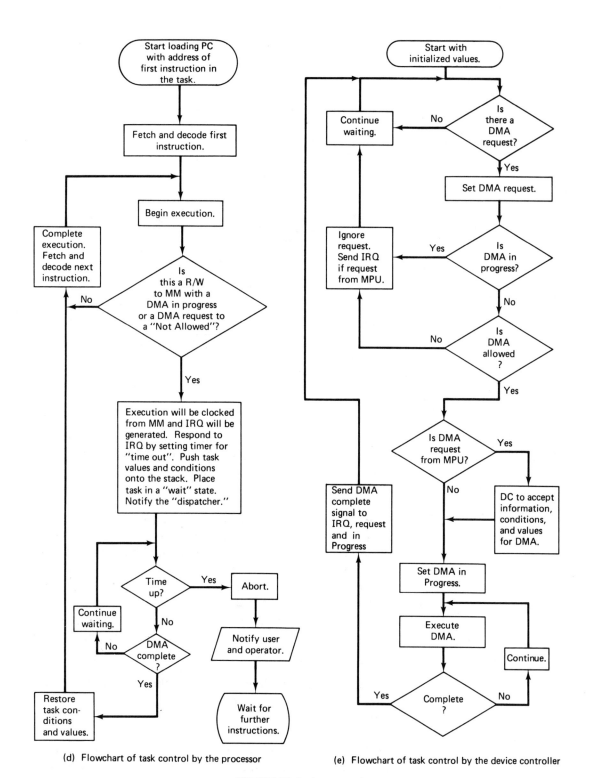

(d) Flowchart of task control by the processor

(e) Flowchart of task control by the device controller

FIGURE VI-2 (continued)

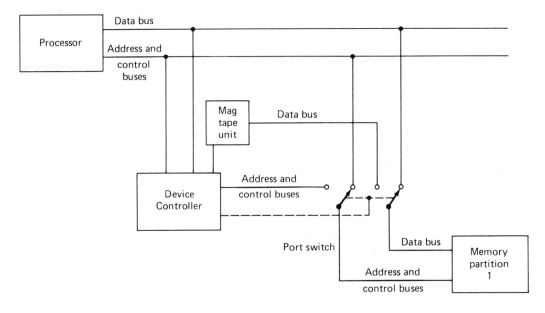

(f) Port switching concept

FIGURE VI-2 (continued)

IOT to be completed, the processor can be switched to another task providing that (give at least three major conditions):

_____

_____

_____

5. Connect the circuitry of Figure VI-2(b). Explain how it is used to "switch ports" and permit data transfers between the device controller and memory. Demonstrate the operation of this control circuitry as you have explained it.

6. Explain each of the flowcharts in Figure VI-2 as they relate to the circuitry in that same figure.

7. Using the conceptual block diagram in Figure VI-3(a), develop and explain a flowchart that depicts how the device controller will copy a new file "Nufile" to disk via DMA. Nufile is to begin at 0B00 and contains 00AA words. Assume that the processor has already added the file to the disk file directory and instructed the device controller to begin the operation (i.e., the file address and word count registers have been initialized).

8. Connect the circuitry of Figure VI-3(b). Explain how it relates to the operations you have just described in your flowchart.

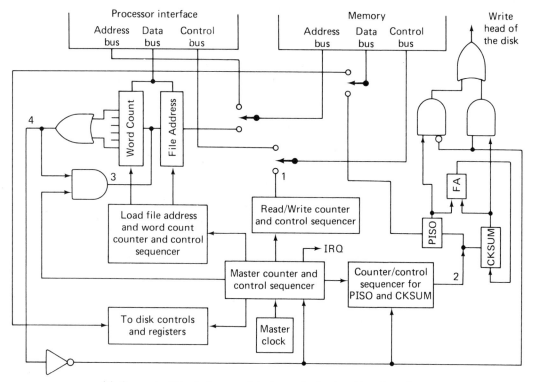

(a) Conceptual block diagram of device controller to address bus of memory

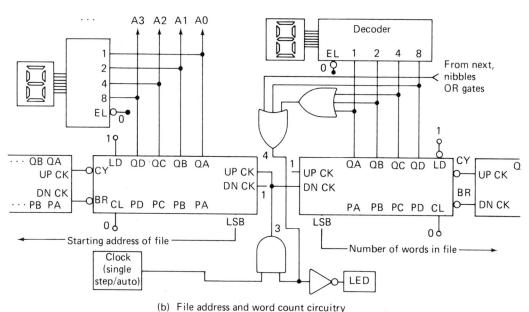

(b) File address and word count circuitry

FIGURE VI-3 Device controller.

193

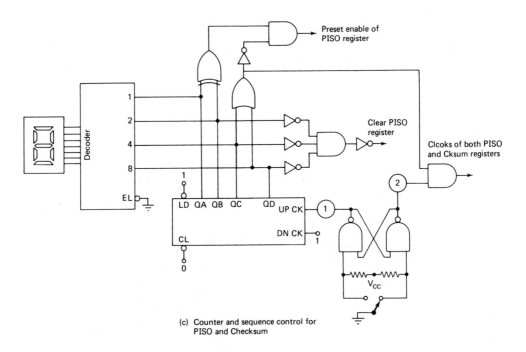

(c) Counter and sequence control for
    PISO and Checksum

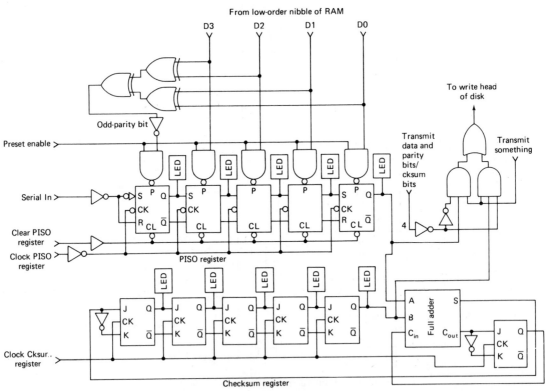

(d) Checksum generation circuitry

194

FIGURE VI-3 (continued)

Demonstrate the operation of this control circuitry as you have explained it.

9. Connect the circuitry of Figure VI-3(c) to that of Figure VI-3(d). Explain how this circuitry relates to the operations you have just described in your flowchart. Demonstrate the operation of this control circuitry as you have explained it.

LIST OF EQUIPMENT AND COMPONENTS USED IN UNIT VI

Equipment:

Oscilloscope: dc-coupled, 10-MHz BW
Power supply: 5 V dc at 1 A

Commonly used logic circuits (see Appendix G):

4 bounceless input switches
12 LED indicators
6 SPDT input switches
8 Mini-DIP SPST switches
2 seven-segment hex displays

Components:

3	7400	quad 2-input NAND
2	7404	hex NOT
1	7408	quad 2-input AND
1	7410	triple 3-input NAND
1	7411	triple 3-input AND
1	7420	dual 4-input NAND
1	7427	triple 3-input OR
2	7432	quad 2-input OR
1	7473	dual JK flip-flops
1	7480	full adder
1	7486	quad XOR
2	7496	5-bit shift register
2	74125	quad three-state driver
2	74193	up/down counter
2	8T97	hex three-state driver
1	6810	1024-bit RAM

Optional components and equipment: Every effort has been made by the author to hold the required costs of the items used in the experiments of this book to a level consistent with the budgets of most educational institutions. Accordingly, the following items are singled out as optional since all but two of the experiments in this unit can be completed without them and since they significantly increase the cost of this course.

The applications notes for these items, available from Analog Devices, Inc., will prove most helpful to the user.

1   8-bit DAC module (AD7524JN, 2-kΩ variable resistance, 1-kΩ fixed resistance, 10-pF capacitor; HP5082-2811 Zener, AD741J op amp, dual power supply: + and – 12 V dc at 1 A)

1   8-bit ADC module (AD7570J; AD311 op amp; 1-kΩ, 3-kΩ, and 200-Ω fixed resist; 1-kΩ variable resist; dual power supply: same as DAC module)

PROBLEMS AND EXPERIMENTS

Memory Transfers to/from Analog Devices

Objectives: By the end of these experiments and the associated problems, you should be able to correctly perform each of the following objectives using only a power supply, logic circuitry, an oscilloscope, and the notes and data obtained from running these experiments and working the associated problems.

1. Explain the meaning of each of the following terms and how it relates to RAM applications.
   a. Hybrid environment vs. digital environment
   b. Sampling oscilloscope vs. traditional oscilloscope
   c. Timing chain based on counters vs. timing chain based on "one-shots"
   d. RAM-to-DAC waveform generator vs. traditional signal generator
2. Using the sampling scope schematics and block diagrams in Figure VI-1, develop and explain a flowchart that depicts how input probe values are tracked, stored, and displayed when the OR2 input is set to "write from probe." The flowchart should also depict how the probe is isolated from the RAM while stored values are recalled from memory for display when the OR2 input is set to "display storage."

   Explain how each of the four timing chain outputs are related to the flowchart.

3. A periodic waveform is to be generated that can be thought of as having eight equal divisions of time in each waveform. During the first division of time, the output amplitude is to be 0. During the second time slice a pulse is to be output with an amplitude of 25% of maximum DAC output. For the third slice, output = 0. Fourth slice, output = 50% of maximum amplitude. Fifth slice, output = 0. Sixth slice, 75% amplitude. Seventh slice, 0. Eighth slice, 100% amplitude. Explain how the circuit of Figure VI-1(a) and (b) can be used to implement this function. Explain what test pattern would be used. Connect the circuitry and demonstrate the accuracy of your predicted test pattern.

Procedures:

1. After reading the narrative on memory operations in digital systems you should be ready to learn how memories can be used in a "hybrid" environment. That is, how these digital memories interact with analog circuits. In particular we will examine techniques of using memories in sampling oscilloscopes and in waveform (signal) generators. Please examine Figure VI-1(c).

2. Note that the oscilloscope probe is an input to an analog-to-digital converter (ADC). The ADC will start to digitize the probe input signal on the trailing edge of F4 from the timing chain. The conversion to an 8-bit value is completed and stored in the ADC's internal latches long before the value of F2 (from the timing chain) enables the ADC's contents to be written into the RAM. Shortly into the F2 "memory write time," the trailing edge of F3 is used to strobe the ADC output contents into the internal latches of the digital-to-analog converter (DAC). The DAC latches can "track" the probe during the ADC's write operations into memory or the DAC can be used to display the digitized values stored in the RAM previously by the ADC.

   The up-counters that select the RAM address are advanced by the leading edge of F1. Typically, the sequence of events is: Disable the ADC Tri-state gates. Start digitizing. Advance to the next address. Enable the write operation from the ADC latches to memory. Enable the transfer from the ADC latches to the DAC latches. Disable the write operation and the ADC Tri-state gates. Start digitizing, and so on. The waveforms and timing are shown in this same figure. If the probe is measuring the periodic analog waveform shown and the samples are taken at the F4 pulse times, then the cathode ray tube (CRT) will display the values sampled as shown. (Actually, an integrator may be used to cause the CRT display to look like the probe input wave except for a slight phase delay that results from averaging the values over the period of the waveform. Thus the CRT waveform might begin at a horizontal point between 0 and 1 on the grid, peak between horizontal grid points 4 and 5, and so on.)

Assume that the counter reads all 0's, CK = 0, Q1 = 1, and Q2 = 0. Refer to the timing chain circuitry and waveforms in the figure and let us analyze the sequencing of the events.

a. When the CK value rises to a 1, the NAND output F4 goes to a _____ level, which sends a _____ edge to start the ADC digitizing process. At this time, F2 = _____, which _____ the DAC Tri-state gates and, provided that a 0 is on the OR2 input, indicating that we are to "write from the probe", also _____ the ADC Tri-state gates. Similarly, F2 causes the RAM to be in a _____ operation at this time (although nothing at the moment is wanting to read the RAM).

b. When CK drops to a 0, we have a trailing edge presented to JK 1, which causes Q1 = _____. This, in turn, presents a trailing edge to JK 2, which causes Q2 = _____. This, in turn, presents a _____ edge to the address counter, which _____ it to (_____)R2. Note that QA out of this counter is shown to advance to a high level for this operation. Also note that F2 is still high, thereby still disabling the Tri-state gates.

c. The clock rises and falls and rises again, which provides time for the ADC to do its job. At this point, CK = 1, Q1 = 1, and Q2 = 1. When the clock falls to 0, this causes Q1 = _____, which causes Q2 = _____ (thanks to the sequence of _____ edges) and now F2 goes to the _____ level. This _____ the Tri-state gates and starts a _____ operation into the RAM. F3 = _____, since all of the NOR inputs are _____.

d. When CK rises to a 1, Q2 = _____ (still) but F3 goes to a _____, presenting a _____ edge to Latch Enable (LE) of the DAC. Hence the ADC contents are copied into the DAC about halfway into the write-to-RAM operation.

e. When CK falls to a 0, Q1 = _____ and Q2 = _____, causing F2 = _____, thus terminating our write operation. When CK rises to a 1, _____ drops to a 0, thus presenting a trailing edge to start the ADC digitizing the next value.

f. Suppose that we wish to leave the CRT tracking the probe when the address counter rolls over from (11, 1111)R2 to (00,0000)R2. No problem. This just means that we are writing over previously stored data.

Suppose that we wish to stop tracking and to display the "stored" waveform. Again no problem. By raising the OR2 input so that "Display Storage = 1" and leaving it there, we would continuously roll over our memory so that each of the 128 locations would be established at the leading edge of F1, read through the DAC Tri-state gates at the trailing edge of F2 and strobed into the DAC latches at the trailing edge of F3.

We need to see this in operation and in just a moment we will proceed to step 3 of our procedures, where we build and verify this memory to DAC interaction. But first consider the advantages of RAM storage oscilloscopes over the more traditional phosphor storage oscilloscopes. If we just had a technique of sharing this RAM with a microprocessor (which of course we do; it is called "multiporting" and is covered in the next experiment), we could search the locations for the biggest values, print them on a printer or CRT screen, calculate times between events, and so on. In other words, with enough shared memory, a microprocessor-based sampling oscilloscope cannot only display the measured waveform but can analyze the stored digital values and can print out on the oscilloscope screen such messages as

"Peak E = 2.95 V, F = 2 kHz"

These messages can be displayed on the CRT along with the waveforms and possibly other analysis messages, such as the correlation coefficient of two waveforms, the mean, standard deviation, and other mathematical values of interest. The traditional analog oscilloscope cannot, in the author's opinion, hope to compete in price, performance, or ease of use beyond the next 5 years unless dramatic breakthroughs are made in manufacturing cost-effective analog components.

a. 0, trailing, 1, disables, disables, read
b. 0, 1, leading, advances, (00,0001)R2
c. 0, 0, trailing, 0, enables, write, 1, 0's
d. 0, 0, trailing
e. 1, 0, 1, F4

3. Let us build and verify the memory-to-DAC interaction discussed in the last procedure. If we can make it work, we ought to be able to make the circuit produce several different types of waveforms, including "reasonable" approximations of sine waves, square waves, triangle waves, and so on. (The word "reasonable" is in quotations not because the technique to be used is faulty, but simply because we will demonstrate it on a 4-bit DAC, which does not have level amplifiers to drive the ladder resistors. Digital gates have a wide tolerance for voltages that are accepted as 1's and 0's. For example, one gate might have a "1" output of 2.67 V and another gate on the same chip might have a "1" output of 3.47 V. Level amplifiers accept these wide tolerances at their inputs and guarantee that their outputs are a known, uniform voltage which can then be supplied to the DAC ladder. If we wanted to build a good waveform generator out of our RAM, we would use at least an 8-bit DAC with level amplifiers.)

Please examine Figure VI-1(a). Its purpose is to allow us to write known data "test patterns" into the RAM, then, without removing power, to modify the circuit to that of Figure VI-1(b) to observe the waveform from the DAC.

A couple of points are in order here. First, since two pieces of equipment or more are to be interconnected (with different power supplies also), you should be sure that their signal grounds are the same. In other words, not only should your wrist strap be connected to the signal ground on the integrated circuits, but the strap should also be connected to the signal ground of your oscilloscope. Second, note in Figure VI-1(a) that D0, D1, D2, and D3 are not shown to be connected to anything but that there are two sets of Tri-state outputs positioned suspiciously close by. For the first test pattern, connect the Tri-state outputs that come from Decoder 2 to the low-order nibble of the RAM's data bus. (Their inputs are connected to the address counter as shown.) Later you will be asked to disconnect these Tri-states from the D0 through D3 lines and to use the Tri-states with switches at their inputs to insert subsequent test patterns. At no time should both sets of Tri-states be connected to write to the RAM.

One last point to be considered involves the Tri-states with their inputs labeled DS0, DS1, and so on. When using these Tri-state gates, be sure that the mini-DIP switches shown in the figure are open. Otherwise, shorts will occur from power supply to ground when data imputs are taken from switches such as PA, PB, and so on. However, if the mini-DIP switches themselves are used for the data entry, no special precautions need be taken.

a. Connect the circuitry of Figure VI-1(a) using the four lines from Decoder 2 to feed D0 through D3. Note that the counter receives pulses to advance from Q2 just as our sampling scope did. The equation for the Tri-state enable function is F2 = _____. Reset the counter to all 0's. Reset the JKs to 0's. Single-step the clock so that Q1 = 1, Q2 = 0. Set EN = 1.

   At this moment F2 = _____, implying that a _____ operation is taking place. The Tri-state gates are _____ and the second display shows the value of _____ _____. Single-step the clock. Now Q1 = _____, Q2 = _____, the counter reads _____ due to receiving F1's _____ edge, F2 = _____, and the second display shows the value of _____. Single-step the clock.

b. Now, F2 = _____, implying that a _____ operation is taking place. Single-step the clock again. Now Q1 = _____, Q2 = _____, F2 = _____, the Tri-states are _____, and the R/W input to the memory is causing a _____ operation to occur. In other words, a (_____)R16 is being written into location (_____)R16. Single-step the clock again. Now Q1 = _____, Q2 = _____, F2 = _____, the Tri-states are _____, and the R/W input to the memory is causing a _____ operation to occur. Note that the counter still contains a (_____)R16. It will not advance until a _____ edge arrives from _____ on the _____ single step of the clock.

c. Based on the preceding observations, we can conclude that each of the first 16 RAM locations will contain a value equal to _____ at the end of _____ pulses from the clock once it is set to automatic mode (free running). Set the clock to automatic and load these 16 values. If the address rolls over, there is no problem, since the same contents are again written into the same locations.

d. Reset En = 0. Disconnect R/W from F2. Now without removing power and the common ground connections of your grounded wrist strap, disconnect the Tri-state gates from the address bus and connect them between the data bus and the DAC as shown in Figure VI-1(b). Complete the necessary connections as shown in part (b) of this figure. Then set EN = R/W = 1.

Before setting the clock to automatic, think for a minute about what you should observe with the oscilloscope monitoring the DAC output. Assuming that you have previously been introduced to DACs and ADCs, you can predict the output waveform as an approximation of a "staircase wave" with 16 distinct steps which correspond to the contents of the 16 different locations. If this output were fed to an "integrator," the 16 "steps" would be averaged out to look like the "ramp" of a sawtooth signal generator. Set the clock to free running and observe the output for a number of different frequencies. Make a mental note of any "steps" that are obviously disproportionate to the other steps and decide which output data lines would profit the most by the insertion of a level amplifier before the DAC. With this in mind, look at Figure VI-1. You are to connect the circuitry of Fig VI-1(a) again. However, do not connect the Tri-state gates between the address lines and the data lines. Instead, connect the Tri-states with switch imputs to D0 through D3.

Now, a rectangular waveform with a 50% duty cycle (percentage of cycle time when wave was at the 1 level) would require the first eight locations to contain the same value (0 or 1) and the next eight locations to contain the complement. Decide what to insert where so that a 25% duty cycle is produced in Figure VI-1(b). (Probably you will want the waveform to go to the 1 level for the first 25% of the period and drop to 0 for the last 75%.) Insert your predicted values, configure part (b), and verify your predictions.

Consider the problem of generating a sine wave. Remembering that a sine wave is at 0% of maximum amplitude at 0°, 180°, and 360° and at 100% of maximum amplitude at 90° (and –100% at 270°), and is at 50% of maximum amplitude at 30° and 150° (and at –50% at 210° and 330°), insert a test sequence to approximate this output. Connect the circuit of part (b) and verify your predictions. [You may want to start by inserting the following sequence of values in the first 16 locations, observing the outputs in part (b) and then modifying the data to accommodate the peculiarities of your 4-bit DAC: (8,A,B,F,F,D,A,8,8,6,3,0,0,3,6,8).]

a. Q1 + Q2; 1, read; disabled, the contents of 000,0000; 0, 1, 0001, leading, 1, the contents of 000,0001

b. 1, read; 0, 0, 0, enabled, write; 1, 1; 1, 0, 1, disabled, read; 1; leading, Q2, next

c. its own address, 64 (four pulses per counter advancement)

PROBLEMS AND EXPERIMENTS

Multiported Memories and Direct Memory Access Operations

Objectives: By the end of these experiments and the associated problems, you should be able to correctly perform each of the following objectives using only a power supply, logic circuitry, and the notes and data obtained from running these experiments and working the associated problems.

1. Explain the meaning of each of the following terms and how it relates to RAM applications.
   a. MTOS vs. memory partition vs. time slice vs. round-robin schedule vs. dispatcher
   b. Processor vs. device controller
   c. Two-ported memory module vs. DMA vs. IOTs
   d. Fence register for paged write protection (from Unit V) vs. Allow DMA flip-flop for a memory module (from this unit)
   e. Time-out-and-abort task vs. checkpoint restart
2. To avoid having the processor idly waiting around for a lengthy IOT to be completed, the processor can be switched to another task providing that (give at least three major conditions):

   _____

   _____

   _____

3. Connect the circuitry of Figure VI-2(b). Explain how it is used to "switch ports" and permit data transfers between the device controller and memory. Demonstrate the operation of this control circuitry as you have explained it.
4. Explain each of the flowcharts in Figure VI-2 as they relate to the circuitry in that figure.

Procedures:

1. After reading the narrative on memory operations in digital systems and completing the experiments and problems on memory transfers to and from analog devices, you should be ready to learn how memories can be used in a multiported DMA environment.

Suppose that three different users want to use the same micro-computer system to perform three different, unrelated tasks at what appears to them to be executed concurrently. (Actually, the users are "time sharing" the processor. That is, the processor is so fast in switching back and forth between the tasks that each user feels that he or she is the sole user of the processor.) One approach to implementing such a time-sharing system is to assign each user his or her own "partition," consisting of a fixed number of memory modules. Then a "multitasking operating system" is written to do at least the following things.

First, the operating system goes to the first partition in memory and begins to execute instructions in that task. Depending upon the priority assigned to that task, only a certain time slice is to be allocated to running the program associated with this task. At the end of the allocated time slice, the operating system generates an interrupt. All task 1 values and conditions are stored on the stack and the *processor* then goes to the second *memory* partition and begins to execute instructions in this second task. At the end of the time slice allotted to this task, all task 2 values and conditions are stored on the stack when the operating system (OS) interrupts the processor to give task 3 a chance. The processor continues to switch between tasks in a "round-robin" fashion (i.e., 1,2,3,1,2,etc.) until all tasks are done. However, there is typically another way in which the processor can be told to switch tasks other than just the expiration of the time slice.

Suppose that the processor has just begun execution of the second task when an instruction is fetched requesting one-or-more memory modules in the partition to be loaded with data from a magnetic tape unit. Now this is a fairly straightforward request that should not require the intelligence of the processor. Also, since the transfer of a large block of data could take quite a while (mag tapes are notoriously slow), there should be no reason for the processor to wait for this transfer to be completed when there are other tasks that it could be attending to. If we just had a "device controller" (DC) that could isolate the address, data, and control buses of the memory partition from the processor and could then supervise the transfer of data from the mag tape to the partition over a second path to memory (often called the second "port" of the partition), we could let the processor service the other tasks and interrupt it when the transfer is completed so that it can return to this task whenever it is ready to do so.

Whenever a processor is bypassed by something that goes directly into memory, a "direct memory access" (DMA) operation is taking place. The conceptual block diagram of such operations are shown in Figure VI-2(f). Circuitry for such operations is shown in Figure VI-2(a). Observe in Figure VI-2(f) that only one of the two paths to memory (ports) can be used at a time. After the processor requests the device controller to supervise the transfer, the processor goes to the next task and the device controller switches the memory port switches so that the memory module's buses now connect to the buses of the controller and mag tape unit and initiates the transfer. Upon the completion of the transfer, the device controller switches the memory path back to the processor and sends a signal to the processor that it is through. This signal notifies a portion of the OS called the "dispatcher" (i.e., it schedules tasks for execution) that the task associated with this partition should be reinserted in the round-robin time-slicing schedule.

Similar task switching can be initiated in any task that would have the processor idly waiting for a lengthy input–output transfer (IOT) (such as "load memory from tape," "copy memory to desk file," etc.) provided that:

a. The processor and its resources are being managed by a multitasking operating system (MTOS).

b. There is more than one path (port or data channel) to the memory modules in the task partition.

c. The IO devices that are to participate in DMA operations have a suitably designed device controller.

Let us examine the device controller in Figure VI-2(a). Study this circuitry for a few minutes to familiarize yourself with the layout. Pay particular attention to the location of the "Allow DMA" flip-flip (No. 3), the "DMA Request" flip flop (No. 2), the "DMA In Progress" flip-flop (No. 1), and NANDS 1 through 8, since these are the portions of the device controller circuitry that switch the memory module between the processor and the mag tape unit. (Other portions of the device controller will be examined in the next sequence of experiments in this unit.) When you have located these components let us see how their initial values are to be established before the task is started into execution. Look at Figure VI-2(c) and we can see the procedural steps. (Remember that a partition may contain several memory modules. Some of these may need to participate in DMA activities at some time during the execution of the task instructions and some may not.)

2. The purpose of the routine shown in Figure VI-2(c) is to establish which memory modules in the partition are to be allowed to participate in DMA activities. After this information is "initialized," a DMA might be used to load the actual program instructions associated with the task. For example, the program may have been previously prepared and then stored on disk so that we can retrieve it and load it back into memory whenever the need arises.

   After the program is loaded into the partition, to keep the processor from accidentally writing into the program (because of another user's runaway program perhaps) the portion of the partition containing the instructions and data that do not change can be "write protected" (as discussed in Unit V). Note that write protection does not keep a module from participating in DMA operations. Therefore, the program could be copied to a card punch or other DMA device if we wanted the computer system to give us a copy of the current program in our partition.

   a. Study this flowchart. Observe that there are two "control" flip-flops that are to be initialized to 0 (i.e., reset) before we begin our program regardless of whether the module is to be involved in DMA or not. These two are labeled _____ and _____. The third control flip-flop is the one that actually determines whether or not DMA operations can occur to the module. This is labeled as _____ and must be _____ if the operations are permissible. To see why this is so, locate the output of this bistable in Figure VI-2(a).

   b. Note that the output (Q3) of "Allow DMA" is connected to two points. It is sent back to the interface to the processor as a "status" line so that the processor can read the interface and see whether or not we want to allow these activities. Q3 is also connected to the input of _____ . Note that the other inputs to this same gate are Q2 of _____ and the Bus Available (BA). In other words, to set the DMA In Progress flip-flop, the permission to participate (Q3 = _____) must exist, a request to participate (_____ = 1) must have been initiated by either the processor or the device controller, and the processor must signify that it has finished its current activities in the partition by a signal (BA = _____) on the bus available line. Once DMA In Progress is set to a 1, the memory module buses will be switched to the Device Controller (DC) and the mag tape unit buses.

   c. From the figure we see that Q1 = 1 causes a 0 to be placed at the inputs of NANDs 4, 5, 6, 7, and 8. Note that the processor's data bus has now been "disconnected" (Tri-states at the high impedance level) thanks to the 1 outputs of NAND _____ and NAND _____. Similarly, the processor's address bus is disconnected by the 1 output from _____, and the processor's Valid Memory Address line is disconnected by the 1 output from _____. In other words, the processor's buses (data, address, and control) are disconnected from the memory module whenever Q _____ = 1.

d. The output $Q1$ of DMA In Progress is connected directly to NAND _____, NAND _____, and _____. If the request for a DMA is still present ($Q2 = 1$), the output of _____ must immediately go to a 0. Note that VMA and the address bus of the Device Controller (DC) are now _____ to communicate to the memory module's VMA and address lines.

e. NAND 1 and NAND 2 are both dependent upon the Data Transfer (DT) and R/W lines from the DC. Assume that we want to read data from the memory. Then $Q1 = 1$, $Q2 = 1$, and R/W = 1 must be established. When DT rises to a 1, signaling that it is time to begin the transfer, the outputs of NAND2 = _____ and NAND1 = _____ enable the Tri-state gates that allow data to flow out of the Memory Module (MM) to the DC.

If R/W was 0 before the DT level was raised to a 1, a _____ operation from the _____ to the _____ would begin when DT went high. The appropriate Tri-states on the DC's data bus would be enabled by the low on _____. This portion of the control circuitry is redrawn for experimentation in Figure VI-2(b).

Note that if the processor is using the MM, the top line (DMA in progress) will be low and therefore all 3 NANDs will be at the 1 level, thereby disconnecting the DC buses from the MMs and allowing transfers between the processor and memory. If the processor has surrendered the buses, a 1 on the top line and a 1 on the request line allows transfers between the DC and MM with each signal on DT. (The direction of the transfer is dependent upon the R/W line.) This is a basic control circuit for two-ported DMA operations. Connect the circuitry and verify the operation as just described. You should be able to explain and demonstrate this circuit as it relates to the other components in Figure VI-2(a).

f. To better understand some of the other features of our two-ported DMA circuit, let us examine Figure VI-2(d) and (e) in conjunction with the schematic.

The first flowchart shows the task control by the processor. Note that, as always, we prepare to execute a program by loading the Program Counter with the location of the first instruction. Then, as usual, the processor fetches the instruction, decodes it, and then begins to execute it. As long as the instruction does not address a module with a DMA presently taking place or the instruction does not request a DMA operation involving a module with a Not Allowed status, the processor continues to execute and fetch instructions during the allotted time slice.

Suppose that an instruction does try to address a module with a DMA in progress. Note that AND3 [Fig. VI-2(a)] has two inputs: one from the module address decode (signaling that the processor wants to communicate with this MM) and the other from a NOT gate which is connected to the output of NAND3 (signaling that a DMA operation is presently taking place since the output of NAND3 is a low). The output of AND3 goes to a _____, which places a _____ on the Interrupt Request line (IRQ) to the processor.

From the flowchart we see that the processor's instruction is blocked. (It cannot get through its disabled buses.) The Operating System and its dispatcher then switch to the next task even though the current task's time slice was not up yet. The current task is now in a "wait" state (waiting for the DMA to conclude). Because peripherals such as mag tape units and memory modules do sometimes fail, the OS may go to a look-up table to see what the maximum time should be for a DMA in this partition. A timer is then set which will interrupt the processor if the DMA is not completed to reset the timer before the time expires. Notice in the flowchart that if the maximum time is exceeded, the processor decides that there is a problem requiring human intervention and it therefore aborts the task (completely removes it from the round-robin schedule) as a lost cause and notifies the user and operator.

Notice that if the DMA currently taking place is completed prior to timing out, the output of OR2 goes high. (Actually, it receives a short pulse.) This high resets $Q2 = 0$ and $Q1 = 0$. It also feeds into _____, which sends the pulse to the processor on the _____ line. This interrupt tells the dispatcher that when the task is entitled to its next time slice, the former values and conditions should be popped off the stack and restored in the processor. This includes a copy of the formerly blocked instruction being placed back in the instruction register (IR). This time, the execution of this instruction will occur unless another request for DMA does not arrive first.

Observe that if the processor requests a DMA operation from a module where such an operation is not allowed, that AND2 will cause the processor to be signaled on the _____ line. This would cause the task to enter the "wait state" and the timer to be set. Upon a time out, the processor would abort the task and notify the user and operator of an attempt to illegally access a protected segment of memory for a DMA.

g. Figure VI-2(e) shows the task control flowchart for the DC. The DC starts with initialized values that tell it how it is to work with the processor and memory in the current configuration and applications of the computer system. Then it waits for a request for DMA activities. The request can come from the processor (bottom input to OR1) or from its own circuitry (top input to OR1). For example, the device controller may be equipped with a feature called "checkpoint restart." With this feature, as the OS switches from one task to another, the DC associated with the preceding task can request a DMA. During this DMA, the key values and conditions of the task are written to a disk file or tape file. Each time the task is granted another time slice, the present tasks are switched and the key values and conditions are written over the old information to update this disk or tape file. Now suppose that a task which requires 10 hours to complete has been running for 9 hours when there is a power failure. If the task is to solve a system of differential equations and the system lacks checkpoint restart, then the operator may have to begin the 10-hour program all over again when the power is restored. However, with checkpoint restart, the task can be resumed (with an hour left to run) at the point of interruption when power is restored.

Back to the flowchart in Figure VI-2(e). Suppose that a DMA request arrives. If a DMA is already taking place, the DC ignores the new request but sends an IRQ signal to the processor. [We just saw what the processor did with that IRQ signal when we examined the flowchart in Figure VI-2(d).] If no

DMA is in progress, the next question should be whether DMAs are allowed in this MM. If the answer is yes, the DC must be concerned with the source. If the processor did not originate the request, the DC itself must have. Since it presumably knows why it wanted to do a DMA, no special instructions, conditions, or values are needed from the processor. It can set its DMA In Progress flip-flop and execute the DMA.

Suppose that the DMA request came from the processor. The processor may want to copy a portion of continuous memory to the mag tape unit. It therefore needs to tell the DC where the information starts and ends. For the DC to be able to accept this information, conditions and values circuitry is required that is not shown in Figure VI-2(a). We will examine this circuitry in the next section. For now, study the flowcharts until you understand and can explain them in relation to the circuitry.

a. DMA Request, DMA In Progress; Allow DMA, set
b. AND1; DMA Request; 1, Q2, 1
c. 4, 5; NAND8, NAND6; Q1
d. 1, 2, NAND3; NAND3; enabled
e. 0, 1; write, DC, MM; NAND1
f. 1, 1; OR3, IRQ; IRQ

PROBLEMS AND EXPERIMENTS

Device Controller Circuits

Objectives: By the end of these experiments and the associated problems, you should be able to correctly perform each of the following objectives using only a power supply, logic circuitry, and the notes and data obtained from running these experiments and working the associated problems.

1. Explain the meaning of each of the following terms and how it relates to RAM applications.
    a. Logical records vs. file vs. disk file directory
    b. Primary memory vs. secondary memory vs. device controller for a disk
    c. Generation and usage of parity bits vs. generation and usage of checksums in a device controller

    d. File address register vs. word count register in a device controller

    e. Soft errors vs. hard errors in copying a disk file back into primary memory

2. Using the conceptual block diagram in Figure VI-3(a), develop and explain a flowchart that depicts how the device controller will copy a new file "Nufile" to disk via DMA. Nufile is to begin at OB00 and contains 00AA words. Assume that the processor has already added the file to the disk file directory and instructed the device controller to begin the operation (i.e., the file address and word count registers have been initialized).

3. Connect the circuitry of Figure VI-3(b). Explain how it relates to the operations you have just described in your flowchart. Demonstrate the operation of this control circuitry as you have explained it.

4. Connect the circuitry of Figure VI-3(c) to that of Figure VI-3(d). Explain how this circuitry relates to the operations you have just described in your flowchart. Demonstrate the operation of this control circuitry as you have explained it.

Procedures:

1. After reading the narrative on memory operations in digital systems and completing the experiments and problems on memory transfers to and from analog devices and on multiported memories and direct memory access operations, you should be ready to learn more about how a device controller accepts information from the processor, performs the indicated operations, and provides error detection and correction while performing its job.

      Suppose that we have just calculated and stored in primary memory the following annual information for a large corporation: a list of all paid expenses for the year, a list of encumbrances (items on order but not yet delivered and paid for), and a list of all income for the year. The data associated with each of these three categories may be referred to as a logical record if all data in each record are stored in contiguous memory. The three logical records for this company together make a "file" for this company. (A file can be any number of related logical records.) Now, suppose that the file begins in memory address A000 and that the three records together contain 01FF words located contiguously between A000 and A1FE. (The "E" is because there is one word in A000.) Further suppose that the task being executed by the processor requests that this file, called "Company A," be copied out to disk. Look at the conceptual block diagram in Figure VI-3(a) and let us study some of the procedures.

Before the processor switches to another task and allows the device controller to supervise the transfer, the operating system will have to look in its "disk file directory" to see where on the disk it wants to put the "Company A" file. When it finds an unused portion of the disk that is big enough to contain 01FF contiguous[1] words, it enters the file name "Company A" and its size in the file directory. It also records in the file directory the exact disk location where the first word of the file is to be stored. This is so that subsequent calls from a task that asks for access to Company A's records will result in the operating system going to the file directory, looking up Company A and returning with the starting disk location and file size. These arguments are then provided to the device controller for the disk. The processor then switches tasks while the device controller supervises loading the file back into primary memory from the disk via a DMA operation.

Let us assume that the disk controls and registers have already been told (via the processor's data bus) where to position the head of the disk to begin writing the file onto the disk. There are different types of disks, but they all use the principle of recording digital data in magnetic form on the concentric circles of the disk surface. For purposes of our study of the device controller, we are assuming that the magnetic recording head is already poised over the selected concentric circle (called a "track") and is to start recording each word of the file in serial form on the track. To minimize the chances of error in this conversion of parallel data stored in electronic form in primary memory to serial data stored in magnetic form in secondary memory, a parity bit will be generated, checked, and stored after the most significant bit of each word. Furthermore, a "checksum" will be generated, checked, and stored at the end of the record.

More will be said about this a little later. For now let us turn our attention back to the simplified block diagram of Figure VI-3(a).

Assume the file address register and the word count register of the device controller have already been loaded with A000 and 01FF, respectively, via the processor's data bus. When the processor

---

[1] The more sophisticated disk systems do not always require a file to be stored contiguously.

switches tasks, the device controller switches the ports connected to the memory module.

a.   The address bus of the memory module is now reading _____ from the _____ register of the DC. The control bus of the memory is now connected to the read/write counter and control sequencer of the DC. The first (see "1" on the diagram) operation performed after the ports are switched is to cause the parallel contents of the first location in the file to be transferred into the PISO (parallel-in, serial-out) register. The second operation to be performed (see "2" on the diagram) is to generate a parity bit and to transfer the data plus the parity bit onto the disk. As the data are being shifted to the disk write head, it is also being sent into a full adder (FA) along with the checksum bits (which were initialized to 0's). The sum of the PISO and the checksum register is written back into the checksum register.

b.   The third operation (see "3" on the diagram) is initiated when the master counter and control sequencer send a pulse into the AND gate which feeds the file address and word count registers. The other input of the AND comes from the _____ gate, which is in turn fed by the Q outputs of the word count register. Since this register presently contains _____ , the OR maintains a 1 on the top input of the AND, which allows the pulse from the master counter to pass through the AND gate. This pulse causes the File Address to increment by 1 to _____ and the Word Count to decrement by 1 to _____ .

c.   Now that the address bus of the memory is set to a new location, we return to point "1" on the diagram, where the master counter signals the read/write control sequencer to transfer the parallel data contained in the new address into the PISO via the memory's _____ bus. The master counter then (see "2" on the diagram) tells the PISO and checksum sequencer to generate a parity bit on the new word and to send the word and the parity out to the disk head. As it is transferred, the serial data are added to the checksum data and the sum is stored back in the checksum register. This register is accumulating the sum of all words in the file. Overflows are likely to occur but will be ignored. We are now back to the third operation, which is initiated when the master counter sends a pulse into the _____ gate.

Since the word count is not yet 0, the output of the

_____ gate is a _____ , thus enabling the master counter pulse to pass through the AND. This causes the File Address to _____ by 1 to a new address value of _____ . The Word Count is _____ by 1 to _____ . Then the sequence of operations is ready to begin again.

d. The sequence continues until the File Address reads _____ , the Word Count reads _____ , and the checksum register contains the sum of all words in the file. Then the master counter sends a pulse to the AND gate. It passes through the AND and _____ the Word Count to _____ . The OR gate then goes to a _____ output for the first (and only) time in the operation. This causes the output of the NOT gate, which is fed by the OR, to rise to a 1. This signal from the NOT tells the master counter and the PISO/checksum counter that all that remains to be done is to transmit the checksum bits to the write head. The PISO/checksum counter will put out enough clock pulses to shift out each bit of the checksum and then it will shut down. The master counter will then switch the ports so that the memory is connected back to the processor once again. The master counter then sends an IRQ pulse to the processor to let it know that the DMA has teminated.

Let us return for a moment to the time when the OR output had just caused the NOT to go to a 1 level. Note that this 1 will be sent not only to the two counters but also to enable the AND, which can now pass the checksum bits through to the write head of the disk. Formerly, the NOT output had been a 0, which disabled the checksum bits and enabled the PISO to be passed through to the write head.

e. Have you thought about what the purpose is of recording the checksum on the disk at the end of the file? Well, suppose that we want to load our memory from this disk file in the future. As we read each word from the disk, we are converting the serially recorded magnetic data on a rotating disk to parallel electronic data for storage in a static RAM. Errors sometimes occur. By generating a parity bit as we retrieve each word off the disk and comparing it to the parity bit recorded on the disk, we have a good chance of catching the error as it occurred if the parity bits disagree, rejecting the word, and asking the disk read head to try the same word again. This is not foolproof, however. If two bits were read in error, there may still be an odd parity generated which agrees with the parity bit recorded on the disk. To catch these kinds of errors, we generate a checksum as we retrieve each word from the disk. At the end of the file, we compare the newly generated checksum to the one recorded on the disk. If they agree, the odds are greatly in our favor that we retrieved the entire file without error. If they do not agree, we try again to retrieve the entire file.

When errors like this disappear upon retrying the read operation, we call the error a "soft error." Hard errors are not recoverable by retrying the operation. One of the biggest causes of soft errors is dirty read/write heads. If, for example, a smoke particle from someone smoking a cigarette in the same room as the computer system (a serious crime that should be punishable by hanging!) is attracted to one of the disk tracks, soft errors can result that cause unbelievable delays and loss time.

a. A000, File Address
b. OR, 01FF, A001, 01FE
c. data, AND, OR, 1, increment, A002, decremented, 01FD
d. A1FE, 0001, decrements, 0000, 0

2. Let us experiment with some of the circuitry that forms the blocks in our conceptual diagram. Study Figure VI-3(b) for a minute. Note that a file address register and a word count register are formed by combining a number of straight-code MSI counters. The file address counters are connected to count up (increment) and the word count counters are connected to count down (decrement). Construct the circuit using one 4-bit counter in each register. Tie the input to the final OR which comes from the next nibble's OR to a 0.

   a. Load the file address counter with a (4) R16 and load the word count counter with a (7) R16. Therefore, if a DMA operation were taking place in a 16-word memory, we could conclude that our file begins at _____ and that we are to copy through _____ to our peripheral.

   At this time the output of the OR at 4 is a _____, which _____ the AND. The output of the NOT is a _____, which would allow the output of the _____ register to be shifted to the write head of the disk [see Figure VI-3(a)].

   b. The DMA transfers from the memory addressed by the file address counter to the disk would continue until the word count circuitry disabled subsequent transfers. Then the device controller would switch the ports so that the processor was again connected to the memory. Practice explaining this operation while referring to Figure VI-3(a). Use the clock and indicators to demonstrate the accuracy of your explanation.

   a. 4, B, 1, enables, 0, PISO

3. Examine and connect the circuitry of Figure VI-3(c) to that of Figure VI-3(d). Use binary switches for D0 through D4 to simulate the inputs from the RAM. Also use switches to simulate the "transmit data and parity bits or transmit checksum bits" and the "transmit something" input.
   a. Clear the six JKs. Set the "transmit something" switch to 1. Place a 1 on the input to the NOT at 4. Note that this is the same NOT that was referred to in Figure VI-3(b) and (a). Place a (6) R16 on the D3 through D0 switches. The odd parity bit from the NOT will be at the _____ level to ensure an odd number of high levels in the data word plus the parity bit. Clear the counter.
   b. Pulses from the counter should cause the PISO to be loaded with the data word plus the parity bit. Subsequent pulses should cause the PISO contents to be shifted out to the write head of the disk while being added to the checksum register contents. Practice explaining this operation while using the circuitry to demonstrate the accuracy of your explanation.

   a. 1

SAMPLE TEST FOR UNIT VI

(Closed book. Closed notes. Use only writing materials; templates; copies of Figures VI-1, VI-2, and VI-3, and logic circuitry.)

1. Explain the meaning of each of the following terms and how it relates to RAM applications.
   a. Timing chain based on counters vs. a timing chain based on one-shots
   b. RAM to DAC waveform generators vs. a traditional signal generator

c. MTOS vs. memory partition vs. time slice vs. round robin

d. Processor vs. device controller

e. Two-ported memory module vs. DMA vs. IOTs

f. Time-out-and-abort task vs. checkpoint restart

g. Logical records vs. file vs. disk file directory

h. Generation and usage of parity bits vs. generation and usage of checksums in a device controller

i. File address register vs. word count register in a device controller

j. Soft errors vs. hard errors in copying a disk file back into primary memory

2. A periodic waveform is to be generated that can be thought of as having eight equal divisions of time in each waveform. During the first division of time, the output amplitude is to be 0. During the second time slice a pulse is to be output with an amplitude of 25% of maximum DAC output. For the third slice, output = 0. Fourth slice, output = 50% of maximum amplitude. Fifth slice, output = 0. Sixth slice, 75% amplitude. Seventh slice, 0. Eighth slice, 100% amplitude. Explain how the circuit of Figure VI-1(a) and (b) can be used to implement this function. Explain what test pattern would be used. Connect the circuitry and demonstrate the accuracy of your predicted test pattern.

3. To avoid having the processor idly waiting around for a lengthy IOT to be completed, the processor can be switched to another task providing that (give at least three major conditions):

_____

_____

_____

4. Connect the circuitry of Figure VI-2(b). Explain how it is used to "switch ports" and permit data transfers between the device controller and memory. Demonstrate the operation of this control circuitry as you have explained it.

5. Explain each of the flowcharts in Figure VI-2 as they relate to the circuitry in that same figure.

6. Using the conceptual block diagram in Figure VI-3(a), develop and explain a flowchart that depicts how the device controller will copy a new file "Nufile" to disk via DMA. Nufile is to begin at 0B00 and contains 00AA words. Assume that the processor has already added the file to the disk file directory and instructed the device controller to begin the operation (i.e., the file address and word count registers have been initialized).

unit

VII

Magnetic Bubble Memory Modules

INTRODUCTION

In the previous units we have concentrated on solid-state, primary memory modules. That is, we have concentrated on memory modules with no moving parts which provide primary rather than secondary storage for a computer system. Until the last decade, secondary mass storage devices have been predominantly constructed as electromechanical devices with many moving parts and therefore a relatively higher maintenance cost and lower reliability than the primary memory systems. However, the disks, drums, and magnetic tape units no longer enjoy the obvious price/performance advantages over their no-moving-parts competition that they once held and the advantages still held by the electromechanical devices for certain applications are continuing to dwindle.

In particular, three types of memory modules with no moving parts are making inroads into applications that were once dominated by

218

disks, drums, and tapes. The three are the core memory modules (which are being moved out of the primary memory systems by the semiconductor RAM modules), the charge-coupled device modules (CCDs), and the magnetic bubble memory modules (MBMs). Of the three it is the author's opinion that the bubble memory systems have the greatest potential for making further inroads into the realm of secondary storage devices. Accordingly, this unit is devoted to the study of bubble memories. Core memories and CCD memories are discussed in the appendices.

Objectives for Unit VII

1. Explain the meaning of each of the following terms and how it relates to MBM applications.
   a. MBMs vs. CCDs vs. traditional mass storage devices with respect to:
      (1) Volatility
      (2) Acceleration/deceleration
      (3) Refresh requirements
      (4) Off-line libraries
   b. Platelet vs. Permalloy track guides vs. permanent magnet vs. orthogonal coils vs. generator vs. detector vs. annihilator vs. replicator vs. transfer gates
   c. Multitrack architecture vs. six basic operational functions for a major–minor organization
2. Explain how the 92,304 bits of the TIB0203-1 are organized into 641 pages of 18 bytes per page.
3. Explain the MBM operations necessary to read the data from page 3 of a TIB0203-1 MBM chip.
4. Explain the MBM operations necessary to write a full page of new data into page 7 of a TIB0203-1.
5. Explain the reasons for sensing impending power failures and for holding the power supplies connected to the MBM chips within regulation until "automatic data positioning to page 0" has been completed.

LIST OF EQUIPMENT AND COMPONENTS
USED IN UNIT VII

The items required to experiment with bubble memories are, at present, sufficiently expensive as to provide at least a tenfold increase in the cost of this course. Since the items listed below are used only in Unit VII, they are considered by the author to be optional.

The applications notes for these items from Texas Instruments, Inc. (see the Bibliography, Appendix H) will prove most helpful to the user.

2	SN75382	MBM coil drivers
2	VSB53	diode assemblies
1	SN75380	MBM function drivers
1	SN75281	MBM sense amplifier
1	TIB0203-1	92,304-bit MBM
1	TSP102F	silicon thermistor
1	SN74LS361	function timing generator

(2-0.1-μF capacitor; 1-470-pF capacitor; 2-3.4-kΩ resistor; 1-1kΩ resistor; 1-4.2-kΩ resistor; 1-374-Ω resistor; dual power supply: + and - 12 V dc at 1 A)

BUBBLE MEMORIES

To appreciate why so many people are excited about the advent of magnetic bubble memories (MBMs) and charge-coupled devices (CCDs) it helps if you share the author's belief that the only "trustworthy" electromechanical computer peripheral is one that is no longer needed because a more reliable, cost-effective solid-state device with no moving parts has replaced the older unit. In particular, the traditional mass storage devices such as the disk, drum, and magnetic tape units are infamous for the number of maintenance problems they present when compared to the number encountered in the solid-state processors.

Both MBMs and CCDs show promise of providing us with solid-state "chips" in DIP form that behave like today's rotating sequential access mass memory devices. Since their announcement by Bell Labs in the late 1960s, a number of firms have made commitments to the MBM technology. Companies such as TI, Rockwell, Hitachi, and others have already incorporated MBM chips into a number of applications. Although at present the chip densities range from about 250K to 1M bits per square inch, there is reason to believe that 1G bits per square inch will be feasible by 1985. MBMs may have an advantage over CCDs in density and in smaller power requirements. Both technologies are young, and just how much if any advantage there really is remains to be seen. However, MBMs definitely have two advantages over CCDs which they will retain. First, the information stored in MBMs is nonvolatile. Second, the information stored in MBMs can be completely halted during a shifting sequence with no worries about acceleration or deceleration. Then data can be shifted in reverse as easily as in the forward direction. (In a disk or mag tape unit, information transfers have to be inhibited while the moving medium is being accelerated or decelerated.) In MBMs and CCDs the storage medium does not move. Only the information does, and it moves in much the same manner as it would in a shift register or ring counter. However unlike the MBM or unlike a ring counter made of JK flip-flops, the information in CCD registers must be continuously recirculated or it will "leak out" (like air from a punctured tire). The real disadvantage of both MBMs and CCDs compared to their electromechanical counterparts is in the area of off-line storage. Neither of the new technologies currently offers a low-cost removable medium, such as mag tape, that permits programs and data that are used only occasionally to be placed in an off-line library to be retained for reloading on an "as needed" basis.

We have briefly discussed a few of the "whys" of MBMs. Now let us examine "what" they are. As shown in Figure VII-0(a), bubble memory manufacturers start with a material capable of supporting magnetic domains. The rare-earth iron garnets are good for this purpose, and more recently certain amorphous materials have been deposited on a substrate such as glass and have given good results. Interestingly enough, some of the MBM materials are grown epitaxially, much like semiconductors.

At any rate, the polarization of the magnetic domains are random in the absence of any externally applied magnetic field as shown in Figure VII-0(a). In this figure the "pluses" indicate polarization pointing into the material, and the serpentine collections of points indicate polarization pointing out of the material toward us. The manufacturers often take a small permanent magnet and attach it to the flat side of the material. Now the material (called the "platelet") has an external magnetic field applied in the immediate vicinity of the randomly organized magnetic domains of the platelet. This tends to align all domain areas of the platelet that were at any kind of an angle to the magnet with the exception of a small percentage of the domain areas that were polarized in the opposite direction and aligned perpendicular to the magnet and the face of the platelet. As shown in Figure VII-0(b), the bulk of the platelet material is now contentedly aligned with the bias field of the permanent magnet and the serpentine domains of the formerly random field have now been reduced to a few round cylinders of polarization opposite to the bias field. These round cylinders of polarization are called "bubbles," and since they represent a magnetic field surrounding certain molecules of the platelet, by providing a moving magnetic field (either by a traveling magnet or by inducing current flow in a manner that simulates the effects of a traveling magnet), these bubbles can be made to "move" in pursuit of the attractive moving flux field. (Actually, the polarized domain is shifted

(a) Top view of symbolic representation of randomized magnetic domains of MBM platelet with NO bias field applied

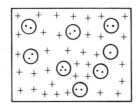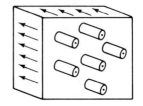

(b) Top and three dimensional views of symbolic representation of cylindrical magnetic domains called bubbles in the presence of an applied bias field

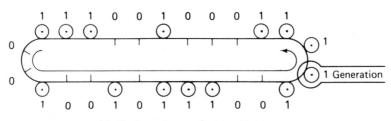

(c) Single-track organization of MBM chip

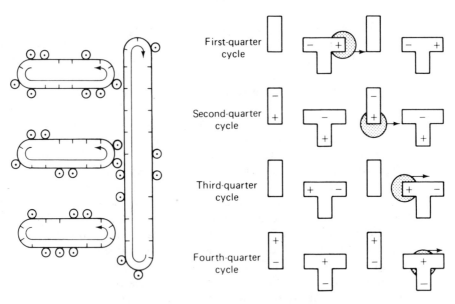

(d) Multitrack organization of MBM chip

(e) Four different views (during four successive quarter cycles of rotating T and I bar fields), showing shifting of a bubble along a track

First-quarter cycle

Second-quarter cycle

Third-quarter cycle

Fourth-quarter cycle

FIGURE VII-0 Magnetic bubble memory fundamentals (Hoffman et al., 1976, p. 80, and Juliussen, 1976, p. 83).

from one set of molecules in the solid-state material to the next. The molecules, of course, are not free to change position in the rigid material.) The presence of a bubble represents a "1" and its absence represents a "0." Bubbles or 1's can be written into the platelet by passing a current pulse of sufficient magnitude through a hairpin-like device parallel to the surface of the platelet. The bubble is induced in the area of the platelet under the "eye" of the hairpin. Similarly, a pulse in the opposite direction can be used to "annihilate" an existing bubble in the area of the platelet under the eye of the hairpin. The trick in making use of these bubbles or "lack of bubbles" is to line them all up in "tracks" so that like a bucket brigade, they can all be marched in the correct sequence across a detector which can read the sequence of 1's and 0's. Figure VII-0(c) shows a track as resembling a bicycle chain where every so many links we will look for an attached bubble signifying a 1 or a lack of a bubble signifying a 0. There is one point along the track where the value is sensed and one point along the track where values can be set or reset.

So far we have discussed the "whys" and the "whats" of MBMs without delving too deeply into the "hows." Let us review this material and then examine how they work.

1. Magnetic bubble memories (MBMs) and charge-coupled devices (CCDs) have the potential to replace at least three traditional mass storage devices in several applications. The three are the _____ , _____ , and _____ . In addition to a reduction in size, MBMs and CCDs offer advantages in reliability and maintenance since unlike the three more traditional mass storage devices, MBMs and CCDs contain no _____ . MBMs have a further advantage over these three in that there is no need to inhibit information transfers while a moving medium (such as a tape or disk platter) is being _____ or _____ .

disk, drum, and magnetic tape units; moving parts; accelerated, decelerated

2. MBMs appear to have an advantage over CCDs in density and power requirements. Two certain advantages of MBMs over CCDs are:

_____

_____

MBM data are nonvolatile and constant recirculation is not required (this recirculation requirement of CCDs is often called the "refresh" requirement).

3. The principal disadvantage of MBMs and CCDs as compared to disks and magnetic tape units is that neither of the newer technologies currently offers a low-cost, _____ storage medium that can be retained in an _____ library for reloading on an "as needed" basis.

removable; off-line (i.e., removed from the computer system)

4. The randomly organized magnetic domains present in a garnet platelet can be aligned into _____ when an external magnetic field is applied perpendicular to the surface of the platelet. In any given "bit position" within the platelet, a 1 or a 0 is indicated by the _____.

bubbles; presence or absence of a bubble

5. Bubbles (i.e., 1's) can be written into the platelet by passing a _____ of sufficient magnitude through a hairpin-like device which is parallel to the surface of the platelet. The bubbles (or lack of bubbles) occupy bit positions which are lined up in tracks. As the bubbles are "marched" in sequence along the tracks by a rotating magnetic field (like the data in a ring counter or shift register), their presence (or absence) can be sensed by a _____ located over a track.

current pulse; detector

There are four basic functions required to operate a magnetic bubble memory (Juliussen, 1976, p. 81). These functions are generation, propagation, detection, and annihilation. In multitrack block organization (Texas Instruments refers to this organization as "major–minor"), two other functions are often required, called replication and transfer.

Generation with the use of the current-carrying hairpin has already been discussed. As shown in Figure VII-0(c), the idea is to rotate the bubble locations under the generation hairpin and to apply a current pulse whenever a 1 is to be inserted in the data stream. To overcome bubble-to-bubble interaction, at least four bubble diameters are allowed between bit locations (Hoffman et al., 1976, p. 77).

Propagation is the process that allows the data bits to be shifted around the track for reading and writing. One technique for accomplishing this is to construct bars shaped like I's and T's along the surface of the platelet where the track is to be located. Four different views of the polarization of this track are shown in Figure VII-0(e). Note that during the first view (which is shown during the first quarter-cycle of rotation), the bubble is located at the right side of the top of the T and is shown to be in motion toward the I. Note also that no field is shown for the "I" bars during this quarter-cycle. The second view shows the same T and I bars but with a 90° rotated field for the T and the bubble has moved to the "+" end of the I bar. The third view shows the same T and I bars of the track but observe that there is a 90° rotation of the T bar and no field shown for the I bar. Note that the bubble was attracted to the right again and is again under the "+" sign. The fourth quarter-cycle is the final view shown of the bubble and these particular bars. Note that the T-bar field has again rotated 90° and that the bubble is still following the "+" marks to the right. In other words, the rotating fields of the I and T bars are acting very much like the individual rollers on a conveyer belt in that the bubble is being "rolled" along the track.

Detection is required to read the data as they pass over the track. To do this, a Permalloy magnetic material is placed at one point under the track. When a bubble (which is usually "stretched" a little before being passed over the detector) goes over the detector, the magnetoresistance of the Permalloy material changes due to the bubble's differing polarity. This change in resistance (if there was a bubble present at this location) or the lack of a resistance change (if the location contained no bubble) is detectable as a millivolt signal.

The annihilator clears a bubble from a location on the track, as has been previously discussed.

Although the architecture of the early MBMs used the single-track approach shown in Figure VII-0(c), the multitrack organization shown in Figure VII-0(d) was not far behind. As shown, there is a major loop fed by a number of minor loops. Data from the minor tracks can be "replicated and transferred" to the major track, or vice versa. A bubble is replicated by stretching its domain and cutting it so that the original remains and the copy (or replica) can be used for scratch pad purposes or for modification. Note that there are implications for on-chip serial-to-parallel or parallel-to-serial conversion in this scheme.

The key to MBMs success in the future probably lies in the manufacturers' ability to increase the density of bits per chip while holding or dropping the price. The thought of 1M bits of storage in the same 14-pin socket a TTL-IC might occupy is a challenging and exciting one.

Before examining the circuitry of an MBM module, let us review some of the major terms and concepts involved.

6. For any MBM the four basic functions required for operation are _____, _____, _____, and _____. For an MBM

with a "major–minor" organization (also called a "multitrack block" organization), there are two additional functions required for operation called _____ and _____ .

generation, propagation, detection, annihilation; replication, transfer

7. Data are written into the MBM by rotating the track of bubble locations under the bubble _____ and applying a current pulse to this hairpin-like loop whenever a 1 is to be inserted into the data stream. The process of eliminating bubbles from the data stream is called _____ .

generator; annihilation

8. _____ is the process that allows the data bits to be shifted around the track for reading and writing. This is typically accomplished by using two mutually perpendicular coils to create a rotating electromagnetic field which causes the bubbles to move serially through the MBM in a manner similar to data in a shift register. As the bubble positions on the track are shifted past the _____ , a change in magnetoresistance indicates that a bubble was present in the bit position.

propagation; detector

9. In a multitrack organization a _____ operation is used to shunt bubbles from the major loop to the minor loops, or vice versa. A bubble can be _____ by stretching its domain and cutting it. Thus the original bubble is retained (i.e., nondestructive readout) and the copy can be directed to the detector.

transfer; replicated

The MBM chip shown in Figure VII-1 is a TIB0203-1 manufactured by Texas Instruments. This chip uses a major–minor loop architecture to provide 92,304 bits of nonvolatile memory. The major loop for data IO contains 640 bit positions. There are 157 minor loops used for data storage, each of which contains 641 bit positions. Because there is a certain risk of manufacturing a chip with one or more defective minor tracks, the user is intended to have access to only 144 of the 157 minor loops that reside on the chip. Each chip is carefully tested at the factory, and on the back of each individual chip the manufacturer lists the hexa-

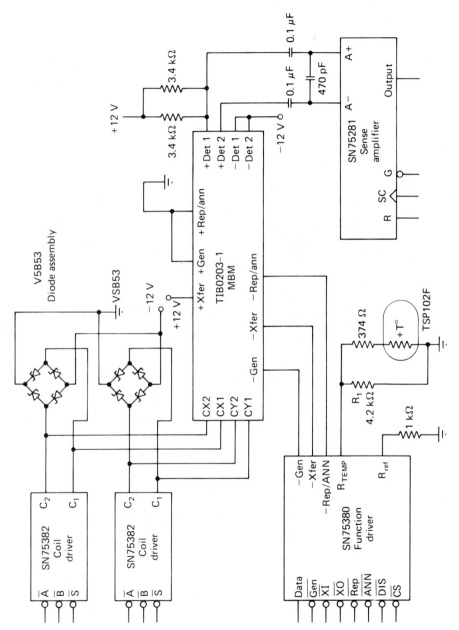

FIGURE VII-1 Schematic of Texas Instruments' MBM module.

decimal addresses of the defective minor loops (13 maximum). The user is then expected to store this information concerning the defective tracks in a read-only memory, which is used to ensure that no attempts are made to read or write data from/to the defective loops.

The data stored in the MBM are considered to be organized into pages. Specifically, there are 641 pages consisting of 144 bits (18 bytes) per page. Thus to read the third page of data stored in the MBM chip would require each of the 144 validated minor loops to be rotated simultaneously until their third bit position was adjacent to the major loop. A "transfer out" signal (XFER out) would then cause the data bit from each of the 144 minor loops to be transferred to the major loop. Now that the desired page of information has been transferred onto the major track, the rotation of the magnetic fields which is caused by the two coil drivers will cause the bit positions to shift serially along the major loop until the first bit of the page passes under the replicate/ annihilate gate. Since this operation is intended to be a nondestructive read operation, a "replicate" signal causes each bubble to be stretched and cut into two bubbles. One bubble is to remain in the original bit position on the major track and will continue to be shifted by the rotating magnetic field along with the other bit positions on the track. The "replica" of the original bubble is shunted onto the detector track and passed under the on-chip detectors, which provide an output pulse to the sense amplifier for each detected bubble. From there the replica bubble is propagated off the chip.

After all 144 bits of the page have been read in serial form, they must continue to be shifted around the major track until at last they are aligned with the 144 minor loops they were transferred from. Now a "transfer-in" signal (XFER in) causes each of the 144 bits to be shunted off the major track back into the third bit position of each of the 144 valid minor tracks. The read operation is now complete.

Note that if the power were removed at any time prior to transferring the 144 bits back from the major to the minor tracks, the circuitry could easily lose the synchronization count, which ensures that bit 0 of page 3 is returned to minor track 0, bit 1 of page 3 is returned to track 1, and so on. Similarly, even if the page 3 data were successfully restored to the minor tracks just before power was lost, the circuitry could easily lose count of which page of data was adjacent to the major loop at the time of power loss. Therefore, it is expected that the user will provide circuitry to sense when power is about to be lost. The power must be held stable until not only the page of data is restored to the correct bit position on the minor loops but until the minor loops are then rotated until the page 0 data is adjacent to the major loop. In this manner when power is restored, the circuitry always expects the stored data in the minor loops to be valid with page 0 in the position under the transfer gates. This data-positioning-upon-power-failure-detection requirement means that the system's power supplies must remain in regulation for at least 12.8 ms after an impending failure is detected. Otherwise, although the data are truly nonvolatile, they become garbled and of no value.

Because of the automatic data positioning requirement and because of the serial reading and writing of data, the TIB0203 operates with a 50 kilobits per second data IO transfer rate. Obviously, this is very slow compared to a static RAM module. However, this data rate is quite competitive with several of the more conventional mass storage devices, and considering that this chip provides 92,304 bits of non-volatile storage in a small 14-pin dual-in-line package, its price/performance ratio is quite impressive. (At the time this book was written, a memory module incorporating this chip could be constructed for a few hundred dollars.)

Suppose that we want to write all new data into page 5. Each of the minor loops would be rotated until their fifth bit position is under the transfer gates. The page is then transferred onto the major loop. As this information is shifted under the annihilate/replicate gate, the old information can be annihilated. At the same time new data are being loaded onto the major track by generating a current pulse to the bubble generator loop each time a 1 is encountered in the incoming serial data stream. When all 144 bits of the page have been written onto the major track, the data are ready to be shifted under the transfer gates. Upon command, the page 5 data are shunted onto the 144 valid minor loops.

The two SN75382s work in conjunction with the diode arrays to provide triangular waveforms that are 90° out of phase with one another to two orthogonal coils on the MBM chip. These signals produce a rotating magnetic field in the plane of the chip which causes the bubbles to move under the Permalloy patterns which define the tracks. Assuming that the gates of the 75382s are enabled by a low on the $\overline{S}$ inputs, the correct field can be generated by applying a sequence of pulses to the $\overline{A}$ and $\overline{B}$ inputs of the two driver chips such that a pulse is applied to the $\overline{A}$ input of the X coil driver. Next, a pulse is applied to the $\overline{A}$ input of the Y coil driver after a 90° interval. After the next 90° interval, a pulse is applied to the $\overline{B}$ input of the X coil driver. The 360° cycle is then completed after a pulse is applied to the $\overline{B}$ input of the Y coil driver during the final 90° of the cycle. The resulting outputs are two triangular ac waveforms which are applied to the X and Y coils of the MBM. (Texas Instruments, Inc., 1978)

The SN75380 function generator is responsible for providing generate, transfer in, transfer out, annihilate, and replicate signals to the MBM chip. The $\overline{CS}$ input selects the chip for memory operations. The $\overline{DIS}$ input can be used to disable the chip's current sink outputs. When an input data bit is high on the DATA input lead and a $\overline{GEN}$ signal permits, a GEN output signal causes a current pulse to generate a

bubble on the major track. Depending upon the timing within the 360°
cycle of the rotating magnetic field, the $\overline{XI}$ input can be used to cause a
transfer in command to be issued to the MBM chip or the $\overline{XO}$ input can
be used to cause a transfer-out command to be issued. Depending upon
timing and the operation, the $\overline{REP}$ input can cause a replicate command
to be issued to the MBM or the $\overline{ANN}$ input can cause the MBM to
annihilate a bubble on the major loop. The R_{ref} input is connected
to a reference resistor, which determines the –Xfer and the –REP/ANN
output currents. The R_{temp} input is connected to a resistor/thermistor
network which provides temperature compensation in setting the –GEN
output current.

The SN75281 sense amplifier senses a voltage change when bubbles pass beneath the magnetoresistive detector elements in the MBM.
The signal from the MBM is passed through an RC network, resulting in
a peak-to-peak signal of about 3 mV. This signal (which typically
contains a great deal of noise due to the in-plane rotating magnetic
field) is applied across the differential inputs A– and A+ of the sense
amplifier. The R input (Restore) is used to set the dc reference voltage
on the coupling capacitors inside the 75281 in preparation for taking a
new data sample. The SC input (Strobe Clock) is responsible for
strobing the sense amplifier output level into a type D flip-flop on the
chip shortly after the signal has reached its peak amplitude. The G
input controls the three-state output gate from the Q point of the type
D flip-flop.

Before turning to the sample exam for this unit, you may wish to
review the description of the MBM module depicted in Figure VII-1.

SAMPLE TEST FOR UNIT VII

*(Closed book. Closed notes. Use only writing materials and copies
of Figures VII-0 and VII-1.)*

1. Explain how the 92,304 bits of the TIB0203-1 chip are organized into 641 pages of 144 bits per page. Name and explain
   the function of all major parts of this chip.
2. Explain the MBM operations necessary to read or to write data
   from/to a MBM chip with a major–minor architecture.
3. Explain the reasons for sensing impending power failure and
   for holding the power supplies connected to the MBM chips
   within regulation until "automatic data positioning to page 0"
   has been completed.

VIII

Where Should We Go from Here?

microprocessors?
computer hardware?
computer software?
telecommunications?
control systems?

Before you began this book, hopefully you had mastered concepts and techniques in number systems, Boolean algebra, combinational circuitry, sequential circuitry, and applications of these. In this book we studied memory interfacing, memory control logic, fixed program memories, sequential access memories, random access read/write memories, stack operations, organization and construction of memory modules, multiported memory modules, device controllers for secondary storage peripherals, and basic software concepts used in programming memories. We examined stored programs in memories and studied the memory operations from the fetching and decoding of a software command through the hardware execution of the command. We studied the effects on both the program control and on the memory when subroutines were encountered, when interrupts occurred, and when files were copied to and from peripherals during direct memory access operations. However, the concepts and techniques that have been mastered thus far are not, as you well know by now, the end of the digital logic world. We have only just begun our study of this large, exciting, and rapidly growing field. Hence the title of this unit: Where should we go from here?

The author feels that the next step toward mastering digital logic is the study of microprocessor architecture. A microprocessor is a central processing unit fabricated on one to four chips. Like any central processing unit, it must contain at least the three functional blocks of circuitry, which together control the interpretation and execution of instructions. These three functional blocks are the arithmetic–logic unit, the control logic unit, and the input–output logic unit. The architecture of the microprocessor refers to the design and structural relationships of its functional circuit blocks. You should now be prepared to begin this study.

After microprocessors should come the study of computer hardware and computer software. There are microcomputers, minicomputers, midicomputers, large-scale computers, and multiprocessor computer systems containing several combinations of computers. Although they all may differ in some respects, they may all be considered to possess two totally interdependent subsystems: hardware and software. The hardware refers to the physical equipment, be it electronic, electrical, mechanical, optical, magnetic, or whatever. The software refers to the collection of programs, procedures, and documentation that work with the hardware to operate the computer system.

The input–output (IO) sections of computers are frequently connected to other computers, to processes being monitored and controlled, and to peripherals (auxiliary machines under the control of the computer, such as floppy disks, cassettes, and data terminals) which are located at some remote site. Such connections introduce the study of problems involved in transmitting digital information from one point to another this interesting field of study is referred to as telecommunications.

Digital logic circuitry plays a unique role in the study of control systems. Various types of control systems include data acquisition systems, supervisory control systems, direct digital control systems, hierarchical computer control systems, and distributed computer control systems. Although they each differ in some respects, they all facilitate operating on inputs until outputs fall within an acceptable range of values. Sophisticated control systems are extremely challenging in that they require an understanding of number systems, digital logic, microprocessors, networks of computers and peripherals, telecommunications, real-time operating systems, applications programming, and control theory. Good luck in your continued studies!

Core Memories

In the late 1960s and early 1970s, memory specialists sometimes referred to core memories as "King Core," because it dominated the primary memory field. When semiconductors moved into MSI and LSI it was largely because of the belief of a few dedicated practitioners that King Core could and should be dethroned. For all practical purposes, this has happened. There are still applications for which core can be as good or better a choice for primary memory as static RAMs, but there is not the undisputed dominance of a decade ago. There now appears to be a concerted effort to revive core as a possible replacement for secondary storage peripherals. After all, if the moving, electromechanical parts of our disks and tape units could be replaced by the more reliable cores on a cost-effective basis, a great service will have been done for the user community.

A magnet core is toroidal in shape, thereby resembling a doughnut. The ferrite cores typically have an outside diameter of about 18 mils and an inside diameter of about 10 mils. This inside diameter is just big enough to allow three wires to be threaded through each core to provide a density of approximately 6K cores per square inch. The industry's "standard" organization is typically a three-wire (two address lines and one line shared between the "sense" and the "inhibit" functions), three-dimensional (all core "planes" have common X and Y address lines and the planes are "stacked" to provide the third dimension), coincident current selection core matrix. (All cores at the intersection or "coincidence" of the selected X address line and the selected Y address line constitute the location of the selected word.) There used to be a linear selection technique, but this has not been popular for some time now.

Let us look at Figure A-0(a) to see how cores work. If a wire is carrying a flow of electrons in the directions indicated, then by pointing the thumb of the left hand in the direction of the electron flow, the curled fingers represent the circular direction of the flux lines of the induced magnetic field. If the wire is threaded through a core and if the wire carries a short pulse of current of magnitude I, where I is just sufficient to induce a magnetic field in the toroidal core, this magnetic field will remain even though the current I has gone. If we look at a clockwise induced field as a stored 0 and a counterclockwise induced field as a stored 1, we see that this core is indeed a memory cell and its contents depend upon the direction of I when it last flowed through the wire threaded through the center of the core. We can also see one of the biggest advantages the core had over the static RAM. The core was theoretically "nonvolatile." (In actual practice the author recalls many frustrating occasions when a power failure would reflect transients into the memory of sufficient amplitude to falsely store bad information in certain locations. Better voltage regulators and transient suppressors were doing a much better job of reducing this problem when the MSI/LSI breakthroughs suddenly changed our memory technology.)

Look at Figure A-0(b) to see graphically how the core is magnetized. Note that if a current of $+I$ is applied to the wires strung through the core, our lines of magnetic flux reach a maximum level above the axis as indicated by point d on the hysteresis curve. This can represent a counterclockwise magnetic field or a 1 stored in the core. If the current is dropped back to 0, the strength of the flux field decreases slightly back to point b on the hysteresis curve. In spite of the slight decrease, the core is still clearly magnetized as a 1 (counterclockwise direction). Note that if we apply a current of $+I/2$, the field increases slightly to point c. If we apply a reverse direction current of $-I/2$, the flux field in the core decreases slightly to point a on the hysteresis curve. However, in the case of both $+I/2$ and $-I/2$, the resulting flux changes were small and the core had no difficulty retaining the direction of its induced field (i.e., a 1). To reset the core back to a 0 (in core

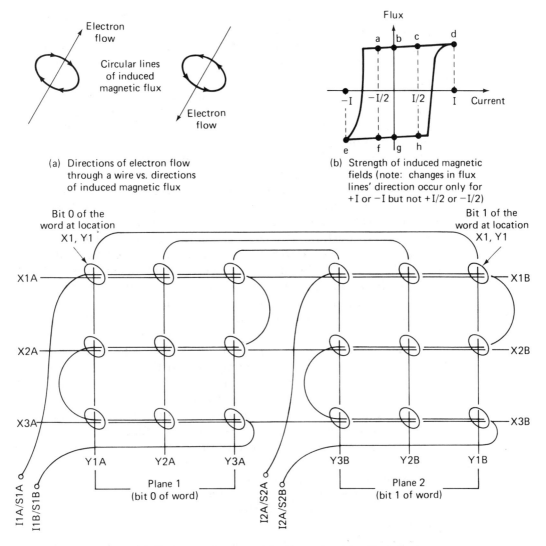

(a) Directions of electron flow
     through a wire vs. directions
     of induced magnetic flux

(b) Strength of induced magnetic
     fields (note: changes in flux
     lines' direction occur only for
     +I or −I but not +I/2 or −I/2)

(c) Core memory arrangement: three-wire, three-dimensional,
     9 words, 2 bits per word

FIGURE A-0 Core memories.

terminology, we "read" it back to 0), we will have to apply a reverse
current of at least *-I*. This puts the core at point *e* on the curve and
indicates that the old flux field has totally collapsed and that a new
clockwise field has now been stored in the core. When the current is
decreased to 0, the induced flux field decreases slightly back to point *g*,
but it is still clearly a clockwise induced field. Applying the "half-

current" signals of $+I/2$ or $-I/2$ can slightly change the strength of the stored flux field but not enough to change the 0 stored there. In short, to write a 1 requires a $+I$. To read to a 0 requires a $-I$. A half-current of $+I/2$ or $-I/2$ will not change the direction of the stored magnetic flux field.

Let us see how a three-dimensional three-wire memory works. Examine Figure A-0(c). Suppose that we have a (1 0) stored in location X 1, Y 1 and we wish to read this value (i.e., bit 1 = 1 and bit 0 = 0). Since the number of planes equals the number of bits in a word, we see that this is a 2-bit word length. Since the number of cores per plane equals the number of words, we see that there are nine words. Notice the 2 bits (cores) at the coincidence of the X 1 and Y 1 address lines. To read the contents of this location, send a $-I/2$ from X 1 A to X 1 B and send a $-I/2$ from Y 1 A to Y 1 B. This means that a total current of $-I$ is flowing through the two cores at the X 1, Y 1 coincidence and that we are destroying whatever contents are stored there with our read operation. Now, if sense bit 0 already contains a 0 (a clockwise induced field), we have moved from point g to point e on the hysteresis curve and there has been no significant change in the flux field. However, at bit 1 we had a 1 stored. Therefore, we moved on our hysteresis curve from point b (before the $-I$) to a to e. In other words, the counter-clockwise field had to be collapsed and a clockwise field had to be formed. If S2A and S2B were connected to the input of a sensitive op amp called a "sense amp," the dramatic change in flux field directions would cause a small current to be induced in this sense amp circuit. This means that even though we did a destructive read operation that read a 0 into both cores, we can catch the fact that bit 1 was a 1 by connecting a bistable to the output of the sense amplifier for the second plane. Similarly, we will connect a bistable to the output of a sense amplifier on the first plane. However, this bistable will contain a 0, since the sense winding for the first plane had no change in the flux field direction of the X 1, Y 1 core to induce a current for the sense amplifier to detect it.

Well, we have done all right so far. At least we have found a way to convert the magnetically stored data to electronically stored data. Now let us see how to write the 1 0 back in to X 1, Y 1. (We always do a write-after-read to restore the contents of a location we only wanted to retrieve data from.) Since we do not have to sense flux changes this time, let us use the same windings in each plane for another function (called the "inhibit" function) during the write cycle. Instead of the windings being used as inputs to a sense amplifier, this time we shall use them to carry a $-I/2$ through each plane where we wish to retain a 0 in the selected core. Since the bistable for plane 1 contains a 0, we will drive $-I/2$ from I 1 A to I 1 B. Since the bistable for plane 2 contains a

1, we will not turn on its inhibit drivers. After our X 1, Y 1 core in plane 1 has a $-I/2$ flowing through its inhibit line, we will drive a $+I/2$ from X 1 B to X 1 A and a $+I/2$ from Y 1 B to Y 1 A. Therefore, the total current through the bit 1 core of X 1, Y 1 is $+I$ and we move on the hysteresis curve from point g to h to d. This creates a counterclockwise field in the core which restores the 1 it contained before we began the read operation.

Look at the total current flowing through the bit 0 core. We have $+I/2$, $+I/2$, and $-I/2$, for a total of $-I/2$, which causes no change in the present clockwise field (a stored 0). We have inhibited the address lines from writing a 1 into the core.

appendix

B

Cache Memories

There are certain applications (such as a multiuser computer system which performs a lot of scientific "number crunching") which are best served by:

1. A central processing unit which is almost continuously busy processing data at the fastest rate possible.
2. A very large main memory capable of storing large programs to be executed by the central processing unit (CPU) and large blocks of data to be "massaged" by those programs.
3. Lengthy "bursts" of time in which new blocks of data can be transferred from the disk directly into main memory without stalling the central processing unit.

One problem frequently encountered in such installations is that the CPU is often capable of operating at much greater speeds than the more reasonably priced memory modules can support. Since the size of the main memory can be quite large in such applications, the cost of building the entire memory to operate with access and transfer rates which match the CPU's capabilities could easily increase the cost of the computer system by 50% or more.

One solution to this problem is to place a small block of very high speed memory (called a "cache buffer" or simply "cache") between main memory and the CPU as shown in Figure B-0. The cache memory operates at speeds comparable to the needs of the central processing unit. By copying into the cache segments of the program currently being executed by the CPU as well as portions of the data currently being massaged by the program, the CPU does not now have to wait on the slower information transfers to and from main memory. Of course, sooner or later the CPU will need a segment of the program and/or data which are not in the cache but still residing in main memory. This implies a need to copy new segments of the program and/or data into

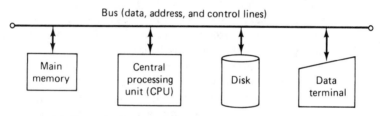

(a) Example of a single-bus computer system without cache

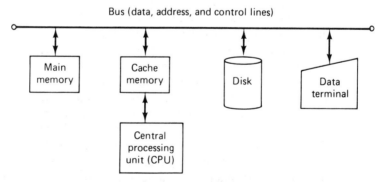

(b) Example of a single-bus computer system that uses a cache
      memory buffer to (1) minimize the mismatch between the
      speeds of the faster CPU and the slower main memory;
      (2) allow more frequent and longer data transfers between
      main memory and disk while the CPU is processing cache
      data

FIGURE B-0 Cache memories.

the cache. If strategies can be implemented which effectively "look ahead" and initiate these transfers so that the vast majority of the time the CPU's needs for instructions and data are met by the cache rather than the slower main memory, then the amount of information processing performed by the CPU can be enhanced by as much as 10 to 50%, depending upon the programs and the hardware (Korn, 1977, p. 43). Another benefit that can result from using a cache is an increase in the number and amount of "burst" times when a disk can copy blocks of new information into the main memory while the processor is busily working with information stored in the cache.

A cache system can enhance the processing throughput of a computer system because the cache takes advantage of the statistics of program behavior (Digital Equipment Corporation, 1977, p. 6-1). Typically the instructions of a program are executed sequentially one after the other or they are being repeatedly executed in small loops. Therefore, if a few hundred instructions are currently stored in the cache and the CPU is currently executing an instruction in the middle of this program segment, the odds are quite good that the next instruction to be executed will also be found in the cache. If the program suddenly causes the CPU to branch past the instructions in the current program segment to a segment of the program still in main memory, the odds are very good that by copying the new segment of the program into the cache, the CPU will be occupied for some time with this new block of instructions in the cache. Similarly, the data to be manipulated by a program also exhibit a high degree of "locality." For example, the variables of a program typically have sequential storage assigned to them by the compiler. A user's programs are often written in a high-level language such as FORTRAN. A FORTRAN compiler will then examine the user's programs and allocate contiguous storage locations to all variables of the same type that occur in these programs. Thus if a user has inserted the instruction "X=Y+Z" in the first few instructions of the program, where X, Y, and Z all contain floating-point numbers, the compiler will probably allocate storage for the variable X next to the storage for the variables Y and Z. Furthermore, if the program calls for the use of a stack or a table of indexed data values, there is a high degree of locality exhibited. (For example, data are pushed or popped from the top of the stack. Therefore, it may be possible to keep the portion of the stack or of a data table that is being frequently accessed in the cache, where the processor can have faster access to the needed data.)

When the instruction or data needed by the CPU are found in the cache, a "hit" is said to occur and there is no necessity to copy new data from main memory into the cache. When the instruction or data needed by the CPU are not in the cache, a "miss" is said to occur and once the needed information is transferred into the CPU for processing, the cache will begin to receive a copy of a new segment of the program or the program's data. The secret of a good cache is to use an allocation mechanism which maximizes the ratio of hits per CPU requests without imposing any changes in the way the user writes his or her programs. This can be implemented by taking advantage of the principle of locality for the instructions and data of a typical program. As an example of how effectively this can be accomplished, Digital Equipment Corporation uses a 2048-byte cache within its PDP11/60 processor. Their statistics (Digital Equipment Corporation, 1977, p. 6-4) indicate that 90% of the memory references that occur in a typical program are for "read operations" and only 10% of the memory references are for "write operations." For these read operations, hits wlll average from 77 to 92%.

appendix

C

Dynamic Rams

The goals of the dynamic RAM designer have some admirable features. For example, we know that all bistables begin as an SR flip-flop. To make this asynchronous bistable into a synchronous bistable, we add extra gates and components. By the time we have a flip-flop suitable for use as a static memory cell, we have a need for a minimum of four to six transistors and we would often prefer to be able to use more. Therefore, when a dynamic RAM designer says he believes that, for a few "small" sacrifices in complexity of use and the addition of "refresh timing," a memory cell can be made using from one to three transistors, our first impression is one of being able to double our density, that is, getting twice as much memory into the same amount of silicon real estate. It is only in the transition from the "theoretical" to the "practical" that these "small" sacrifices begin to concern us.

The principle is very simple and very old. Place a charge on a perfect capacitor and it will be retained indefinitely (or as long as needed), representing a stored value of 1. Discharge the capacitor and we have a stored value of 0. Now add to this our knowledge that the input to the gate of an MOS transistor has a great deal of capacitance and the temptation to try dynamic memories becomes stronger. The problem is that the MOS gate input "leaks" its charge away. Therefore, before it has deteriorated to an unrecognizable level we need to shift it through circuit elements that sense what the charge is intended to be and then amplifies and recirculates a full charge back to the capacitor. By recycling through this refresh operation about 500 to 1000 times per second, we have a good chance of retaining whatever information the cell is supposed to contain. This refresh cycling can usually be done under the control of a four-phase clock, as we shall see in a minute. But for now consider the plight of the microprocessor, large-scale computer, device controller, or whatever, that wants to read these stored data when they are in the process of being refreshed. Similarly, consider the problem of wanting to enter new data when the old data are currently being recirculated about the closed loop. To be certain of the results, the read or write operation will have to wait until refreshing is done. Therefore, to make a long story short, although the dynamic RAMs have a better density than the static RAMs, the need for external refresh circuitry plus designing interfaces to make allowances for waiting until the appropriate instant in a refresh cycle to read or write data plus the frequent requirement for three power supply values rather than the 1 needed by a static RAM does much to offset the density advantage of the dynamic RAM.

Examine Figure C-0 and note the parasitic capacitances, which are dotted in since these are not physically distinguishable as "real" capacitors. This figure shows only one cell in a dynamic memory. However, the inverting refresh amplifier is typically time-shared among 16 to 32 cells (Korn, 1977, p. 47). Assume that a value is stored in the cell and we want to examine the refresh operation. First the Read Bus is used to charge C2. Then Read Select is enabled. Now if C1 had no charge, then Q2 does not conduct from the source to the drain leads, which means that C2 could not discharge to ground. Therefore, a 1 is fed into the inverting refresh amplifier, and when enabled by a control pulse, this amplifier has a 0 output. When a Write Select pulse turns on Q1, the 0 from the inverting amplifier's output further ensures that there will be no charge on C1. (In other words, both sides of the capacitor are at ground potential.) Well, this shows you how a 0 is recirculated; now let us see how a 1 is recirculated (refreshed).

Again we begin our four-phase refresh cycle by pulsing the Precharge line to charge the parasitic capacitance C2. Now, since a 1 is stored in the cell, this means that C1 is charged. If enough of the charge still remains after leakage (and it is theoretically supposed to), Q2 is turned on and C2 will have a discharge path to ground as soon as the

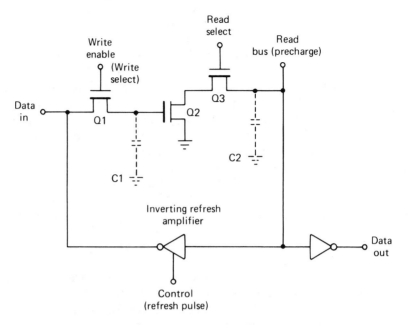

FIGURE C-0   Dynamic RAM cell.

Read Select pulse turns Q3 on. This means a 0 (from the discharged C2) will be presented to the input of the inverting refresh amplifier when the refresh pulse to its control line enables it. Therefore, the output of the inverting amplifier will be a 1 when it is enabled. (But not a "lower" level that is still acceptable as a 1. This is a higher level than is typically encountered for a 1, much the same as we expect from a level amplifier output to a DAC ladder.) This means that when a Write Select pulse turns on Q1, the 1 output from the amplifier recharges C1 back to the 1 level it was losing due to leakage. (Remember that this operation is going on 500 to 1000 times per second while a flip-flop in a static RAM would just sit there and retain the value at the Q output until we asked for it.) So much for the refresh operation; let us examine a read operation.

Assume that a refresh operation has just been completed and that a microprocessor wants to read the contents of the cell. As usual, the Precharge pulse is used to charge C2. When the Read Select pulse comes along if a 1 is stored in C1, then Q2 and Q3 provide a discharge path to ground for C2 and a 0 is presented to both the input of the inverting refresh amplifier and to the input of the inverter, whose output drives the data output line. Since the processor wanted to read the cell contents, this is its chance. Similarly, if a 1 had not been stored at C1 prior to the occurrence of the Read Select pulse, then C2 could not have discharged and a 1 would have been fed into both inverters. So much for the read operation; now let us examine a write operation.

Assume that a processor wants to write either a 1 or a 0 into the cell. During the refresh operation, C2 is charged as usual. Then a Read Select pulse gives C2 a chance to discharge or stay charged, dependent upon the status of C1. The result of this is passed along to the input of the inverting refresh amplifier as always. However, since the processor is waiting to write new information into the cell, the refresh pulse is inhibited from enabling the amplifier. Instead, the data input (which had to be gated out or "disabled" prior to this operation) is now enabled to charge C1 (or to allow it to discharge if a 0 is to be inserted) when a pulse on Write Enable turns Q1 on. When the Write Enable and the Data Input signals are gone, we now have a newly inserted 1 (charged C1) or 0 (discharged C1), which will go through the refresh operation until it is time to insert new data into the cell.

In closing, it is only fair to point out that the cell we have just discussed is essentially the same architecture as the 1103. This was the dynamic RAM organized as a 1024×1 memory matrix that, perhaps more than any other influence, convinced a very large segment of the memory manufacturers that a cost-effective replacement for King Core had at last been found. By the end of the first year of producing the 1103s, the undisputed dominance of magnetic-core technology for memory systems was over. Since this "emotional shock" required the more conservative members of our digital specialists to make an "attitudinal adjustment" of sorts, the way was paved for a comparatively smooth and rapid acceptance of the LSI static RAMs a year later. For that we can be grateful to the dynamic RAM. Also, you will find in Appendix D that it led directly to the much more important CCD.

appendix

D

Charge-Coupled Devices

The material in this appendix assumes that the reader has completed the preceding materials on bubble memories and dynamic RAMs.

Charge-coupled devices (CCDs) were announced in 1970 by Bell Telephone Laboratories (Crouch et al., 1976, p. 76). Since that time, companies such as Intel and Fairchild have begun manufacturing and marketing these DIP chips. The chips can be used to form solid-state memory modules that are intended to replace magnetic drums and fixed-head disks.

The principles of CCDs are extensions of those encountered in our study of dynamic RAMs. In a dynamic RAM each cell uses a capacitively stored charge to represent a content of 1. Since the quality of the capacitance of MOS devices is poor, the charge leakage makes it necessary to "recirculate" or "refresh" each cell's contents every few milliseconds. In CCDs the idea is to organize these cells into ring counters (i.e., shift registers with the data from the last cell fed back into the first cell). Thus in a 256-bit ring counter arrangement, instead of the

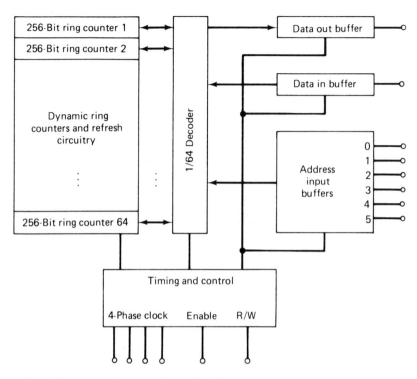

FIGURE D-0 Block diagram for a 16K CCD organized as 64 registers of 256 bits each.

refresh cycle being used to recirculate each cell's contents as it would in a 256-bit dynamic RAM, the contents of each cell are sensed, amplified, and shifted into the next adjacent cell. As you would expect, more than one ring counter can be kept recirculating simultaneously in a CCD chip. Figure D-0 shows a block diagram of a 16K-CCD chip similar to those manufactured by Intel in their 2416 series. The chip is organized into 64 ring counters of 256 bits each. A four-phase clock is used (as it was in our study of dynamic RAMs) and data may be read from the last cell of any of the ring counters at the end of a shift-and-refresh cycle. The particular ring counter that is to be read or written is selected via six address lines. Since the data transfer rate can be considerably faster than the refresh rate, it is not uncommon to read or write 8 or 16 ring counters in rapid succession at the end of a shift-and-refresh cycle. Note that the six address lines can only select, via the 1-of-64 decoder, which one of the ring counters is to be involved in a transfer at a given instant. These address lines cannot keep track of which one of the 256 bits in that ring counter is being read, for example. This must be done by external circuitry such as we studied in the sections on device controllers in Units V and VI.

A final reminder may be in order as to where in the memory hierarchy CCDs fit as opposed to where dynamic RAMs fit. Dynamic RAMs are intended for use as primary memory devices. The author feels they are inferior to static RAMs in this application, for reasons that have already been stated. CCDs, on the other hand, are intended for use as mass memory devices. The recirculating memory contents of the ring counters behave in a very similar manner to the rotating disk or drum devices that have traditionally been used for these mass memory devices. The lack of moving parts and the continuing trends toward lower costs for semiconductor devices make the CCDs, in the author's opinion, superior to the more traditional electromechanical devices if (1) volatility is not a major concern (see Unit VII on bubble memories), and (2) a removable medium for off-line storage is not needed for the application being considered. The comparison to an organization of ring counters composed of static cells is not a viable one at this time because of the density requirements, and hence the price per bit of CCDs is considerably lower.

appendix

E

Content Addressable (or Associative) Memories

For at least the last 20 years various members of the computing profession have written descriptions of a type of memory that would be much better suited than conventional RAM for the processing of information which can be logically grouped into rows and columns of a collection of tables. Unfortunately, such a memory (called "associative" or "content addressable") has been prohibitively expensive to produce for the vast majority of the desired applications and only since the advent of large-scale integrated circuits (such as the Signetics 8220) has the price of production of such memories shown any potential to drop to a feasible level for inclusion in a general-purpose computer system. As a result, volumes have been written describing different software techniques which enable the programmer to use RAM to "simulate" an associative memory. Almost all commercially available software packages that allow the user to search tables of values, sort values, insert/delete values, and so on, rely heavily on one or more versions of these rather cumbersome and relatively slow "simulation" processes.

249

To better understand the organization of a content addressable memory (CAM) module, let us examine an application. Suppose that a company maintains a data base (a collection of interrelated data with defined and controlled accesses) for a few thousand employees. For each employee there exists information in the computer data base which includes (in the order given) the employee's name, social security number, address, job classification, department, years with the company, and salary. These seven "attributes" correspond to column headings for a personnel table. Data on each employee will occupy one row of the table (in data-base terminology, each row is often referred to as a tuple). If the company needed a list of all engineers in the organization, the attribute "job classification" is used as the "key" to search the data base and print out the tuple (row of information) for each employee classified as "engineer." If the company needed a list of all engineers in the marketing department, there would be two keys used to select the tuples to be printed. That is, the attribute "job classification" must equal "engineer" and the "department" must also equal "marketing" within the same tuple before the tuple is to be selected for printing. Consider how this search process would have to be conducted if the data are stored in RAM. First, the data for each attribute for each employee must be assigned to an address in the RAM. To retrieve the data stored as the attribute "job classification" for each employee requires supplying the unique address for this attribute for each employee. Then the data at this address will be compared to the key "engineer." If a match is found, the program must then supply the unique address for the attribute "department" for that same employee. These retrieved data must be compared to the key "marketing." If a match is found, the program must supply all addresses in the tuple so that the information for this employee can be printed out. Obviously, this sequential process of determining and supplying one address at a time, then retrieving the contents and comparing the contents to the search key, and so on, is a somewhat lengthy and involved process.

By using a CAM the processor has no need to determine and supply addresses for sequential, one-mailbox-at-a-time access. Instead, the processor writes the keys "engineer" and "marketing" into the positions of an Argument Register which correspond to the positions within a tuple for the attributes "job classification" and "department." Next, the processor writes information into a Key Register which masks out consideration of any other attributes for the forthcoming search. (For example, all bits in the Key Register associated with the employee's name attribute are reset to 0's, whereas all bits in the Key Register associated with the job classification attribute will be set to 1's.) Then the processor will issue a command on a control line to the CAM called "Associate." At that time every tuple in the CAM has its job classification and department attributes examined and compared to the keys "engineer" and "marketing." This operation of search and compare is done completely in parallel at the moment the "associate" command is given. Furthermore, each tuple in the CAM has an associated bit in the CAM's Match Register that will be set if a perfect match to both keys is found. Thus if the company has 30 engineers employed in their marketing department, the associate command will cause the two attributes of every one of their few thousand employees to be searched and compared simultaneously. There will be only 30 bits set in the CAM's Match Register at the end of this operation. Each of the 30 tuples will then be copied out to the processor in sequence as the next operation.

Note that the tuples of data selected to be copied out to the processor were selected based upon their content rather than their address. (Hence the term "Content Addressable Memory." The term "associative" comes from the fact that data entry, query, updating, and so on, are operations associated solely with data content of the tuples.) The processor does not know or care where (i.e., an address) the selected tuples are stored in the CAM. The processor only knows that it can now request the CAM to send it each tuple which matched the keys. Obviously, CAMs are much more expensive than RAMs since the controller is more complex and since each bit cell of each tuple must not only read/write control and storage but must also contain the logic circuitry to compare its value with that of a stored argument. Therefore, CAMs can only be cost-justified in those applications in which search time is very critical and must be short.

Figure E-0 shows a block diagram of a CAM module with M tuples of N bits each. If the "name" attribute is intended to store names up to 20 letters long using ASCII code of 8 bits per letter, bits A1 through A160 could be set with the ASCII code for "SMITH, JAMES W." (unused bits would be reset) if we wanted to enter this name as a key into the Argument Register. If this is the only key value to be searched for, the K1 through K160 bits of the Key Register will be set to 1's and all other bits of the Key Register will be reset to 0's (thus masking out any consideration of the other attributes for this particular search). Suppose that there is only one James W. Smith in this company and the tuple containing his data is stored in tuple 2 of the CAM. When the processor sends an "associate command" to the CAM, the first 160 cells of every tuple will be simultaneously compared to the first 160 bits of the Argument Register. Since there is perfect agreement for all 160 bits only for tuple 2 (i.e., $A_1 = C_{21}$, $A_2 = C_{22}$, ..., $A_{160} = C_{2\text{-}160}$) M2 will be the only bit set in the match register by this associate operation. When the processor then asks for any tuples with a match for this key (a "read" request to the CAM), the CAM memory controller will then copy all N bits of this tuple to the processor.

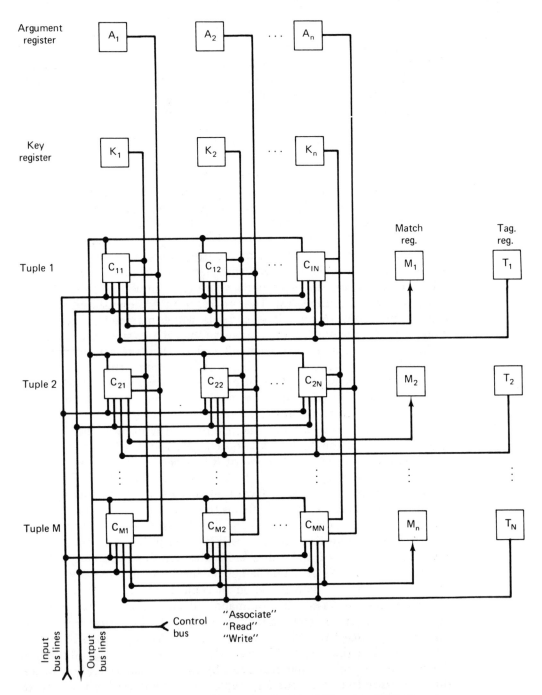

FIGURE E-0 Associative memory module: "*M*" tuples of "*N*" bits each.

Suppose that James W. Smith resigns from this company. The personnel who maintain the data base would use the processor to search the CAM for this name. Again, the M2 bit will be set to signify that a match was found. However, instead of issuing a read request, the processor would send a signal to reset T_2. This is a bit in the Tag Register which indicates whether tuple 2 contains active information. As long as Smith was working for the company, his Tag bit contained a 1 and his tuple of data was examined in every search operation that took place. Now that he is no longer employed by the company, his Tag bit contains a 0, which disables his entire tuple from being examined in subsequent searches (which means M2 will be reset to 0 and remain at this level while T_2 contains a 0).

Suppose that Mary S. Jones is a new employee to be added to the data base. The CAM memory controller can determine whether or not the CAM has any available space by examining the Tag Register. (If the register contains all 1's, then all tuples are active and there is no memory space available in the CAM.) When the processor requests to write the tuple for Jones into the CAM, the CAM controller scans the Tag bits until the first 0 is encountered. The tuple information is then written from the data bus into the selected tuple. Assuming that tuple 1 contains data on an employee that is still active with the company, the tuple for Mary S. Jones would be written into tuple 2 and T_2 would be set to a 1. All subsequent searches would then examine the appropriate attributes of this tuple.

appendix

F

Glossary

analysis of digital systems: The process of determining input–output characteristics by separating the whole system into its component parts or elements.

automata theory: The study of the processing of information between the input and the output terminals of systems (Givone, 1970, p. 1).

bus: A group of connections that carry information between various portions of a digital system. The address bus is used to establish a communications link between the portions of the system that are to be involved in the information transaction. The data bus is used to convey the information. The control bus is used to synchronize the operations on the other buses.

bytes: A defined number of bits. Typically 8 bits.

character: A single-digit symbol that appears in numbers of a number system.

checksum: Summation of digits or bits according to some predetermined rules. Primarily used for error detection.

combinational logic: Those digital circuits whose outputs at any time t are dependent only on the inputs present at time t.

control systems: Control systems operate on the inputs of a system until the outputs of the system fall within an accepted range of values.

cycle time: A read cycle time is the interval of time between the start and end of the cycle which accesses the intended memory cell or cells and retrieves the information stored there. Similarly, a write cycle time is the time interval between the start and end of the cycle which accesses the intended cell or cells and stores new information there.

digital computers: Systems containing at least the following: memory, arithmetic-logic unit, controls, and sections for input and output.

dynamic RAMs: Form of random access read/write memory that uses capacitive changes which require periodic refreshing because of leakage.

EROM: Erasable read-only memory. A form of fixed program memory that can be reprogrammed by the user. When desired, the EROM can be removed from the original application, bulk erased, and reprogrammed.

firmware: Software instructions and/or data that have been stored in ROM.

fixed program memory: Memory contents are not intended to be altered during normal operation. Includes ROMs, PROMs, and EROMs.

hard errors: Not recoverable by retrying the operation.

hardware, computer: The physical equipment of a computer system, be it electronic, electrical, mechanical, optical, magnetic, or whatever.

intermediate storage (scratch pad) in a computer system: Refers to temporary storage used by the computer for intermediate values that occur during a calculation routine or other operation.

interrupt: Any signal that causes the suspension of a running program so that another program segment will be executed.

location: Refers to a position or address in memory.

loops: In programming or other methods of problem solving, a sequence of instructions to be repeatedly executed until a predefined exit condition is satisfied.

LSI: Large-scale integrated circuitry. Each chip contains 100 or more gates or circuitry of similar complexity.

main memory: (See primary storage)

mass storage (secondary memory or secondary storage) in a computer system: Stores data in a form that is not directly readable by the electronic gates and registers of the computer. Instead, the devices, such as disks and drums, must be interfaced to the gates and registers of the computer with circuitry that is responsible for making the data readable by the gates and registers of the computer.

memory (storage) in a digital system: Refers to any device into which information (data) can be entered, retained, and accessed and retrieved for future use.

module: A circuit module is a packaged functional hardware unit designed for use with other components. (ANSI definition)

MSI: Medium-scale integrated circuitry. Each chip contains more than 10 to 12 but less than 100 gates or circuitry of similar complexity.

nibble: A defined collection of 4 bits.

N-tuple: A combination of binary inputs.

peripherals: Auxiliary machines under the control of the computer such as disks, floppies, cassettes, and data terminals.

primary storage (main memory) in a computer system: Stores data in a form that is directly readable by the electronic gates and registers of the computer.

process: A system in which deliberate guidance or manipulation of inputs is used to achieve the desired outputs.

process variable: A condition, such as pressure, light, voltage, or temperature, that exists in a process and that has a value which is subject to change.

programming: The arranging of both the data and the sequence of steps which will operate upon the data to solve a given problem.

PROM: Programmable read-only memory. A form of fixed program memory that can be programmed for the first and only time by the user.

random access read/write memory: Contents can be accessed in any order for either retrieval or storage with similar access time for each location. Includes static and dynamic RAMs.

ROM: Read-only memory. A form of fixed program memory that is programmed by the manufacturer at manufacturing time.

scratch pad memory: (See intermediate storage)

secondary memory or secondary storage: (See mass storage)

sequential access memory: Access to memory contents is limited to passing through a fixed sequence of locations. Includes shift registers and CCDs.

sequential circuits: Circuits with outputs that depend not only on present inputs but also on some memory of past inputs.

shutdown circuits: Circuits that "shut down" operations in an orderly fashion whenever a predetermined set of conditions are met.

soft errors: Recoverable by retrying the operation.

software, computer: The collection of programs, procedures, and documentation that work with the hardware to operate the computer system.

SSI: Small-scale integrated circuitry. Each chip contains a maximum of 10 (some sources prefer 12) gates or circuitry of similar complexity.

static RAMs: Form of random access read/write memory that uses bistables for memory cells.

storage: (See Memory)

strobe: Data are strobed to the circuitry if a clock pulse or sequencing pulse is required either to store data in or to present data to a portion of circuitry.

synchronous circuits: Have outputs that can change only with the introduction of appropriate inputs and a clock pulse or a sequencing pulse.

synthesis of digital systems: The process of combining component parts or elements to form a whole system, with predetermined input–output characteristics.

system: A group of interdependent elements acting together to accomplish a predetermined purpose.

system's crash: The shutdown of operations in a disorderly fashion.

VLSI: Very-large-scale integrated circuitry. Each chip contains 1000 or more gates or circuitry of similar complexity.

volatile memory: Refers to memory that loses its contents if power is removed.

word: A group of characters to be accessed as a unit and retrieved (or stored if the memory is RAM) as a unit.

G

Equipment and Components Recommended for the Majority of the Experiments in This Book

Equipment:

> Oscilloscope: dc-coupled, 10 MHz BW
> Power supply: 5 V dc at 1 A

Commonly used logic circuits: The schematics for these circuits are given later in this appendix. The components are included in the list of components that follows. The author suggests that these circuits be constructed and left intact for use throughout the course.

> 4   bounceless input switches
> 12   LED indicators
> 6   SPDT input switches
> 8   mini-DIP SPST switches
> 2   seven-segment hex displays

Components:

Quantity	Type	Description
8	7400	Quad 2-input NAND
1	7402	Quad 2-input NOR
6	7404	Hex NOT
1	7408	Quad 2-input AND
1	7410	Triple 3-input NAND
1	7411	Triple 3-input AND
1	7420	Dual 4-input NAND
1	7421	Dual 4-input AND
3	7427	Triple 3-input NOR
2	7432	Quad 2-input OR
2	7473	Dual JK flip-flops
1	7475	Quad D flip-flops
1	7480	Full adder
1	7486	Quad XOR
2	7496	5-bit shift register
1	74121	One-shot
3	74125	Quad three-state drivers
2	74154	4-to-16 line decoder/demultiplexer
2	74193	4-bit up/down counter
2	8T97	Hex three-state drivers
2	9368	Hex display decoder/driver
2	F9368-97	Seven-segment common-cathode display
12	MV5020	LED
1	6810	1024-bit RAM
12		1-kΩ resistors ($\geqslant \frac{1}{8}$ W)
22		2.2-kΩ resistors ($\geqslant \frac{1}{8}$ W)
10		SPDT switches
1		Mini-DIP set of eight SPST switches
1		0.001-μF capacitor
1		20-kΩ variable resistor

Optional equipment and supplies referred to in this book: These items are used in less than 10% of the book's experiments. Yet their expense could easily approach 1000% of the cost of all other items used. Hence they are designated "optional." A list of these components is given in units VI and VII.

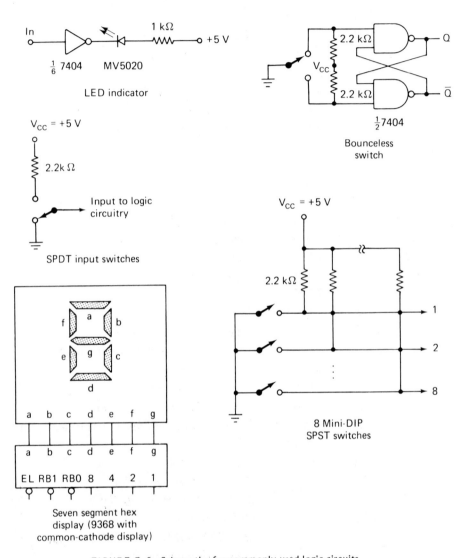

LED indicator

Bounceless switch

SPDT input switches

8 Mini-DIP SPST switches

Seven segment hex display (9368 with common-cathode display)

FIGURE G-0   Schematics for commonly used logic circuits.

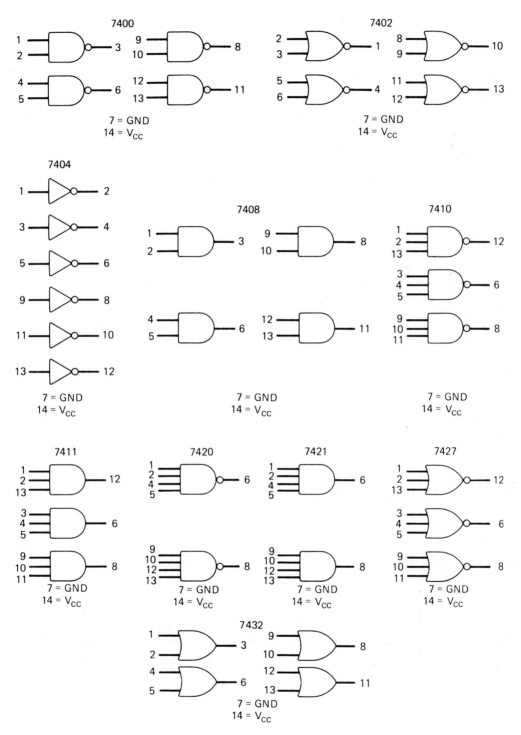

FIGURE G-1 Pin numbers.

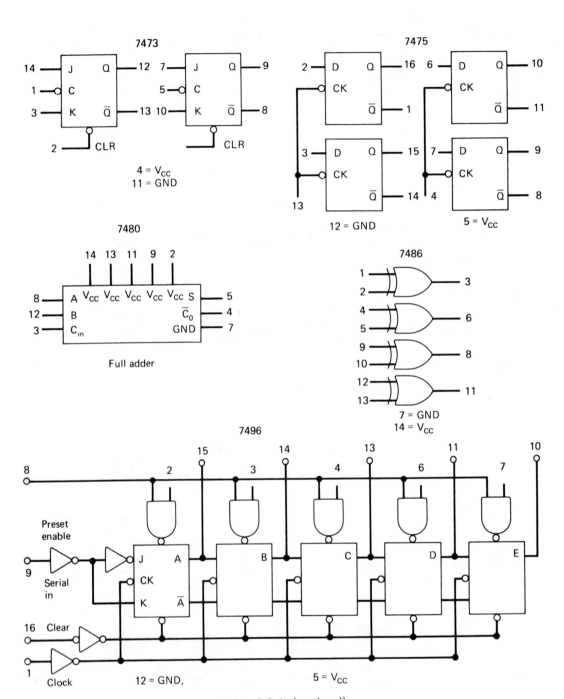

FIGURE G-1 (continued)

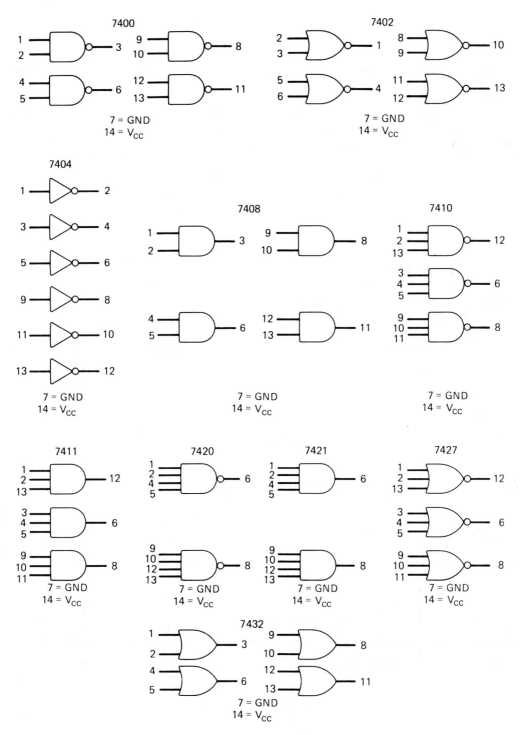

FIGURE G-1 Pin numbers.

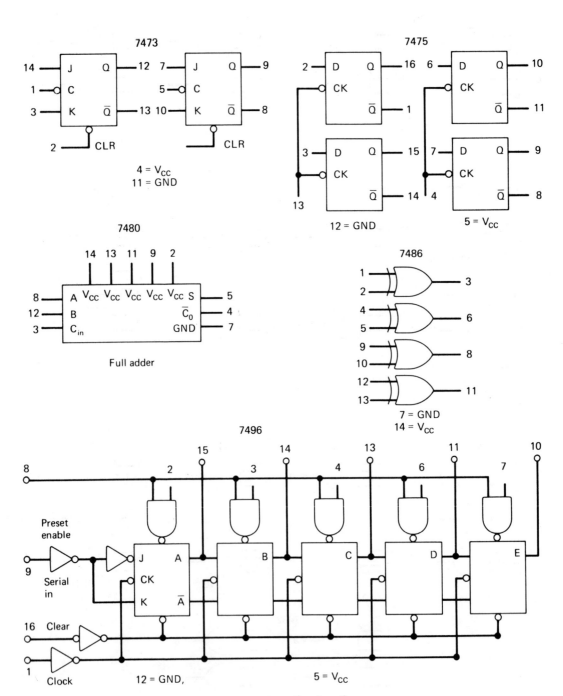

FIGURE G-1 (continued)

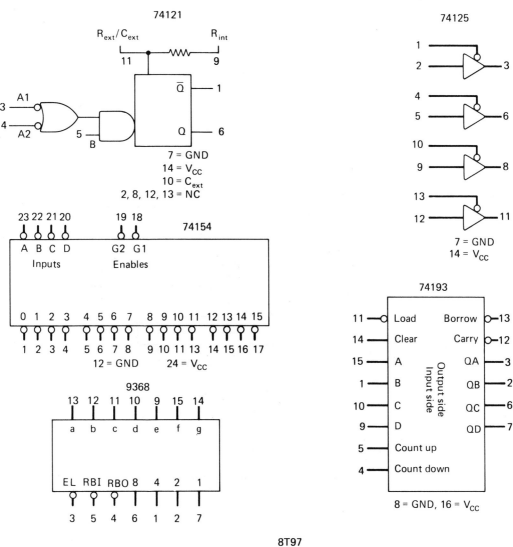

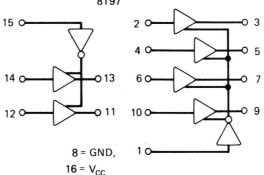

FIGURE G-1 (continued)

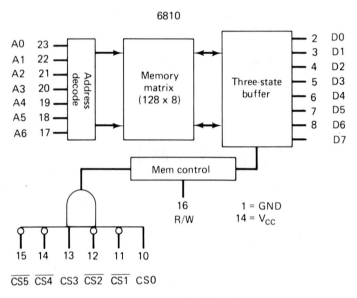

FIGURE G-1 (continued)

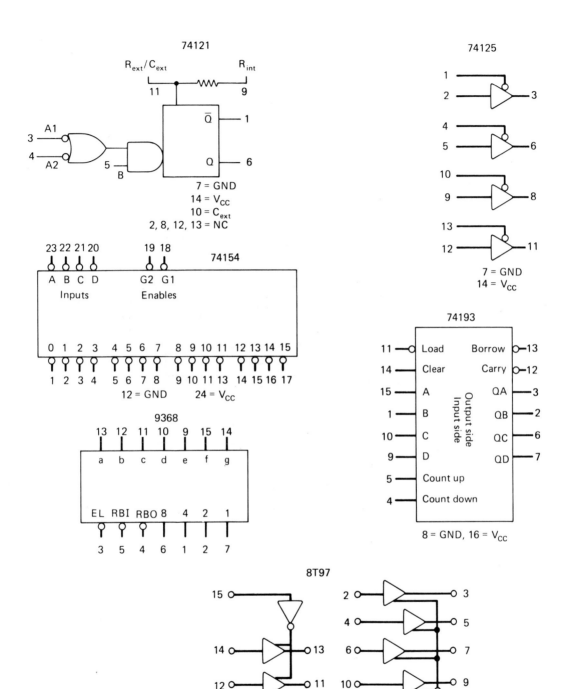

FIGURE G-1 (continued)

6810

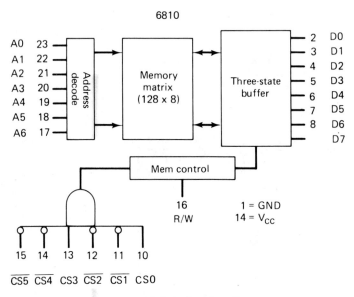

FIGURE G-1 (continued)

264

appendix

Bibliography

American National Standards Institute, *American National Standard Vocabulary for Information Processing.* ANSI, 1970.

Bartee, T. C., *Digital Computer Fundamentals.* New York: McGraw-Hill, 1972.

Chorafas, D. N., *Systems and Stimulation.* New York: Academic Press, 1965.

Crouch, H. B., J. B. Cornet, and R. S. Edward, "CCD's in Memory Systems Move into Sight," *Computer Design*, vol. 15, no. 9 (Sept. 1976).

Digital Equipment Corporation, *Introduction to Programming.* Maynard, Mass., 1970.

Digital Equipment Corporation, *PDP11/60 Processor Handbook.* Maynard, Mass., 1977.

Forsythe, A. I., T. A. Keenan, E. I. Organick, and W. Stenber, *Computer Science: A First Course.* New York: Wiley, 1969.

Givone, D. D., *Introduction to Switching Circuit Theory.* New York: McGraw Hill, 1970.

Hoffman, E. J., R. C. Moore, and T. J. McGovern, "Designing a Magnetic Bubble Data Recorder, Part 1: The Component Level," *Computer Design*, vol. 15, no. 3 (March 1976).

IBM Corporation, *Data Processing Glossary*. Poughkeepsie, N.Y., 1972.

Institute of Electrical and Electronics Engineers, Inc., *IEEE Standard Dictionary of Electrical and Electronics Terms*. New York: Wiley, 1972.

Intel Corporation, *Intel Data Catalog*. Santa Clara, Calif., 1975.

Juliussen, J. E., "Magnetic Bubble Systems Approach Practical Use," *Computer Design*, vol. 15, no. 10 (Oct. 1976).

Korn, G. A., *Minicomputers for Engineers and Scientists*. New York: McGraw-Hill, 1973.

Korn, G. A., *Microprocessors & Small Digital Computer Systems for Scientists and Engineers*. New York: McGraw Hill, 1977.

McKay, C. W., *Digital Circuits: A Preparation for Microprocessors*. Englewood Cliffs, N.J.: Prentice-Hall, 1978.

Mano, M. M., *Computer System Architecture*. Englewood Cliffs, N.J.: Prentice-Hall, 1976.

Millman, J., and C. C. Halkias, *Integrated Electronics: Analog and Digital Circuits and Systems*. New York: McGraw-Hill, 1972.

Motorola Semiconductor Products, Inc. *McMOS Integrated Circuits Data Book*, U.S.A., 1973.

Signetics Corp., *Digital/Linear MOS Applications*. Sunnyvale, Calif., 1974.

Texas Instruments, Inc., *Bipolar Microcomputer Components Data Book for Design Engineers*. Dallas, Tex., 1977.

Texas Instruments, Inc. *TIB0203 Magnetic Bubble Memory and Associated Circuits*. Dallas, Tex., 1978.

Index

Index

Index